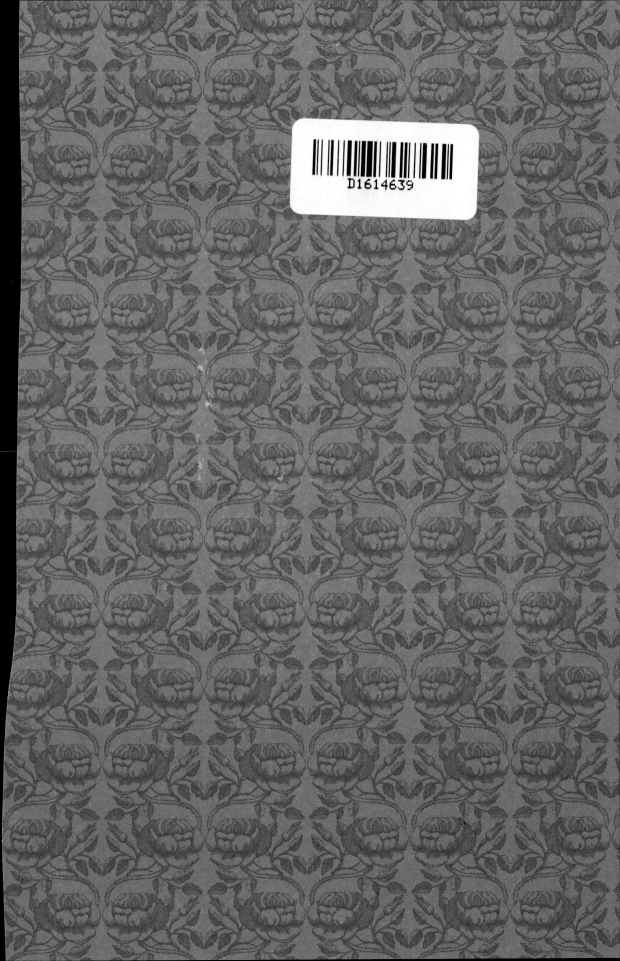

CLARA

Clara Bryant Ford

CLARA
Mrs. Henry Ford

by
Ford R. Bryan

Ford Books, Dearborn, Michigan, 2001

05 04 03 02 01   1 2 3 4 5
ISBN 0-8143-2998-5
Library of Congress Preassigned
Control Number 2001 131442

Designed by Mary Primeau

This book is dedicated to the hundreds of working volunteers who during the past thirty years and more have made it possible to keep a presentable Fair Lane open to the public. Their thousands of hours of donated time tending the gardens and escorting visitors — often on precious Sundays and holidays — are contributions warranting grateful acknowledgment.

Contents

Foreword

"Behind every successful man is a woman" the old saying goes, and that certainly was true with my great-grandfather and his remarkable wife Clara. Her steadfast belief in her husband, through some difficult years, truly demonstrates her stalwart character. Yet because Clara chose to fulfill a traditional supportive role, little has been written about her. Ford Bryan has filled this historical void. Ford is well known to our family as an outstanding historian, and once again he has produced a meticulously crafted account. The task of piecing together the bits and pieces of a quiet woman's life to provide us with a complete story could not have been easy. We thank Ford Bryan for giving us this insightful profile of a remarkable woman.

Edsel B. Ford II

Acknowledgements

Members of the staff of the Benson Ford Research Center of Henry Ford Museum & Greenfield Village have contributed greatly to my ability to assemble material for this book. Permission to access the stacks of the Ford Archives was granted by Judith Endelman, Charles Hanson, and Terry Hoover. Valuable assistance in ferreting out suitable accessions was constantly provided by Catherine Latendresse. Assistance in locating and ordering appropriate photographs has been provided by Cynthia Read Miller, Carol Wright, Mia Temple, Alene Soloway, and Melissa Haddock. The high quality of photographic imagery appearing in the book can be attributed to Allan Harvey of the Henry Ford Museum Photographic Studio.

Jeanine Head Miller of the Henry Ford Museum staff has been a consistent source of encouragement, as has Alice M. Nigoghosian of Wayne State University Press. Hubert J. Beudert, now associated with the Cranbrook Educational Community, continues his strong moral support as he has through three of my previous publications.

Bryant family members who have been especially helpful include Mrs. Melvin Kennedy Bryant of Indianapolis, Indiana; Mrs. Carol Bryant Lemon of Winter Haven, Flordia; Mrs. William H. Raymond of Adrian, Michigan; and Mr. James Bryant of Lake Angelus, Michigan.

In finalizing the book, L. Kay Richardson and Wendy Warren Keebler have provided the editing, Mary Primeau did the designing and typesetting, and Alice Nigoghosian has been my publishing consultant. To all these people and many more who helped in the process, I am deeply grateful.

Introduction

*A*t the beginning of the twenty-first century, it is hard to imagine what life would be like without Henry Ford's radical innovations in industry. Ford made possible much of the technological progress achieved in the past one hundred years. Among Ford's firsts are the moving assembly line, affordable automobiles for the masses, vertical integration of all aspects of his industry from raw materials to the shipping of finished products, and fair wages for all employees. And the financial legacy of the Ford Foundation has provided untold wealth for many charitable causes.

Ford himself appeared larger than life to most Americans of his era. Indeed, he may well have been the first prominent citizen in the United States to become a truly global public figure. His brief, no-nonsense comments received immense public scrutiny from the press and endeared him to the little man, even when the comments were ill informed or, on occasion, dead wrong. Although shy by nature, he did not hesitate to use his prominence (and his wealth) to espouse his own opinions and preferences on many issues, ranging from war to music. David Lewis, one of Ford's most astute biographers, has pointed out that Ford learned early to exploit his popularity with the public and turned it into a bonanza of free publicity and advertising.

The Ford legend — the "rich man with a poor man's tastes," the captain of industry who was on the side of the little man — becomes the Ford enigma as one digs deeper into his personal life. His generosity is legendary, yet he was more generous when he was poor than he was after he had achieved his wealth. In later life, he was famous for promoting vegetarianism and holding elaborate meatless banquets based on soybeans, yet his family grocery bills included large orders for chops and steaks of all kinds. And this champion of the little man was notorious within his company for his brutal firing habits; the victim would find his office cleaned out and the phone line cut, and Henry Ford would be nowhere to be found for an explanation. Ford insisted that his employees be sober, hardworking men devoted to their families, yet his relationships with his father, William, and his own son, Edsel, were hardly models of familial piety. Last but not least, no one who knew Henry doubted his devotion to his wife, Clara. He was quoted as saying about marriage, "Pick a good model and stick with it," yet there is evidence that Ford may have strayed and fathered an illegitimate son.

Whereas Henry lived in the limelight, Clara chose to remain in his shadow. The two times she objected to his opinions were notable—in both instances, Henry bowed to her wishes.

And therein lies the tale of this book. Who was Henry's beloved "Callie," née Clara Jane Bryant? She was married for fifty-nine years to a man who called her "The Believer," and on many occasions he tested her belief in him sorely. She never objected in the early years of their marriage when Henry moved from job to job and moved his family from house to apartment to house. As a grandmother, she opened Fair Lane to a child rumored to be Henry's and encouraged the boy to play with her grandchildren. And she watched in bitter silence as her husband treated Edsel, their only child, with cruelty and scorn because Henry considered him too "soft" in business. Edsel died at the age of forty-nine of stomach cancer that had developed from ulcers and possibly a case of undulant fever.

The private lives of Clara, her husband, and their families are the focus of this book. Despite the publication of more than a hundred books on Ford and his industrial empire, rather less has been published about the family members who were not immediately involved in the day-to-day business of Ford Motor Company. In particular, little attention has been paid to Clara and her family, the Bryants, and little has been published based on the family's personal papers. Their behind-the-scenes influence and involvement in the development of Henry Ford's business during both his early days and his later periods of success have not been previously documented.

Despite this gap, the researcher has an embarrassment of riches to work with, thanks to two remarkable resources. First, hundreds of boxes of personal papers are available at the Research Center of the Henry Ford Museum & Greenfield Village in Dearborn, Michigan. These papers were given to the center in 1964 by the Ford Archives, which had retrieved them from the Fords' Fair Lane residence in Dearborn following the death of Clara Ford in 1950. Henry and Clara Ford saved almost every piece of paper, regardless of importance—a forty-cent newsboy's receipt might be found alongside a million-dollar bank statement. These personal papers literally filled the indoor swimming pool at Fair Lane after they had been boxed for archiving. The Research Center also holds the private office papers of Henry Ford and the business papers of Ford Motor Company.

The second resource is the result of one of the first major efforts to record personal reminiscences of a well-known figure in a scholarly manner. Associates, friends, and acquaintances of Henry Ford were interviewed following the deaths of Henry and Clara Ford. These interviews were taped and transcribed, creating an extensive oral history of both Henry's and Clara's lives as well as Ford Motor Company. This project was conducted by Professor Owen Bombard of Columbia University and was sponsored by Ford Motor Company during the mid-1950s.

Oral history is one of the oldest forms of historical documentation. Scholars ignored it for many decades in favor of more objective and "scientific" sources. In the second half of the twentieth century, it regained popularity even among academic historians, because of its ability to convey a more tangible sense of what life was like at a particular point in time. One can only marvel at the foresight of Henry Ford II, Henry's grandson, in initiating and supporting Professor Bombard's oral history research into his family and its company.

Approximately three hundred personal reminiscences were recorded, resulting in more than three hundred bound volumes. Although the primary goal was to obtain information about Henry Ford and the development of his company, a considerable number also contain statements concerning Clara. These interviews provide rare insight into the personalities and private lives of Henry and Clara.

In the few written accounts published about Clara, she is portrayed as a completely guileless person who lived a fantasy existence as an exceptionally devoted housewife with simple thoughts and simple needs. The real Clara was far more complex and down-to-earth, she wanted what was best for Henry and her family, and she was capable of being less than kind in achieving it.

It is possible that the overabundance of research material may have led to a certain lassitude on the part of some authors. Many of the books on Ford have mined the same material over and over again, offering little that is new in either information or insight and recycling the most "quotable quotes" from the oral history records. As a result, readers of previous books about Ford are surely familiar with Clara's habit of darning Henry's socks well after the Fords had become very wealthy (and the fact that Henry detested wearing darned socks). However, Clara's charity work among poor blacks in the rural South, for example, is not well known.

It has been my intention to draw specifically on archival materials that have not been made public before. Material was gathered from a hundred or more boxes and a thousand or more folders. Individual accessions in the Research Center number more than one thousand, varying in size from as little as one folder to more than three thousand boxes in each. Information for this book was taken from so many of these sources that including a reference to each item was impractical, but a listing of the major sources used is given. Unless otherwise noted, photographs are from the collections of the Henry Ford Museum & Greenfield Village.

The material in this volume is arranged chronologically. Because so many excellent and thorough books have been published on the history of Ford Motor Company, it is not my intention to retell its phenomenal rise here. However, chapters begin with time lines listing major events, including milestones in the company's development. A chronology of the company's history is also provided in an appendix.

After all this research, do some mysteries regarding Clara, Henry, and their families still remain? If the truth be told, there are probably more now than there were before. What we do have, however, is a richer and more intimate portrait of two individuals—one who lived in the limelight and one who lived in the shadows.

Chapter 1
Early Years in the Country

Michigan in the mid-1800s was a wilderness with great promise. Life on the frontier was rugged, but the cheap, fertile land attracted many immigrants. Clara Jane Bryant and Henry Ford both came from successful pioneer families; they grew up on prosperous farms about ten miles northwest and west of Detroit. The Bryant and Ford homesteads were about five country miles apart; the Bryant home was in Greenfield Township, and the Ford home was in adjoining Springwells Township.

Melvin S. Bryant, Clara's father, was born in Greenfield Township, Michigan, in 1835; he was the son of a Canadian immigrant. His wife, Martha Bench, and her parents had emigrated from Warwick, England, when Martha was eight. Melvin and Martha had ten children, all of whom grew to maturity. In order of age, they were Frederick, Edward, Clara, William, Harry, Kate, Milton, Marvin, Eva, and Edgar LeRoy.

The first five Bryant children (including Clara) were born in a house at the intersection of Grand River Road and Greenfield Road in Wayne County. Clara was born on April 11, 1866, and baptized on August 19, 1866, by the Reverend William E. Armitage of St. John's Episcopal Church in Detroit. When Clara was four, her family moved to a forty-acre farm on Monnier Road, about a half mile north of Grand River. Eight years later, a large brick home was built on that property to accommodate the growing Bryant family.

Much of what we know about the Bryants comes from Edward Monnier, a neighbor of the Bryants who was approximately the same age as Clara. Edward characterized Melvin Bryant, Clara's father, as a hardworking farmer who was considerably more productive than any of his seven sons. Edward and Clara attended school together in the crowded one-room Greenfield Township District No. 3 School (some

July 30, 1863
Henry Ford is born

April 11, 1866
Clara Jane Bryant is born

December 31, 1885
Henry and Clara meet

April 11, 1888
Henry and Clara marry

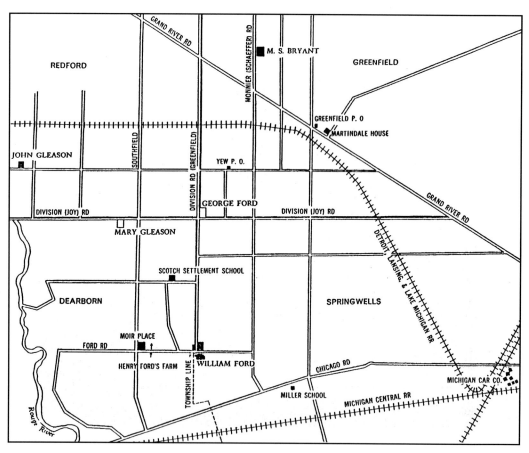

Map showing places
related to Henry and
Clara's activities,
1883–1891.

of their teachers also taught Henry Ford at the Scotch Settlement School, which was four miles south). Because there were eight grades in one room, at times two teachers taught simultaneously. Both the Greenfield and Scotch Settlement schools used very popular, moralizing McGuffey readers.

Clara was "a nice, good-looking girl, a popular and smart girl," according to Edward Monnier. As the eldest daughter in a farm family of twelve, Clara learned the rudiments of cooking and cleaning early. Putting three meals a day on the table for eight or more hungry farm workers (it was common practice to provide meals for hired help) without the benefit of refrigeration or electricity made for a long workday. Keeping a large family clean and neatly dressed for their labors without running water was another Herculean chore.

When Clara turned fifteen in 1881, she was confirmed at St. James Church in Detroit by the Reverend S. S. Harris, D.D., Bishop of Michigan. The following winter (1881–82), she was in the seventh grade

The Bryant home. Located on Monnier Road about a half mile north of Grand River Avenue, it was built in 1880 and was the third house in which Clara lived as a girl. The earlier ones were smaller and of frame construction. Clara was fourteen years old when the family moved into this brick home. In 1888, Henry and Clara were married in the front parlor with the bay window. Sometime after the death of Clara's father in 1917, the house was torn down; the hardware and bricks were saved and later used in the construction of the Martha-Mary Chapel in Greenfield Village. (P.0.188.12855)

Greenfield Township District No. 3 School on Monnier Road as it appeared about 1900. All ten children of Melvin and Martha Bryant attended this school, and it was the only public school Clara attended. Built in 1865, it accommodated as many as seventy-four pupils. They were taught by a female teacher if a qualified man could not be found. At times, two teachers taught simultaneously in the same crowded room. In 1874, when the surrounding acres were pastureland, the tight board fence was erected to keep out the cows. The children often ate their lunches across the road under a spreading maple tree. In 1877, a woodshed was built; two years later, a bell was installed. In 1892, the school tax was raised to purchase an unabridged Webster's dictionary; in 1894, a flagstaff and flag were added. One teacher was Samuel Raymond, who taught Eva and Roy Bryant and later married Clara's sister Kate. A new brick school building was constructed in 1903. (B.32426)

Mary Litogot Ahern Ford. This is the only known picture of Henry's mother; he searched in vain for another. In 1842, Mary Litogot was orphaned at the age of three; she had three brothers. Margaret and Patrick Ahern, a childless couple living in a log cabin on a ninety-one-acre Dearborn and Springwells Township farm, adopted her. Mary attended the Scotch Settlement School one mile north of the Ahern farm. William Ford helped build a frame house for Patrick Ahern in 1860. During that time, William became well acquainted with Mary. On April 21, 1861, when Mary was twenty-two and William was thirty-four, they were married. (P.0.188.2707)

William Ford. This rather proper and solemn photograph, taken in the 1890s, shows Henry's father as a somewhat formidable character. William Ford (no middle name) was born in a small dry-stone cottage on twenty-eight acres of leased land in Ireland near the town of Clonakilty in County Cork. His father was John Ford, his grandfather William Ford. He was trained as a carpenter before coming to America with his family in 1847. William eventually obtained half of his father's eighty-acre farm in Redford Township, Michigan, purchased another eighty acres in Dearborn Township, and acquired another ninety-one acres by marriage to Mary Litogot Ahern. A prosperous farmer, by 1876 he was a staunch and respected citizen of Wayne County. (P.0.360)

The Ford homestead was built in 1860 by Patrick Ahern with the help of William Ford. Henry Ford was born here on July 30, 1863. The farm was on the southeast corner of what are now Greenfield and Ford roads in Dearborn. The house was restored during the 1920s and moved to Greenfield Village in 1944, where it is now open to the public. Buildings of Henry Ford Village, a retirement community sponsored by Ford Land Development (a subsidiary of Ford Motor Company), now stand on the original property. (P.0.3055)

at Franklin School and showed exceptional ability in penmanship. Clara finished her eight grades of schooling in 1883 at the age of seventeen.

William Ford, Henry's father, emigrated from Ireland in 1847; he joined relatives who had emigrated earlier, starting in 1832. Mary Litogot Ahern, Henry's mother, was an orphan whose Old World roots are obscure. Her surname suggests either Dutch or Flemish origin; in later life, Henry would search in vain for more information on her family. William and Mary Ford had eight children, all of whom were born in a frame house on the south side of Ford Road. Half of the house was in Springwells Township and the other half in Dearborn Township (the road dividing the two townships had not yet been built). Henry is said to have been born in the Springwells side of the house.

At the time of Henry's birth, William Ford was not a citizen of the United States. It was not until July 19, 1865, two months after Appomattox, that William declared his intention to become a citizen. Mary's youngest brother, John Litogot, had been killed at Gettysburg; even at the young age of two, Henry felt his mother's grief. This was probably the source of Henry's enduring dislike of war.

Of the eight children born to the Fords, only five grew to adulthood. Henry was the oldest surviving child, born July 30, 1863; he was preceded by an infant son who had died in 1861. John, Margaret, Jane, William, and Robert followed Henry. On March 18, 1876, Mary Ford delivered a stillborn son; she died eleven days later from complications. Henry was thirteen at the time; he was especially grief-stricken by his mother's death. He later recalled that "the family was like a watch with-

Scotch Settlement School, summer 1906. Henry Ford sits at the right with his friend and neighbor Joseph Rycraft. They may be recalling their school days. Henry started his schooling in this building in 1871 and quit in 1879, having finished six grades (he also attended Miller School in Springwells Township for a year or so). At least thirty Fords attended this school, including Henry's mother. Henry purchased the building in 1923, when it was replaced. Henry used it as a nursery school promoting advanced methods of teaching. In 1929, it was one of the first buildings to be relocated to Greenfield Village, where it was used as part of the Edison Institute school system until 1962. It is now open to tourists. (P.0.411)

out its mainspring." Henry would often affirm that he had held his mother very dear. In 1877, Henry's youngest brother, Robert, died; Henry felt as if his family were falling apart. Margaret, Henry's nine-year-old sister, took over much of the housekeeping.

Henry started public school in January 1871 in the one-room Scotch Settlement School in Dearborn Township. His seat mate was Edsel Ruddiman, and his teacher was Emily Nardin. Miss Nardin boarded with Henry's parents. However, for several years, Henry, his brother John, and his sister Margaret followed their favorite teacher—John Chapman—to the Miller School in Springwells Township. Chapman was paid forty-five dollars a month, five dollars more than other teachers, because he was a strict disciplinarian. The Ford children were allowed to change schools because their farm lay in both townships. Henry ultimately finished school in the early summer of 1879 at Scotch Settlement, having completed the sixth grade. He was sixteen years old.

William Ford was a hardworking farmer, and his three sons and two daughters served him well. Henry's contribution, however, must have come more in the form of technological rather than physical help. Henry's mechanical leanings were well known to the farmers in the general neighborhood. Many had concluded that the Ford boy was not only lazy but a bit crazy as well. A schoolmate from Scotch Settlement (one of the Monniers) later said:

> You know that little devil was the laziest bugger on the face of
> the earth. I worked with him and his father on his father's farm
> as a hired hand. Henry would work along all right until about
> ten o'clock in the morning, and then he would go to the house
> for a drink of water. He would go and get the drink of water,
> but he would never come back!

Henry did indeed spend a good deal of his time "tinkering," which his father readily admitted.

Machinery fascinated Henry far more than farming did. After finishing the farm work in the late fall of 1879, Henry walked into Detroit without permission from his father. He stayed temporarily with his aunt Rebecca (his father's oldest sister) as a boarder and obtained work at the Michigan Car Company Works, where streetcars were built. But he was fired after only six days.

William then arranged for his son to become an apprentice machinist at the James Flower Brothers Machine Shop; William knew the owner and hence could keep track of Henry. Apprentice wages were only $2.50 for a sixty-hour week, while room and board was $3.50. Henry made up the difference working evenings repairing watches in a jewelry store. His apprenticeship at Flower Brothers lasted nine months.

Henry became a close friend of Frederick Strauss, another Flower Brothers apprentice. In his reminiscences, Strauss said that Henry was never a good manual worker himself, but he was a likable fellow who could get others to do work for him. Henry was always trying to get someone else to help him build something. For several years following their first meeting in 1880, Strauss occasionally machined experimental parts for Ford; sometimes he was paid, sometimes not.

In the fall of 1880, Henry got a job at Detroit Dry Dock Engine Works. The pay was only two dollars a week, even less than his pay at Flower Brothers, but the giant plant provided a much greater variety of manufacturing operations. Henry's experience at this company can be considered his graduate mechanical education. In the spring of 1882, he returned home to the farm, satisfied with his basic knowledge of machinery and factory operations.

That summer, Henry operated a small portable steam threshing machine—the Westinghouse Agricultural Engine—for James Gleason, a neighboring farmer. Henry, then nineteen, soon established himself as an expert in its operation and maintenance. John Cheeny, road agent for Westinghouse, called on Henry to operate and repair engines manufactured and sold in Michigan and northern Ohio. Henry spent the summers of 1883 and 1884 running these engines. The winters were spent in his shop at the homestead, where he is said to have tried to build a "farm locomotive" but with little success.

When threshers came to a farm to harvest oats or wheat, as many as twenty men might be involved. The machinery crew of perhaps four or five came with the engine, water wagon, and separator. Neighboring farmers furnished wagons and teams to haul bundles of grain from the fields to the grain separator, and the wives went to work preparing a giant feast for the men's noon meal. Henry operated only the engine. The owner of the threshing equipment collected three cents per bushel for threshed oats and four cents for wheat. Henry and other machinery operators were paid their wages out of the engine owner's payment.

While working for James Gleason, Henry became enthralled with Christine, James's charming daughter. Christine's brother Fred recalls that Henry proposed marriage to Christine, but she chose to marry a more mature suitor, Joseph Sheffery, who owned a blacksmith shop, horses, and a carriage. Henry did not even have a bicycle at that time.

Winter gave Henry the opportunity to further his education. On December 1, 1884, he enrolled in the Goldsmith, Bryant & Stratton Business University in downtown Detroit (no connection with the Melvin S. Bryant family). Just what courses he took is not known, but he was probably exposed to at least the rudiments of penmanship, bookkeeping, mechanical drawing, and general business practice. It was a small amount of business training that he received during a few months that winter and the next, but he certainly made the most of it in later life.

The long Michigan winters had also allowed Henry time to develop a social life. Dancing was quite popular; young people met and danced at places such as Coon's Tavern on Plymouth Road and other road houses and inns on Grand River Avenue. One of these, Martindale's Four Mile House, which was four miles outside of Detroit, was not far from the Bryant home. Henry went to dances from the time he was nineteen; Clara was sixteen then and did not attend dances until a bit later.

According to Alfred Monnier, special dances were held in Greenfield on holidays such as New Year's, Easter Monday, and Thanksgiving. These informal and crowded affairs sometimes lasted until dawn. Boys paid $1.25 for the supper and dance. Girls, who were

Clara Jane Bryant in 1888. This portrait is often referred to as Clara's wedding portrait. Although taken sometime in 1888, it was not taken at her wedding. There are no known photographs of Clara as a child. (P.0.392)

Henry Ford at age twenty-three. Sometimes referred to as Henry's wedding portrait, this photograph was actually taken on September 20, 1886, a year and a half prior to his wedding. The photographer was McMichael of 153 Woodward Avenue in Detroit. (P.0.422)

often brought by their brothers, did not pay. Raw oysters or oyster stew were commonly served around midnight, after which the dancing continued. A downstairs bar offered hard and soft drinks.

Henry Ford and Clara Bryant first met during the 1885 New Year's dance at Martindale House. Clara's brother William brought her to the dance. Annie Ford, Henry's cousin, introduced him to Clara. Edward Monnier remembered that "Henry wasn't forward at that age. He was a little shy." Clara seems not to have been impressed by Henry that first evening. At a later dance, they were again introduced, this time by Henry's older friend Alfred Monnier. Henry showed Clara his watch, which displayed both standard time and sun time. Clara sensed this boy was "different" from the others.

Henry was twenty-one, and Clara was nineteen. The two were impressed by each other, Clara with Henry's unique mechanical talents and Henry with Clara's serious and appreciative disposition. Henry was the eldest of five children, and Clara was the eldest of the three Bryant sisters; being eldest in hardworking farm families gave them both a sense of leadership. Henry grew up as the leader of his brothers and other male companions, and Clara was well trained in household management. Both were familiar with the roles of organizer, sibling adviser, and peacemaker, and these family characteristics persisted throughout their lives.

Clara was not a complete stranger to Henry's family; Margaret Ford, Henry's sister, had been Clara's friend for years, and Clara's brothers were friends of Henry.

While courting, Henry and Clara no doubt participated in the typical rural entertainment of that time, including evening husking bees. Corn was husked by moonlight, and the farmer's wife served a late hot meal for her guest workers. In the house, the rug was removed to make space for dancing. Those who could play musical instruments were called upon to perform, and Henry may have played his Jew's harp. Henry greatly appreciated fancy "fiddling" and could play violin to some extent, but he never became proficient at it.

Running James Gleason's threshing machine in the summer once got in the way of Henry's courtship. Edward Monnier recalls one Sunday evening when Henry came pounding on the door of the Monnier house about midnight, waking the whole household. Henry had promised Clara that he would take her to Put-in-Bay, a small island in Lake Erie that was a popular destination for all-day steamboat trips during the summer months, the next day. He cajoled his mechanically oriented friend Alfred into operating the steam engine for him that Monday. Edward reported that his brother operated the engine with no trouble whatsoever.

Henry took Clara to dances at Martindale House. He often rode horseback because his father not only kept farm horses but also boarded horses for Detroiters. Later, Henry bought a cutter to provide enjoyable winter riding for both Clara and himself.

Apparently, Clara had other beaus, and it is likely that her brothers often took her to dances before she met Henry. Martha Bryant, Clara's mother, thought Clara was too young to get married, so the couple waited until April 19, 1886, when Clara was twenty, to get engaged. On Valentine's Day before their engagement, Henry wrote the following love letter to her. His penmanship was excellent, thanks to his training at Goldsmith, Bryant & Stratton Business University. His spelling and grammar, however, needed improvement.

Springwells Feb 14th 86

I again take the pleasure of writing you a few lines. It sems like a year since I seen you. It don't seem mutch like the cutter rideing to night does it but I guess we will have more sleighing. There is a great many Sick in this neighborhood i have called on five sick persons this

Mr. & Mrs. Bryant,
request your presence at the marriage
ceremony of their daughter
Clara,
to
Henry Ford,
on Wednesday, April 11th, 1888,
at 7.30 P. M.,
at their residence,
Greenfield, Mich.

Henry and Clara's wedding invitation. (D.32)

afternoon three in one house. John is going back to school tomorrow I hope you and your folks are all well. Clara Dear you did not expect me Friday night and I think as the weather is so bad you will not expect me tonight, but if the weather and roads are good you look for me. Friday or Saturday night for the Opera or Sunday night or Monday night at the party and if your Brother has got some one else let me know when you write but I guess I will see you before then. Clara Dear, you can not imagine what pleasure it gives me to think that I have at last found one so loveing kind and true as you are and

I hope we will always have good success. Well I shall have to Close
wishing you all the Joys of the year and a kind Good Night.

May Floweretts of love around you bee twined.
And the Sunshine
of peace Shed its joys o'e your Minde
From one tht Dearly loves you
H.

These were happy years for both Henry and Clara. The music, the dancing, and the gaiety of those times remained indelibly in their memories. Later, when there was money to spend, Henry and Clara would invest extravagantly in ballrooms and musicians to resurrect the old-fashioned music and dancing they remembered so well from their youth.

After Henry was engaged to Clara, William Ford tried to encourage Henry to consider farming as a lifetime occupation. In 1886, William offered him the use of an eighty-acre farm with an inhabitable house, which William had purchased from George Moir in 1865. Henry accepted the offer and paid the taxes on the Moir farm beginning in 1887, but he had no intention of raising crops. There were plentiful woods to clear, so Henry set up a portable circular sawmill powered by a steam engine. Not only did he sell lumber from his own farm, but he also arranged to cut lumber for neighboring farmers. Henry also used the steam engine to pull stumps. On occasion, his betrothed rode faithfully by his side. The ride must have been rough and noisy, but Clara, a frontier farm girl, was not easily frightened.

Before the wedding, the Bryant and Ford brothers and sisters fixed up the old Moir farmhouse for Henry and Clara. Henry built a small workshop on the farm to hold the equipment moved from his machine shop on the Ford homestead.

The Bryants were churchgoing Episcopalians. The Fords were nominally Episcopalian, although they did not adhere strictly to any one denomination and from time to time attended various Protestant churches. Henry did not attend any church regularly, and apparently he never fully appreciated the traditional Christian sermon. On March 7, 1888, barely a month before their marriage, Henry was hastily confirmed at Christ Church, Dearborn, by Reverend Samuel S. Harris, D.D.; the certificate was signed by Thomas R. Reid, Rector. Later in life, Henry built several chapels for schoolchildren and attended chapel with students and teachers, but he declined to hire an ordained minister for them.

Henry and Clara were married on her twenty-second birthday, April 11, 1888, at the home of her parents. The marriage is recorded in

The Moir House. Henry and Clara moved in following their wedding on April 11, 1888, and lived here for about a year before building the Square House, which Clara designed. This photograph was taken after Henry had restored it in 1942; the house has since been demolished. (P.0.5431)

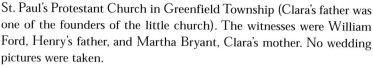

St. Paul's Protestant Church in Greenfield Township (Clara's father was one of the founders of the little church). The witnesses were William Ford, Henry's father, and Martha Bryant, Clara's mother. No wedding pictures were taken.

As Henry continued in the lumber business, he and Clara began to design a larger house that would be built of lumber from their own farm. They called it the "Honeymoon House" or the "Square House," and Clara determined the exact dimensions of the rooms and took charge of interior arrangements. Henry, along with a finishing carpenter known as Mr. Traverse, did the general carpentry. For the year 1889, Henry paid only 75 cents for fire insurance on the Moir farm buildings, but by 1891, taxes on the eighty-acre farm were $29.44, and the property was valued at $6,000. There are bills showing that several hundred dollars were spent on furniture, hardware, and blacksmithing during 1890; they were addressed to Henry Ford, Jr., because another Henry Ford—an older and better-known uncle—also lived in Dearborn.

After thirteen months in the old Moir house, the couple moved into the Square House. Many are convinced that the Square House was the most attractive home in which the Fords ever lived. Clara was content living on this large, substantial farm that was close to her friends and family. She must have been delighted when Henry bought her an organ so that she could play the music they both loved, and she was especially fond of her flower and herb gardens. Gardening would remain a lifelong passion for Clara.

The Square House. Built by Henry and Clara on the Moir farm in 1889-90, this is the house Clara had to leave when Henry decided to work in Detroit. Clara designed the interior (kitchen 12 by 15, sitting room 14 by 14, parlor 18 by 14, bedroom 10 by 14). Henry sawed much of the lumber and helped with the carpentry. The silo and barn behind the tree at the right indicate that this photograph was taken while the farm was operated as the "Dairy Farm." (P.0.592)

Henry, however, was still thinking of machinery. In the late summer of 1891, he confided in Clara that he thought a gasoline engine could be used to power a horseless carriage. He had examined and repaired an Otto gasoline engine for Eagle Iron Works in Detroit, and he drew a sketch of how it would work for a horseless carriage on the back of a piece of sheet music that Clara had been playing.

Henry could be very convincing. In his enthusiasm, he had already taken a job in Detroit without Clara's knowledge. He was to be a night maintenance man at the Willis Avenue Substation of Edison Illuminating Company for a salary of forty dollars a month and many machines to explore. Henry explained to Clara that he needed this job to learn more about electricity. A man had been killed at the substation (one wonders if Henry told Clara this), and a replacement was needed quickly. Henry knew the substation chief, John R. Wilde, from their days together at the Flower Brothers machine shop. Wilde was aware of

Henry's experience with a 100-horsepower Beck steam engine, the type used to drive the generators at the substation, and so Henry was chosen for the position.

Clara was stunned at the thought of leaving the house she and her husband had designed and built together; they had lived there for less than two years. Later, she confided to her sister-in-law Margaret that she found the move heartbreaking, but she did not want to thwart Henry's ambitions. Henry's father, William, also must have been deeply disappointed. Nevertheless, the young couple arranged to move to Detroit.

Chapter 2
From House to House
in Detroit

Henry rented half of a double house at 618 John R Street in Detroit for ten dollars a month. With help from Clara's brothers, the couple moved some furniture from the Moir farm to that address on September 25, 1891, in a hay wagon. Henry's working hours at the Edison substation were from six p.m. to six a.m., a twelve-hour shift; he started the job that evening. Henry was twenty-eight.

Edison Illuminating Company had been founded in 1886; by 1891, it furnished perhaps a thousand residences with electric lights and more than five thousand lights for street illumination. Although there was competition, Edison's position was strong, and Detroit, a city of two hundred thousand, had grown 80 percent during the previous decade.

The substation where Henry worked was at Woodward and Willis avenues, a new section of the city about a mile and a half north of City Hall. Although 618 John R Street was at least ten blocks from the substation, Henry presumably walked to work. His sprightly step would have gotten him to work faster than the last of the horse cars that plodded up and down Woodward Avenue. On his way, he might have seen his brothers John (age twenty-six) and Will (age twenty), who operated a milk and egg route in Detroit. Clara bought from them.

Moving into a small rented residence in downtown Detroit was quite a change for Clara, but she could not have felt completely alone. Two of her brothers lived in Detroit: Edward at 387 Milwaukee East and Harry at 963 16th Street. Harry married Nellie Pierce of Detroit that same year. Two other Bryant brothers were boarding in Detroit: Fred at 311 Cass Avenue and William at 11 Gilman Street. Both were listed in the Detroit City Directory as milk peddlers; their milk probably came from the Monnier Road farm.

Henry's star at Edison rose quickly. During his first month at the

September 25, 1891
Henry and Clara move to Detroit

November 6, 1893
Edsel Ford is born

Spring 1896
Ford's first car, the Quadricyle, is completed

April 17, 1897
Henry Ford applies for a patent for a carburetor

August 5, 1899
Detroit Automobile Company is formed

August 15, 1899
Henry Ford quits Edison Illuminating Company

618 John R Street. Henry and Clara moved here from the Square House in September 1891. The Fords lived in the right half, which is shown as a laundry in this photograph taken fifty years later. Rent was ten dollars a month—one quarter of Henry's starting salary at Edison. (P.0.188.26465)

Washington Boulevard, circa 1915. Henry rented a room in this apartment building in downtown Detroit in 1892. Called the Parsons Building, it was in the middle of the block, between the Cadillac Hotel and Edison's main powerhouse. Henry is said to have occupied a room to the left of the main entrance steps. The rent was twelve dollars a month. (188.3818)

substation, the Beck steam engine broke down after a heavy electrical load at a Sunday church function. The damage was severe, and lights would have been off in the area for several days, but Henry repaired the engine in record time. His pay was increased to forty-five dollars a month on the first of November, and in December it rose to fifty dollars.

Finding a residence in Detroit seemed to be a problem. The duplex on John R Street was not really suitable. In early 1892, just a few months after coming to the city, Henry and Clara moved to a room at 7 Washington Boulevard in downtown Detroit. That summer, Clara may have gone back to her parents' farm to help her mother; during warm weather, she certainly would have been more comfortable in the country. In October 1892, Henry and Clara moved to an apartment over 162 Cass Avenue, another downtown location; the rent was fifteen dollars a month.

Henry and Clara may have considered building a house in Detroit. On June 29, 1892, they purchased a vacant thirty-foot residential lot from John Adam Moeller for three hundred fifty dollars. The lot was in a subdivision on Moeller Avenue (now Philadelphia Avenue), located one block east of Russell Street in Hamtramck Township. The location was not very desirable; it was next to an alley and adjacent to the Detroit, Grand Haven, and Milwaukee Railroad tracks (now Grand Trunk). The Fords sold the lot on November 14, 1894, to McLelland and Anderson Savings Bank for one hundred seventy dollars.

To augment his salary, Henry taught classes in machine tool practice at the YMCA during the winter of 1892–93. This earned him an extra $2.50 per session. (No doubt, he also used the school shop to do some machining on experimental engine parts for himself.) On February 10, 1893, Henry bought a bicycle; he paid twenty-five dollars down and still owed fifteen dollars on it.

The Fords moved again in May 1893, this time to 570 Forest Avenue, a few doors down from Clara's younger brother Harry and his family. Clara was expecting a baby in November and probably wanted to be close to part of her family. Harry's wife, Jo, had recently had a baby, and Clara used her doctor. Rent for the new house was fifteen dollars. In July, Henry was transferred to the main Edison Powerhouse at Washington and State streets; his salary was still fifty dollars a month.

In preparation for both the baby and winter, Clara purchased a second-hand Peninsular base-burner stove from Wm. H. Byrne hardware store on October 4, 1893. The price was $20.85; a collar and damper for the stove pipe cost another forty cents. A balance of ten dollars was due the next month.

Henry took care of fuel for the stove. He bought forty-five pieces of sixteen-inch beechwood blocks and thirty-five pieces of sixteen-inch split blocks for two dollars from Bruno Gladewitz, a wood, coal, and

570 West Forest Avenue. The Fords lived here from May to December 1893; Edsel was born here in November. This photograph was taken much later than 1893; the elderly gentleman on the front walk is said to be John A. Wallace, who lived here at the time the photograph was taken. (P.0.4473)

kindling dealer who also sold sawdust and shavings from his milling operations. A half ton of chestnut coal was purchased for $3.25, with fifteen cents added for carrying it in.

Henry was also buying another type of fuel during this period. Between June and October 1893, Standard Oil Company delivered gasoline to Forest Avenue in fifty-two-gallon barrels for 7.5 cents per gallon. Although he did not have a workshop at this address, he must have been experimenting somewhere in Detroit with gasoline engines. According to Frederick Strauss, his friend from Flower Brothers, Henry did not spend a lot of time at the powerhouse but was more likely to be with friends downtown. He often worked on his own projects on Edison property and Edison time—always being "on call," of course. This was not especially appreciated by Edison top management.

With a baby on the way, Henry considered changing jobs. He wanted to earn more money, both to provide for his family and to continue with his engine experiments. His 1893 Dearborn Township taxes

Henry with the lightweight bicycle he purchased in February 1893. It has no fenders or chain guard; Henry is wearing clips around his ankles to keep his trousers out of the sprocket. He is no doubt proud of having this up-to-date mode of transportation. (P.0.423.B)

for the Moir farm were $44.55; fire insurance was $3.15. Taxes for the Moeller subdivision lot were $0.29.

Edsel Bryant Ford, Henry and Clara's only child, was born on November 6, 1893. He was named after Edsel Ruddiman, Henry's class-mate at Scotch Settlement School. Dr. David H. O'Donnell, who had delivered a baby for Clara's sister-in-law down the street, came to the house on a bicycle, his doctor's bag tied to the handlebars. The young doctor was not yet sufficiently established to have a horse and buggy.

Dr. O'Donnell reported that Clara "was a wonderful patient. Mr. Ford was in the house during the delivery. He didn't get excited and

Edsel and Clara. This is probably Edsel's first photograph; he is only a few months old. Clara would be twenty-eight. (P.0.801)

William Bryant and his wife, Anna Wolfertz Bryant, 1890. They had one child, Florence. William was two years younger than Clara. He was in the barber supply business for a while and later worked on streetcars in Detroit. He was active in the Masonic Lodge. (P.0.1030)

didn't bother me a bit. A lot of young fathers bother the life out of a doctor, you know." The cost of delivery was ten dollars, and a live-in nurse, Mrs. Kelly, was employed at four dollars per week to care for Clara for two weeks. For some years following, Clara, Henry, and sometimes Henry's father went to Dr. O'Donnell for checkups. The doctor later treated baby Edsel for a case of bronchial pneumonia, but otherwise the family's health was good.

There was other family news as well. On November 8, 1893, Clara's brother William announced his engagement to Anna Wolfertz. Another brother, Milton, had recently moved in with Harry Bryant's family, which was just down the street on Forest Avenue. Milton was working as a clerk at Harvey's Sons, a drug manufacturing firm, and attending the School of Pharmacy at Detroit College of Medicine.

A few days after Edsel's birth, Henry's pay was raised to ninety dollars a month, and on December 1, 1893, he was made chief engineer at the main downtown Edison plant at Washington and State streets. The winter of 1893–94 was unusually severe; Henry sometimes found it difficult to get back and forth to work in a hurry when necessary. The distance from Forest Avenue to the main Edison powerhouse was about twenty-five blocks. The streetcars were not on time, and often they were

58 Bagley Avenue, date unknown. Henry, Clara, and Edsel lived in the left
half of this duplex from December 1893 until July 1897. Behind the house is
the woodshed where Henry assembled his first vehicle, the Quadricycle. The
"contraption" was first driven on the streets of Detroit in the early morning
hours of June 4, 1896. (P.0.619)

too crowded to board. After his promotion and hefty raise, Henry had to do something to keep his employer happy.

Clara was just beginning to feel a bit at home with five-week-old Edsel when Henry announced they were to move again. She must have been horrified at the thought of preparing her family for the move. Henry promised that the movers would take care of everything, including laying carpets, placing furniture, and hanging curtains. Their new residence, half of a duplex at 58 Bagley Avenue, was very close to Henry's job at Edison's main powerplant. By December 15, the young family was ensconced at Bagley, where rent was twenty-five dollars a month.

Henry was especially pleased with the Bagley premises; there was a brick shed in back that could serve as a home workshop. His responsibilities at Edison allowed for plenty of time to tinker in the Edison boiler room and chat with cronies about experimental work on gasoline engines. Across the alley from the Edison building was a storage building; Henry and his friends rented it for use as a machine shop to try out Henry's experimental engines. Henry was probably not spending much time with Clara and Edsel.

On Christmas Eve 1893, Henry made a breakthrough on his gasoline engine. He was so excited that he dragged the little engine into the kitchen, clamped it to the drainboard of the sink, and asked Clara to help him fire it up. To Henry's delight, it roared to life, no doubt belching smoke and fumes.

There is no written record of Clara's reaction, but it is safe to say that most women would be sorely put out by such an intrusion. They had moved less than two weeks before. Clara had given birth to Edsel less than two months before, and the baby was sleeping in a room next to the kitchen. This was to be their first Christmas with the new baby, and the Bryant family was coming from Greenfield the next day. Clara was in the middle of preparing a big Christmas dinner for her family. A gasoline engine in her kitchen could not have been part of her Christmas Eve plans. Clara's patience with her husband's tinkering seems to have been boundless.

Clara's sister Kate and her niece Nettie Bryant (ages twenty-three and twenty) came for a weeklong visit during this period. Nettie relates that Clara often made trips to the little shed behind the house to visit Henry. "Henry is making something, and maybe someday I'll tell you," Clara told them.

Despite his work in the shop, Henry always found time for tomfoolery. Once Kate and Nettie found all the doorknobs in the house covered with butter, courtesy of Henry. On another occasion, they were tiptoeing up the stairs after returning from a party late at night, when a scary object came rolling down toward them. It turned out to be a bundle of clothing in which Henry had put several bricks. The girls had

Clara's sister Kate and her husband, Samuel Raymond, circa 1895. Kate became the mother of three boys and a girl. Sam operated a Ford dealership in Adrian, Michigan, and later served in the Michigan Senate from Lenawee County. Kate died on September 17, 1949; she is buried in Adrian. (P.0.1034)

their fun, too. One morning, they put salt in Henry's shoes, but Henry felt the coarse grains and emptied his shoes. The girls then tried finely ground pepper. Henry's feet got so hot at work that he had to hurry home and change his shoes.

By 1894, Henry was making one hundred dollars a month as chief engineer at Edison and was the highest paid of some fifty employees. He had three assistant engineers, one of whom was classified as a machinist. His friend George Cato, an electrician, earned eighty dollars a month. James Bishop (who later joined Henry in the automobile business) was classified as assistant inspector, with a salary of thirty-five dollars a month. Meter boys at Edison received only fifteen dollars a month.

Henry made friends easily, and on November 29, 1894, he joined the Palestine Masonic Lodge with his coworkers George Cato and James Bishop (Henry's father had been a Mason). He also befriended his elderly neighbor at Bagley, Felix Julien, who became fascinated with the goings-on in the shed. Julien realized that Henry needed more work space and began storing his wood and coal in the house rather than in his half of the shed.

Henry's many experimental automotive parts were fabricated at or next door to the Edison shops, with Henry supplying most of the materials and his friends most of the labor. The final assembly of his first suc-

Henry and the Quadricycle, October 1896. Since the first trial run in June, Henry had boxed in the engine on the rear of the vehicle. The Quadricycle was sold for two hundred dollars; later, Henry bought it back from a third party for sixty dollars. It is now encased in glass at the Henry Ford Museum. Several replicas have been made, which are occasionally driven. (P.0.833.89114)

cessful vehicle—the Quadricycle—took place in the brick shed behind the house on Bagley in the spring of 1896.

As a child, John Dahlinger (of whom we shall learn more later) often played with Henry's grandchildren. Dahlinger reports that Clara was fond of telling her grandchildren about Grandpa Henry's little mistake. He had fully assembled the Quadricycle without thinking to measure the shed door.

> [Henry] came running into the house to get her and to wake up his little son Edsel so that he too could witness the glorious event. Mrs. Ford worried a little about the noise that would be made in the middle of the night, but then she had a worse worry. As she watched in horror from the back door of the house, she saw her husband crash through the walls of the barn with a pickax as he enlarged the doorway enough to get his little masterpiece through.

Creating an impromptu garage door was the evening's only real problem. Once freed from the shed, the Quadricycle rode off into the streets of Detroit and into history.

During 1884, 1895, and 1896, the cost of Henry's numerous experimental auto parts put a strain on the family budget. Strelinger, one of Henry's major hardware suppliers, limited his credit to fifteen dollars. Clara knew that materials for the car were eating up all the family's surplus above necessary home expenses. She confided in her sister-in-law Margaret Ford that her only concern was the immediate one: Henry needed parts for his work, and she wanted to be sure there was sufficient money in the bank to pay for them. Despite her faith in Henry, Clara wondered more than once if she would ever live to see their bank balance restored.

Henry's hardware bill from Strelinger during July 1895 came to $12.37, but household needs could not be completely ignored. In January 1895, a couch was recovered by Thomas O'Toole, upholsterer. In May, forty-two yards of carpeting were cleaned by the Detroit Steam Carpet Cleaning Works for $1.26. On December 16, a Champion Garland range was purchased from R. Byrne & Co. With a new zinc, the price was thirty-one dollars; the Fords paid ten dollars down. They were buying their coal from Alexander Malcomson, who would later be one of Henry's backers. Taxes on their Dearborn farm for 1895 were $50.11. During this period, Henry subscribed to the *Detroit Evening Journal* at forty-five cents a month.

Music was important to Henry and Clara all of their lives. Despite their strained finances, on November 22, they treated themselves to a piano; the price was $375 on a five-year plan, with monthly payments

Edward L. and Laura Bell Bryant with their two youngest children, Emily
Doris and Lloyd, 1895. Lloyd died of acute appendicitis and peritonitis in
1902 at age eleven. Edward was Clara's older brother. He and Laura Bell
reared a large family here and were still living in this house when Edward died
from pneumonia on April 29, 1913, at age fifty. (B.37783)

of $10. Interest on the unpaid balance was 7 percent. It would take them years to pay it off.

Henry had enrolled in an electrical course at the National School of Electricity, but he dropped out by December 1895 without paying all of his tuition. It is not clear whether he withdrew because of short finances or because he did not find the course worthwhile.

Alexander Dow, Henry's new boss at Edison Illuminating Company in 1896, wanted Henry to stop his experiments with a gasoline car and pay full attention to his job at the utility. In July 1896, Dow made it a point to introduce Ford to Thomas Edison in New York, believing that Edison would talk Ford out of gasoline as a motive power. Edison, however, encouraged Ford. When Henry returned from New York, he enthusiastically told Clara, "You won't be seeing much of me for the next year." Instead of being upset, Clara seems to have joined Henry in his enthusiasm. In later years, Henry and Thomas Edison became very close friends.

While living at 58 Bagley, Henry, Clara, and Edsel sometimes would eat at the very nice basement dining room of the Family Hotel on Clifford Street facing Park Place. One was served soup, meat, potatoes, a vegetable, coffee, and dessert for fifteen cents. Harry C. Needham, a friend who sometimes ate there with the Fords, recalled: "We walked to the cigar counter and paid our fifteen cents, and Henry did the same." Eating out must have been a treat for Clara.

Things mechanical always appealed to Henry, so it is not surprising that he purchased a camera in 1896. He was snapping pictures right and left, and many have survived; they are approximately two by four inches in size, and remarkably clear. Among the very first are snapshots of his trip to New York, where he met Thomas Edison. Dozens of the photos are of Clara and Edsel, and also of the Bryants at their farm. Henry must have carried his camera with him on weekend outings; he does not appear in any of the photos himself.

Henry often drove Clara and Edsel out to the Bryant and Ford farms in the Quadricycle. Their first arrival at the Ford homestead in the noisy contraption created quite a stir. Henry's father refused to take a ride in it, but his sister Margaret did: "After I had ridden in the car, I wondered more than ever at the cool confidence and nerve which Clara displayed in trusting herself and Edsel to Henry's little car for the first ride into the country."

In 1896, at age seventy, Henry's father, William Ford, prepared his will. He left the Moir farm to Henry, forty acres east of the homestead to John, forty acres across the road from the homestead to Margaret, and forty acres east of Margaret's acreage to Jane. Will was to inherit the homestead's fifty-one acres. Henry was to pay two hundred dollars to each of the others for having received the largest parcel.

The Bryant women at the Bryant farm, circa 1896. From right: Clara watching Edsel; Clara's mother, Martha; Eva standing behind Edsel; and Kate to the far left. Henry undoubtedly took this picture. (P.0.970)

Mary Ward and John Ford, Henry's brother, about the time of their marriage in 1895. Henry very likely took this photograph. The John Fords lived on the Dearborn land inherited from William throughout their married life; they were not particularly intimate with Henry and Clara. John operated a real estate business and was a city councilman at the time of his death in 1927. He and his wife are buried in Grand Lawn Cemetery in Detroit. (0.1122)

Henry's brother John had married Mary Ward in 1895; they lived about a mile from the homestead. Will married Frances Ann Reed on October 27, 1897. At that time, William Sr. retired with his two daughters, Margaret (age thirty) and Jane (age twenty-eight) to a rented house at 582 West Grand Boulevard in Detroit. Will and his wife stayed on the homestead farm.

Margaret and Jane kept house for their father in Detroit. Margaret took embroidery lessons, which served her well; needlework became her lifelong pastime. Jane, the more gregarious of the two, helped with the housework and shopping, although she was rather sickly. Clara sometimes joined them to attend the theater or take a trip to the country.

During the summer of 1897, Clara, Edsel, and William visited Henry at the Edison plant. William often went downtown alone to follow Henry's progress with his horseless carriage. He is said to have frequented Jimmie Burns's Saloon, having a drink and a sirloin steak before tracking down his son. Several sources say Henry's father liked to stand inside and watch the traffic on Washington Boulevard. He became quite proud of Henry's position with the Edison Illuminating Company and Henry's acquaintance with so many prominent Detroiters.

On the Ford homestead, 1896. Taken by Henry, this photograph shows the family standing in the middle of Ford Road in front of the homestead. From left: Henry's jovial sister Jane, Henry's other sister Margaret, Clara, and William Ford, Sr. Henry, Clara, and Edsel may have driven out to the farm from Detroit on the Quadricycle. (P.0.972)

Fred and Johanna (Jo) Bryant, date unknown. Jo and Fred were married in 1894 in Adrian, Michigan. They operated a milk and cream business in Detroit, then left Detroit to operate the Wellington Hotel and Marina on Lake St. Clair. Jo kept inviting all the Bryants to their hotel for hunting and fishing. Henry did not have the patience for fishing, but he enjoyed duck hunting until he became an ardent bird protector some years later. (P.0.1025)

Henry was developing a second car in the little basement shop next to the Edison plant where he worked. He was getting rough parts from blacksmith J. Allen Gray, who insisted on payment for each piece before he started the next. The bill was given to Henry, who then took it to his friend, Detroit Mayor William Maybury, who wrote a check to cover the cost. Ford's little shops at the Edison location were not complete enough to supply all of the machining necessary for his engine experiments. In early 1897, he located a storefront at 151 Shelby Street for his machinist friend Frederick Strauss. Ford paid the rent of thirty dollars a month and furnished Strauss with at least a hundred dollars' worth of tools for machining engine parts. According to Strauss:

> Henry had so much time on his hands that he didn't know what to do around the shop. He was always down where I was. Henry never used his hands, to tell the truth. He never came to work until after nine, either. He never could get around in the morning.

The milk business was not doing well in Detroit. By 1897, Clara's brother Edward, who lived at 857 Milwaukee, had switched to cabinet-making. Fred Bryant had also gotten out of selling dairy products; he moved his family to Algonac, Michigan, on Lake St. Clair, where he became proprietor of the Wellington Hotel, a large waterfront establishment on Harson's Island. Harry Bryant and his family joined the Fred Bryants in 1898 and operated a store at Anchor Bay on the same Lake St. Clair Flats. The entire Bryant family took advantage of the recreation facilities on the water. The men, including Henry, were all good hunters. Ducks and geese abounded on the Flats, and fish were plentiful.

In June 1897, Henry moved his family to a cheaper residence at 72 East Alexandrine Avenue, a mile and a half north of the main Edison plant; rent was only fifteen dollars a month. They were moved with horse and wagon by Mr. Leonard of Leonard Brothers Storage Co. Henry had a shop in a barn at that address, where he again induced Strauss to help him with work, beginning in July 1897.

Bills for hardware and plumbing supplies for Henry's experimental engine parts are very conspicuous during this period. Henry continued to work at the Edison plant during 1898, using the rented basement quarters next door for automotive work and for garnering financial support. After trying this and that and discarding many trial parts, he finished his second car early in 1898. It was considerably better than the Quadricycle, which he had sold to his friend Charles Ainsley for two hundred dollars to help with the expenses for the new car.

On April 7, 1897, Henry applied for his first patent, which

72 East Alexandrine Avenue. Edsel, now between three and four years old, sits with his mother on the porch steps. Henry took this picture. The Fords lived here for three years. There was an old barn behind the house where Henry could work. This is where William Ellis cut the grass all season for $1.50. (188.4756)

described a carburetor; the patent was assigned to his sponsor William C. Maybury and was issued on August 30, 1898.

Henry's second successful auto was operational in 1898, and he used it. He often drove it out to the Bryant farm via the Grand River Toll Road. Charlotte M. Prindle, a gatekeeper on that road, said that Henry tried to avoid paying:

> We saw Henry Ford coming with his contraption. We really didn't know what to call it. We could hardly believe our eyes. He was going out to the Bryants', which was on what we call Monnier Road. I thought he was a smart man because, as I remember, I thought they were bicycle wheels on the contraption, which they might have been.
>
> The tollhouse was at Grand River and Wyoming avenues, and streetcar tracks were being laid along Grand River. We had a pole that you swing around to let people through. When we went to bed at night, we would close the gate, and if anybody came along, they would have to wake us up. We would lie down dressed, you might say. This pole was closed that day that Mr. Ford came along. My mother shut the gate on him, and he politely bounced around on the streetcar tracks and went around the toll gate and didn't pay the money.
>
> I didn't have much trouble with him. He paid me, but I had a little better chance of catching him. I told Mr. Ford he would have to pay toll, and he didn't object. I suppose he thought, why should he pay toll to drive over a plank road? It was oak plank on one side and the other was dirt road. You paid the two cents for the upkeep of this plank road so that you wouldn't have the mud to drive through.

In Henry's defense, country roads in Wayne County were in dreadful condition. This toll road provided an alternative in its early days, but it was not kept up. Of course, no roads had been built at that time for motor vehicles.

Newell Collins, son of Henry's first teacher, Emily Nardin, reported a more courteous encounter during this period:

> My earliest personal contact with Mr. Ford was in the '90s, when I was driving the old top buggy down the Grand River plank road. The little mare was spirited and took a rather dim view of Mr. Ford's vehicle. But Mr. Ford was most kind; he stopped his horseless carriage, got out, took the mare by the bridle, and led her past, for which I was duly grateful.

DETROIT, MICH., *Sept 1* 1898

Mr Ford

72 Alex Ave E

In account with **GEO. FORSYTH,**

DEALERS IN

GROCERIES, MEATS, POULTRY,

711 WOODWARD AVE., COR. SELDEN.   Fruits and Vegetables.

Aug 2	1/2 L Chops 24	24
6	C Liver 20 G Sugar 25 J C Crackers 5	50
	Sardines 10 Salmon 18 & Cutlet 15	43
15	C Salmon 18	18
17	1/4 L Chops 20 Bread 5	25
	Bananas 20	20
20	Chicken 48 Crackers 8 Peaches 13	69
	Tomatoes 5 & 5/2 R Lamb 88	93
22	Bread 8 1 gt Peaches 10	18
	1 gt Tomatoes 5 F Wafers 15	20
23	Chops 27	27
24	Sugar 25 3 Beef 30 Sausage 10	65
29	Bread 1/2 L Chops 24	29
	Pots 20 G Sugar 25	45
		$ 5 46
	July Bill	8 10
		$ 13 56
Sept 6	By Cash	8 10
	Rec Payment Oct 12/98	$ 5 46

Clara's grocery bill, August 1898. There was an unpaid balance of $8.10 from
July that was paid on September 6; the August bill was paid on October 12.
(D.78)

Henry and Clara lived at 72 Alexandrine until October 1899. Clara regularly purchased her groceries from George Forsyth, whose store was one block down Woodward Avenue at the corner of Selden. She visited the store every two or three days, and her monthly bills were usually between five and ten dollars.

The Forsyth store had an unusually wide selection from which to choose. The variety of foods Clara bought was phenomenal; she was obviously doing considerable canning as well as cooking from scratch. In July 1897, she purchased a crate of cherries ($1.10) and granulated sugar ($0.50). Other fruit in season included a bushel of peaches ($1.40) and a bushel of plums ($0.50). Fruits in small quantities included apples by the peck, tomatoes, bananas, cranberries, grapes, currants, oranges, lemons, strawberries, red raspberries, huckleberries, prunes, raisins, pineapple, citron, coconut, and mixed nuts. Vegetables regularly purchased were potatoes by the half bushel, onions, celery, peas, cabbage, turnips, carrots, beets, lettuce, radishes, asparagus, cucumbers, and pickles.

In later life, Henry became a health nut; he abstained from sugar and espoused both the soybean and a vegetarian diet. Clara's account with Forsyth, however, included the following on a regular basis: porterhouse steak, veal cutlets, leg of lamb, lamb chops, lamb stew, baked ham, pork chops, pork sausage, Vienna sausage, chicken, liver, and occasionally salt pork. Seafoods included salmon, sardines, and oysters.

Of course, there were staples: flour, cornmeal, sugar, rice, eggs, cheese, crackers, macaroni, and spaghetti. Baking powder, yeast, starch, lard, and suet, along with vanilla, vinegar, allspice, cloves, and sage, were also on the list, but Clara purchased fresh bread for the table almost daily (an older Henry also preached against the evils of freshly baked bread). Forsyth also supplied Clara with stove polish, matches, kerosene oil, and Lava soap for especially dirty hands. In the spring of 1899, D. M. Ferry flower and vegetable seeds were also on her list. It is unclear where Clara planned to grow them; she and Henry moved out of the house on Alexandrine by October of that year.

Despite Clara's prowess in the kitchen, Henry did not have a discriminating palate. It is doubtful that he appreciated the effort Clara made to provide all those appetizing meals; later in life, she would complain about Henry's lack of interest in well-prepared food. Because of his job at Edison, he missed many meals at home; instead, he regularly patronized an all-night lunch stand, the "Owl Night Lunch." His favorite meal there was a glass of milk and a piece of pie. The stand was a four-wheel horse-drawn enclosed wagon at Michigan Avenue and Griswold; it was open for business from evening until daybreak. Because Detroit restaurants typically closed at eight in the evening, this spot was a popular all-night downtown hangout. (In 1927, Henry purchased the

Owl Night Lunch Wagon. Henry patronized the "Owl" during his years at Edison Illuminating. It was pulled to and from the curbside at Michigan and Griswold by "Reddy," John Colquhoun's bay horse. It opened at six p.m. and departed at daybreak. There were stools inside the wagon and a window for take-out service. The wagon is now in the Henry Ford Museum. This photograph was taken about 1935, when the wagon served hamburgers, frankfurters, buttermilk, and pop for five cents to visitors to Greenfield Village. (P.0.188.22427-A)

wagon from its owner, John M. Colquhoun, who had operated it until 1926. It is now on display in the Henry Ford Museum.)

In the fall of 1899, Milton was apprised of the situation at the Bryant homestead by Marvin, who at age twenty was still on the farm. Life on the farm had changed little since Clara left:

Greenfield 10.29.99

Dear Brother Milton,

We are getting along fairly well with our work, we put in 14 acres of wheat so that made us a little late with our husking, have husked about 500 bu and have only a little over one third husked, it goes rather slow as I have to do it all alone. Had 406 bu of oats and 55 bu of wheat, wheat here was very poor, have got 27 hogs of which 13 are nearly ready for market.

Kate came down, stayed two weeks, she was sorry she did not see you, Roy went home with her he has been there 3 weeks Wednesday. Last thursday Pa and Ma went out to see her for the first time, expect them home sometime this week. I reckon Pa will shoot all kinds of game, hunting around here is good, there are lots of quails.

Milton Bryant, circa 1901. Ten years younger than Clara, "Doc" Bryant graduated from the Detroit College of Medicine as a pharmacist in 1898. He worked for five years for the Peter-Bauer Drug Company of Louisville, Kentucky, as a drug salesman. In 1902, he offered to act as manager of racing activities for Henry Ford. He returned to Detroit and spent three years in the creamery business, after which he sold Ford Model T automobiles. On May 15, 1912, he married Bernice Robertson of Traverse City, Michigan. He later became owner of the Grand Traverse Auto Company, the Ford agency in Traverse City. In 1924, he was elected state representative from that district. He died on March 16, 1928, at age fifty-three, following a hernia operation performed by a surgeon from Henry Ford Hospital in Detroit. The Milton Bryants at that time had two children—Jean and Richard—both by adoption. (64.167.102.4)

Have you been hunting this season? I haven't, but expect to go duck hunting when the work is done. Fred is shooting every day, one day he got 85.

Our dancing Club has organized two dances, and tell you what, we have fine times, we have Finneys music it is swell, and wish you were here to attend them. I am going to the halloween party to Mr. Kemptons tomorrow Eve.

I tell you what Milt he is a great old sport, after you went away, we went down town and had a great old time.

Lizzie Browne was married last Wednesday.

Henry is getting along OK as far as I know. They have moved, they live at 1292 Second St.

The Bryant sisters—Clara, Kate, and Eva—about 1900. This picture is perhaps the first to show Clara's love for tall and elaborate hats. (P.0.851)

Clara's brother Harry Bryant with his wife, Nellie, and their second son Harry Jacques Bryant. Harry and Nellie were married in Detroit in 1891. Melvin, their older son (who probably took this picture), was born at 525 Forest Avenue in Detroit not long before Edsel was born. Clara stayed with her sister for the delivery. After operating a store at Anchor Bay on Lake St. Clair, Harry and Nellie moved to Boise, Idaho, where they operated a Ford dealership for many years. (B.29246)

Eva had had a falling out with her fellow, but he is out tonight so presume they will make up. I hope so for he is a fine young man, do not mention it when you write to her. Well this will be all for tonight, hoping to hear from you soon I am as ever your brother Marvin. Remember to the boys.

This letter contains the first hint that Clara's younger sister Eva was going to be a problem. The farm was too dull for her; a year or two later, she moved to Detroit and relished city life.

Henry was now working days and receiving good wages at Edison, but he continued to spend considerable time on his "carriage." He obviously planned on making automobiles his career. In July 1899, he took wealthy lumber merchant William H. Murphy for a ride in his second car. They drove trouble-free to Farmington and Pontiac and then back to Detroit. The demonstration took three and a half hours, covered sixty miles, and gained Henry the confidence of a strong financial backer.

On August 5, 1899, the Detroit Automobile Company was formed under Murphy's leadership; there were eleven stockholders, including Ford, who was designated mechanical superintendent with a salary of $150 a month. The manufacturing plant was to be at 1343 Cass Avenue at Amsterdam.

That same month, Alex Dow, Henry's boss at Edison, gave him a hard choice: either Edison or automobiles but not both. Henry resigned on August 15, 1899, turning down a promised salary of nineteen hundred dollars a year as general superintendent of Edison. After years of tight budgets and rented houses, refusing that handsome salary must have been a painful decision. Henry was gambling that he could make a successful horseless carriage, and Clara was right beside him.

Chapter 3
Business and
Racing Ventures

Having given up his well-paid job at Edison Illuminating, Henry was now on his own. In October 1899, soon after Edsel started public school at age seven, the Fords moved to 1292 Second Boulevard, not far from the shops of Detroit Automobile Company. This move marked the beginning of a period of turmoil.

Thanks to Henry's friendship with Mayor Maybury, the stockholders of Detroit Automobile Company included several of the most influential names in Detroit. James and Hugh McMillan owned railroads, steamship lines, iron smelters, Detroit Drydock Company, and Michigan Car Works. William McMillan was vice president of Union Trust Company. Dexter M. Ferry owned Ferry Seed Company. Thomas Palmer was a lumber baron and U.S. senator. George Peck was president of Michigan Savings Bank and Edison Illuminating Company.

The company's first product, a delivery truck, was completed in January 1900. Being considerably heavier than the Quadricycle, the truck required large carriage tires. These were bought from Harvey S. Firestone, a salesman for the Columbia Buggy Company on Jefferson Avenue in Detroit. It was the first of many tire purchases by Ford, who later bought them by the thousands from Firestone Tire & Rubber Company of Akron, Ohio. Harvey Firestone and Henry Ford not only did a great deal of business together, but they also became lifelong friends.

Major stockholders of the new company were pushing for a variety of vehicles and were in a hurry to make profits. Henry, however, was beset with a number of engineering problems. His experience to date had not included making more than one car at a time. Several cars were produced, but they were not of the quality that Henry wanted, and they were priced too high to sell.

By November 1900, the Detroit Automobile Company had ground

January 1900
Detroit Automobile Company produces its first vehicle

January 1901
Detroit Automobile Company is dissolved

October 10, 1901
Henry Ford's first racer beats Winton's "Bullet"

November 30, 1901
Henry Ford Company is formed

March 10, 1902
Henry Ford leaves Henry Ford Company

August 20, 1902
Henry Ford and Alexander Malcomson sign a Memorandum Agreement

October 25, 1902
Henry Ford's 999 racer wins the Manufacturers' Challenge Cup

June 16, 1903
Ford Motor Company is incorporated

Detroit Automobile Company. The factory on Cass Avenue is where Henry met his first real manufacturing challenge. The first vehicle, a delivery wagon, is in front. The business was well financed and the facilities adequate, but Henry did not have the experience to produce more than one vehicle at a time. (P.0.3064.)

to a halt, having spent almost eighty-six thousand dollars. Henry received his final check for seventy-five dollars from Murphy, the treasurer, on October 29, 1900. The company was officially dissolved in January of the next year.

Henry no longer had a steady source of income for his family. Their furniture was sent back to the Moir farm for storage, and on October 29, 1900, Clara paid eleven dollars for room and board to a Mrs. Hewitt for that week. On October 24, Edsel had given his address to his school as 36 Clifford Street; later that month, he gave his grandfather's address, 582 West Grand Boulevard.

Henry and Clara were not penniless at this stage, but they were smart enough to realize that hard times were coming, and they took pre-

Margaret Ford Ruddiman, circa 1900. Henry's sister Maggie was four years younger than Henry. She married James Ruddiman in 1900; they had one daughter, Mary Catherine. In 1909, James Ruddiman died; Henry and Clara arranged for care of Margaret and her daughter until Mary Catherine's death in 1992 at age ninety. Mary Catherine never married. (P.0.3184)

ventive action. Clara would not allow her family to suffer physical hardship if she could possibly avoid it. No matter how inconvenient, moving in with family to cut down on living expenses must have been an acceptable option.

At this time, Clara had no relatives who could accommodate them. Fred Bryant and his family had moved to Harson's Island in Lake St. Clair in 1897 and were soon followed by Harry Bryant and his family. Edward Bryant, now a cabinetmaker, did live in Detroit but had a house full of children. Milton Bryant was in Kentucky, and Marvin, Eva, and Roy were still on the Monnier Road farm with their parents.

On November 7, 1900, Henry's sister Margaret, who had been living with her father and sister Jane in Detroit, married James Ruddiman; the couple took up residence on the sixty-acre Ruddiman farm at the corner of Warren and Southfield roads. James had attended the Scotch Settlement School with the Ford children; he was well known in the Dearborn community and had served as township treasurer during 1884 and 1885.

582 West Grand Boulevard. Henry, Clara, and Edsel shared this house with Henry's father and sister Jane during 1901. Henry's father was seventy-six years old, so it is assumed that he occupied the ground-floor apartment. (188.26460)

Henry's father, William, was still living in Detroit at 582 West Grand Boulevard with his daughter Jane in a two-family house. William must have been financially comfortable and physically active at this time. In July 1900, he traveled by train to California to visit his brother Henry. William wrote to his daughter Margaret and to Clara, describing the goldmines and sawmills in the mountains northeast of Sacramento.

On January 8, 1901, Henry, Clara, and Edsel moved into the other half of William Ford's house, bringing their furniture back from the Moir farm. The building had upstairs and downstairs apartments; William paid the rent for both. Given William's age, the younger Fords probably lived upstairs.

Moving from house to house—none of them her own—must have been very trying for a woman with Clara's homemaking instincts.

Living with her father-in-law may have been even more of a strain, but Clara was not one to complain. (Appendix 2 contains Clara's daily diary from January 1 to May 15, 1901.) During this period, Clara also stayed with her sister Kate for the delivery of Kate's first child. It was a difficult time, but Clara remained on an even keel and did her best to take care of her family.

Several times in her diary, Clara mentions being lonely because of Henry's absence. He was working long hours on a new venture. Clara didn't whine about the situation but just made note of it.

Despite the shutdown of Detroit Automobile Company, Henry still had friends in Detroit. Some of the former stockholders retained a portion of the Cass Avenue building so that Henry could develop a car independently. Now he concentrated on a racer. His specialty was engines, and he was convinced that racing would attract the attention necessary to establish him in the automotive field.

Henry told his family that he would be spending many nights on a cot at the Cass Avenue plant. Working around the clock and with the part-time assistance of his friends Ed Huff, Oliver Barthel, and Harold Wills, Henry completed a lightweight two-cylinder, 26-horsepower racer in 1901. This car is said to have cost more than five thousand dollars to build, and William Murphy paid much of this. By midsummer, the racer was almost ready, and Henry took Clara, Edsel, and Clara's mother, Martha Bryant, to Niagara Falls by train. Family finances may have been tight, but Henry and Clara were not down to their last penny. Henry had been working hard, and living with his father was probably a strain; under these circumstances, a vacation was money well spent.

Kate Raymond, Clara's sister in Jasper, Michigan, wrote her brother Milton a newsy family letter on August 18, 1901. The following excerpt deals with Henry and family:

> We had the pleasure of entertaining Clara, Henry and Eds. last Sunday. They gave us quite a surprise, came on auto—stayed until Mon., left here at 11 AM and arrived in Det at 5 PM. They stopped and made Mrs. Seidel a short visit on the way back and made three stops from here to Det. I think they made splendid time, dont' you, we think it is about 80 miles from here to Det.

> Edsel is growing quite a little. I think Clara is awfully fleshy, but Henry is awfully thin. She, Edsel, and Eva had been in Buffalo all week and just returned on Sat eve.

Clara was becoming plump, and she remained so for much of her life. Her cooking skills (plus Henry's uneaten dinners) must have been a source of continual temptation. A close friend of Clara's in later life,

Henry's two-cylinder, 26-horsepower racer, summer 1901. Henry is at the wheel, and "Spider" Huff is on the running board ready to hang out as ballast on curves. The racer had a wheelbase of 96 inches. In October 1901, Henry beat Alexander Winton at Grosse Pointe, winning on thousand dollars, a punchbowl set, and considerable notoriety. (P.0.188.10038)

Clara Snow, related the following incident that reveals much about Clara Ford:

> The Fords were a fairly prosperous farm family. I remember somebody said to Mrs. Ford one time something about that. Mrs. Ford had said that she was dieting, not too much, but she was using not so much butter and not so much cream or quite so much sugar. This woman said to her: "Too bad, and just when you've gotten to where you could afford it."
>
> Mrs. Ford bristled right up and said, "Well, I've always been able to afford enough to eat."

Henry was never a big eater, but his thinness during this period was the result of skipping meals and working long hours on the racer. All that hard work was about to pay off. On October 10, 1901, he challenged Alexander Winton, the well-known Cleveland automobile manufacturer and racer. Winton's "Bullet" was a heavy 40-horsepower vehicle that had won several championship races in the United States.

The race was held at Grosse Pointe, Michigan, on a one-mile dirt track with a high wooden fence around it. Six thousand people were in attendance, including Clara Ford, Alexander Malcomson (the coal dealer), and Malcomson's secretary, James Couzens. The champion bicycle racers Tom Cooper and Barney Oldfield were also there. Each of these people would play a role in Henry's future success.

Wellington Hotel and
Marina, St. Clair Flats.
Fred and Jo Bryant were
the proprietors; they often
invited family to visit.

Henry was not favored to win. The trophy, a cut-glass punchbowl set, had been chosen by Winton's mechanic "because he figured [it] would look well in the bay window of the Winton dining room," according to W. A. Simonds. The punchbowl went home with Clara and Henry instead, along with a one-thousand-dollar cash prize.

In the ten-mile race, Henry averaged a speed of nearly a mile a minute. Ed Huff probably earned his nickname "Spider" during this race; he hung on the running board as ballast and leaned out to balance the car on turns. The crowd roared with delight at this victory of a local engineer over an established champion. Henry was in shock. Harry C. Needham, a witness, was close enough to hear Ford say, "Boy, I'll never do that again. That board fence was right here in front of my face all the time. I was scared to death, and I'll never do that again." He never did race again on a circular track.

To celebrate, Henry bought a new Winchester rifle for $13.73 on October 15 and organized a duck-hunting expedition to the St. Clair

332 Hendrie Avenue. Henry, Clara, and Edsel moved into the apartment at the left of the double entrance in late fall 1901, after Henry won the race with Winton, and stayed until 1905. Henry's father and sister Jane moved into 338 Hendrie, just three doors down in the same building. Henry's father died here in 1905. (188.26463)

Flats, where Fred and Harry Bryant operated hotel and boat rental businesses. Henry got on well with Clara's brothers and often spent time with them. In fact, he was beginning to spend more time with them than with his own brothers.

Henry may have found the race a sobering experience, but Clara was enthusiastic. On December 3, 1901, she wrote her brother Milton:

Did you get the paper I sent you? If so, you know how Henry has been covering himself with glory and dust. He rec'd a beautiful cut glass punch bowl for winning his first race. I wish you could have seen him. Also you should have heard the cheering when he passed Winton. The people went wild. One man threw his hat up and when it came down he stamped on it, he was so excited. Another man had hit his wife on the head to keep her from going off the handle. She stood up in her seat & screamed "I'd bet fifty dollars on Ford if I had it!"

Henry has worked very hard to get where he is. That race has advertised him far and wide. And the next thing will be to make some money out of it. I am afraid it will be a hard struggle. You know rich men want it all. He went to NY last month to take in the automobile show. He met Fournier the French racer, found him a fine young fellow. He met lots of personal friends and lots that knew him by reputation only and was given the glad hand by everybody. We are keeping house again and are very happy to be alone. We have

a very nice cozy little house. We did not build on account of Henry
building the racer. He could not see anything else. So we will have to
put up with rented homes a little longer. We got Edsel a bicycle for his
birthday. He rides it to school and thinks it is fine. He and Henry
both have raglan overcoats. Edsel thinks he is as big as his father. You
would laugh to see him imitate Henry. Eva is thinking of going to
NYC in the interest of embroidery—there is an art school there that
she wishes to attend for a short time if she can. She is very ambitious.

The race against Winton had produced a bonanza of publicity for
Henry as an automotive engineer, but Clara was smart enough to realize that there was still much to do before they could depend on it for a
living. Her brother Milton would soon become involved in trying to
help them make the transition.

Clara's brief reference to her younger sister Eva raises the question
of whether embroidery school was what truly interested Eva about New
York. Eva was not only ambitious but also restless.

Henry and Clara must have felt more secure financially after the
race; Edsel's bicycle and the raglan coats were expensive purchases. In
late November, they moved out of his father's residence; Clara's pleasure
at this turn of events is obvious from her letter. They rented a brick ter-
race home at 332 Hendrie Street for sixteen dollars a month and purchased a range and other household items for the new residence.

Two months later, William Sr. and Jane moved into an adjacent ter-
race apartment at 338 Hendrie. There is some indication that Henry and
Clara were not pleased with this development. When they lived together on West Grand, William had pestered Henry with questions about his
work when he came home, even though Henry was tired and hungry.

The thousand-dollar prize money was certainly welcome, but it was
still not clear where the next check was coming from. Clara was doing
all the housekeeping and cooking herself. Helen Gore, a neighbor's
child who was a little younger than Edsel, described the Fords' life on
Hendrie Street:

> It [the house] had three rooms downstairs with a living room,
> a dining room, and a kitchen. The stairway went up out of the
> dining room. I think there were two or three bedrooms
> upstairs. I remember there was a skylight in the hall, because
> we used to like to sit up there in the rainstorms and look at the
> rain patter on the skylight. Mrs. Ford had no help in her home
> on Hendrie. She did all the cooking. We used to always hang
> around her back door waiting for the big sugar cookies. Edsel
> used to have a little table in the kitchen and we used it to have
> great fun when she would make soup. She used to put the alpha-
> bet in it. That was how I learned the alphabet. We used to pick

Dec. 24. 1901

Dear Santa Claus.
I Havent Had Any
Christmas Tree In 4
Years And I Have
Broken All My
Trimmings And I want
some More I Want
A Pair Of Roller
Skates And A Book I
Cant Think Of Any
Thing more I want
You To Think Of
Something more
Good By.
Edsel Ford.

Edsel's 1901 letter to Santa. (D.82)

out the letters of the alphabet. We used to take an ironing board and put one end on a chair in the front room and use it for a slide. These were things we did in the daytime; Mr. Ford wasn't around then. We used to see him a little bit in the evening, but he was pretty busy and didn't have much time for play.

Throughout the oral history records, Clara is remembered fondly by the children who knew her. She seems to have had a special touch of kindness and patience for youngsters.

Clara's thrift was often mistaken for poverty. On Christmas Eve 1901, Edsel wrote a letter to Santa Claus that was later interpreted by some historians as proof that the Fords were destitute during this period, but this was not the case. Sidney Olson researched the supply of Christmas trees in Detroit that year. For a population of 286,000, there were only 15,000 trees, and the prices were high. According to Helen Gore, Edsel did have a Christmas tree, along with ornaments, presents, and candy.

Given Henry's much enhanced reputation for engineering design, William Murphy and other members of the former Detroit Automobile Company had formed the Henry Ford Company on November 30, 1901. Ford was named chief engineer and given one-sixth of the company stock, valued at ten thousand dollars, but there is no record of wages.

The new company's goal was to build a lightweight runabout with a price of about one thousand dollars. Henry, however, still had racing fever, in spite of his white-knuckled view of the board fence at Grosse Pointe. After that race, he had declared, "Put Winton in my car, and it will beat anything in the country." Now, Henry wanted to build a giant four-cylinder racing car and spent most of his time designing an engine for such a car. Although Murphy had financed the two-cylinder racer, he did not want Ford working on a larger racer. To Ford's annoyance, Murphy began to consult Henry M. Leland, a highly respected mechanical engineer. Leland and Ford did not see eye to eye.

Clara's brother Milton, a salesman for Peter Bauer Drug Company in Louisville, Kentucky, was looking for a career change. He was anxious to become Ford's racing manager, and he had both Clara's and Henry's support. On January 6, 1902, Henry wrote Milton on company stationery.

If I can bring Mr. Fournier in line there is a barrel of money in this business, it was his proposition and I dont see why he wont fall in line if he dont I will chalenge him until I am black in the face, as for managing my end of the racing business I would rather have you than any one else I know of. My Company will kick about me following racing but they will get the advertising and I expect to make $ where I cant make c at manufacturing. We are writing to Mr. Fournier.

Clara also wrote to Milton that same day:

We rec'd your letter Saturday and was glad as well as surprised to hear from you so soon. You did not lose any time when you did get back, as you seem to be pretty well informed in regard to race tracks and other things. Henry thinks what you have done is all right. We have just heard that Mr. Fournier has not gone to Paris yet, but will go some time this month. We will write him and trust that he will get it before he goes. In regard to the contract, Henry thinks he had better have the Louisville race first and see how you come out, and then you can tell better what you can do. We both realize that you will be able to do it. Henry says that whatever you do he will be there with his car to challenge any one. Will write you as soon as we hear from M. Fournier. Will send magazine with account of Fournier's race from Paris to Berlin.

Henry says the track does not need to be so hard, that what is good enough for horses to practice on is good enough for him. Do you not think that a good deal of enthusiasm will have been spent after the Derby races? Do you think the people would turn out as well?

Marve was up to supper Saturday night he is pretty blue, has advertised his milk business for sale, says he does not now what he would do if he sells out. Henry and I both say that if there is any thing that you can do to get him away from the girl to do it. He says he has lost so many customers that paying the higher price for milk he cannot make enough to pay him to continue. I expected Eva this week but she has not come. Perhaps she danced herself sick at the New Years ball. Well I cannot go out to see as Edsel has the mumps has been quite sick but is better today. Hoping you are well and not over working on acc't of your visit.

Apart from the racing business, it is obvious that Eva was turning into a social butterfly, and Clara did not approve. This would later cause some consternation in the Bryant family. Marvin Bryant's business troubles would later be resolved.

More evidence that Henry and Clara had never been penniless comes in early 1902, when Henry arranged to purchase the Dearborn homestead property from his father for four thousand dollars. Henry's brother Will and his family were to move out of the homestead so that the house could be moved; Greenfield Road was being extended southward.

In early March 1902, the wealthy bicyclist Tom Cooper, who had witnessed Ford's defeat of Winton, asked Ford to build him a racer. Cooper had made his wealth from winning bicycle races and represent-

A pensive Edsel Ford at age nine, 1902. Clara was buying books for him to read and encouraging him to correspond with his aunts. He wrote to his aunt Kate near Adrian, Michigan, his aunt Eva after she moved to California, and his aunt Maggie in Dearborn. In return, he received long letters from them and many postcards from various friends and places. His playmate Helen Gore sent him a card from vacation: "I want you to know I remember you." James Couzens, who liked Edsel very much, sent several cards from Europe while on an extended vacation there in 1907. At age ten, Edsel would be driving one of his father's Model A cars. Early cars were simple to drive, but coping with horse-drawn vehicles in the city could be a problem. (P.0.832)

Belle Isle picnic, 1902. Henry took this well-known picture (one of his best) of the Bryant women on a sunny summer afternoon. Seated from left to right are Wallace and Doris Bryant, children of Clara's brother Edward who lived at 857 Milwaukee in Detroit, and Edsel Ford, seated next to his mother, who is wearing a white blouse and bowtie. Standing in the foreground is Kate Raymond's one-year-old son, Russell. The three ladies on the right, seated behind the goodies on the bench, are Clara's mother, Martha, and sisters Eva Bryant and Kate Raymond. (P.0.821)

ing bicycle manufacturers. But a new racer was a sore subject at the Henry Ford Company, and on March 10, 1902, Henry was forced out. His agreement with the company was that it could no longer use his name; he would get the unfinished drawings for the big race car and nine hundred dollars in cash. Ford's two-cylinder racer remained with the company and was sold for two thousand dollars. The company's name was changed to Cadillac Automobile Company; Henry Leland became chief engineer.

Ford and Cooper arranged with young Barton Peck for working space in his bicycle repair shop downtown at 81 Park Place in May 1902. Barton was a bicycle and automobile racing buff and the youngest son of George Peck, president of Edison Illuminating Company. (Ford is reported to have been a "mender of bicycles" during this time.) Ford's major projects were two racers, the "999" for himself and the "Arrow" for Cooper; the racers were named for fast railroad express trains. According to John Wandersee, a worker there in late 1902, the small frame building housed both the Ford-Cooper auto shop and a blacksmith shop of sorts. Henry was around most of the time, always wearing neatly laundered blue overalls. Wandersee's pay was ten cents an hour.

In the meantime, Milton Bryant had drawn up a lengthy "Memorandum of Agreement" that outlined an arrangement in which Ford, Cooper, and Bryant would equally share proceeds from racing schedules arranged by Bryant, who would be manager and handle all funds. In a June 14, 1902, letter, on Ford & Cooper stationery and signed by Cooper, Milton was told "it was not our intention to engage a manager but simply thought it would be a good chance to make some money by getting together and running a few meets."

Milton later learned that the American Automobile Association had strict rules regarding who could hold races and who could participate. Milton was not eligible as an organizer. This was unfortunate, because Clara did not trust Cooper. If Henry was going into racing, Clara wanted someone she could trust to handle whatever money was involved, and in those days that generally meant family.

Milton wrote to Clara in May, asking for a testimonial to bolster his standing with his current employer. She replied on May 13, 1902:

> I rec'd your nice letter, also the "Brain Ease." Henry has his letter heads all down town. Have told him to bring me some. Have not had reason to use "Brain Ease" yet but will gladly send you a testimonial. If Henry brings me the paper tonight will send it right away and if he forgets I will write it on plain paper as you are in a hurry.

Although Clara had not used Brain Ease, she was glad to oblige her brother. She wrote the testimonial on stationery from the defunct Henry Ford Company and dated it January 3, 1900:

> I have been troubled for years with Headache and Neuralgia a relative of mine advised me to use Brain Ease. I did so and had immediate relief. I can recommend Brain Ease, to all persons suffering with the same. If this testimonial will be of value to you I will gladly grant permission of its use.

It is curious that Clara chose to use the old Henry Ford Company stationery, given the availability of "Ford & Cooper" stationery. It is not clear what kind of formal business agreement Henry Ford and Tom Cooper had at this time, if any, despite the stationery.

HENRY FORD COMPANY.

BUILDERS OF HIGH-GRADE

AUTOMOBILES
AND

TOURIST CARS.

MAKERS OF

AUTOMOBILE
SPECIALTIES
AND

SPARK COILS.

OFFICE AND FACTORY.
1343 CASS AVE.

DETROIT, MICH. *Jan 3rd 1900*

Peter Bauer Drug Co.
Louisville Ky
   Gentlemen

I have been troubled for years with Headache and Neuralgia a relative of mine advised me to use Brain Ease. I did so and had immediate relief. I can recommend Brain Ease to all persons suffering with the same. If this testimonial will be of value to you I will gladly grant permission of its use.
  Respectfully,
    Mrs Henry Ford.
      Detroit Mich.

Brain Ease testimonial.
(D.200)

On August 20, 1902, Ford made a deal with Alexander Malcomson, the Detroit coal dealer, to market a motor car of simple design. Harold Wills had made drawings for such a car. Malcomson and Ford's Memorandum Agreement provided for the equal sharing of Ford's racer, then under construction, together with Henry's patents and shop equipment. Malcomson agreed to furnish five hundred dollars immediately, and additional funds as necessary to complete a sample commercial vehicle. The partnership was to place the sample vehicle on display for the purpose of raising capital in the formation of a corporation for the manufacture of the vehicle.

Under this agreement, Wills was to receive one hundred twenty-five dollars a month to be split fifty-fifty with Ford. This meant that Ford was working as an employee for Malcomson, who was paying the bills. In October 1902, there were ten employees, in addition to Ford and Wills, working in the little shop. Each of the hourly employees was paid sixteen dollars for fifty-one hours of work a week.

The first race Ford and Cooper entered was the Manufacturers' Challenge Cup on October 25, 1902, at Grosse Pointe. Working directly on the cars were Ford, Harold Wills, Ed Huff, Charles Beebe, and Gus Degener. The 999 — Ford and Malcomson's racer — was equipped with four seven-inch cylinders and developed horsepower of between 80 and 100. When it was ready for testing, Ford, Cooper, and Huff each tried driving it, but none was willing to drive it in the race. Cooper asked his friend Barney Oldfield, the bicycle racer who had never driven a motor car, to drive it. Barney practiced out of town for one week with Ed Huff coaching him. On the day of the race, Ford's friend "Night Owl John" used his horse to pull the racer from the city to the track; the car was far too noisy to drive in the city.

Barney Oldfield in the 999 won the five-mile race with a lap to spare; his time of 5:28 was an American record. The field of four included the famous Winton, who vowed that he would build a racer that could beat the 999. Ford retorted, "I'll build another machine that will go him one better if I have to design a cylinder as big as a hogshead. I am bound to keep the record in Detroit. "

The 999. Oldfield is gripping the steering lever, and Henry is standing beside him. This racer had twice the displacement and three times the horsepower of the one Henry had beaten Winton with just one year earlier. Oldfield drove it to victory on the Grosse Pointe racetrack on October 25, 1902. (P.0.833.2908)

After the race, Cooper left Detroit with the Arrow, a near duplicate of the 999. To Clara, it was good riddance. On October 27, 1902, she wrote to Milton:

I wrote you some time ago and have rec'd no answer, but think I promised to write again soon and tell you if Henry went to Cleveland to take part in the races. Well he did not, as his machine was not tried. I was very glad and so was he. I suppose you have heard of Winton's Pups. In the Cleveland race Mr. Harkness of New York beat the Pup and won the cup and after it was over they disputed the weight of the machine, and took the cup away from him. And a number of other things of the same type have come up that have disgusted Henry.

Well our races took place at last after being postponed twice. Henry sold his machine to Cooper two weeks ago, and thinks himself lucky to be rid of him. He caught him in a number of sneaky tricks. He [Cooper] was looking out for Cooper and Cooper only. He turned out to be just what you suspected of him. I am glad we are rid of him. I would not like you or Henry to travel with him. He thinks too much of low down women to suit me. His chum Barney Oldfield is going to run Henry's rig and Cooper his own. They are going to run races on their own.

Henry's rig beat again. Winton's rig was very bad. Sometimes it would not start at all, and the rest would have to go back and start over again. Henry called them down good and proper for it. And again Winton's rig would start up fine and get 1/4 around and perhaps 1/3 around and then stop. Mr Harkness of N.Y. and Winton started a twenty mile race. Winton gave up on the eighth round. I will send you papers that will tell you the exact truth.

Will Bryant was over tonight to talk over the races. He lives in our neighborhood. Ma, Edsel and I have been out to Kates, had a nice time. We went to Toledo then took Electric car, much pleasanter way than the old. Roy is getting on nicely in school. Eva is getting along slowly. Henry gave Roy a nice little gun, and they do a lot of target shooting. Pa is best shot. Hoping you are well and that you will write me soon and tell me about your self. I am your loving sister.

Clara's interest in her husband's affairs was keen and well informed. In particular, her distrust of Cooper (hence her desire to get Milton involved) seems to have been justified. Henry must have been quite comfortable discussing business with her and probably respected her opinions on such matters. Clara was learning the auto business along with him.

A few days after the race, Malcomson wrote the following letter to Henry:

I was very sorry I did not leave the letters for the News & Journal as agreed but wish to assure you it was not intentional on my part. Mr Couzens tells me Mr Wills is getting around and I am glad to hear it. Hope you will get everything running in good shape at the Shop, so that the work can be pushed at all possible speed. Our salvation for next Season will be in getting the machine out quickly and placing it on the market early, it is pleasing that you have been so successful thus far in getting the right kind of help. Mr Couzens and I called at the Shop last week and found quite a change, it is taking on quite a business aspect. Anything you may need while I am away will be attended to by Mr. Couzens, he can analyze the situation thoroughly. I did not see it myself but am told the Journal did you justice this week. Leave for New York tonight. Remember me to Mr Wills.

Henry's business focus after the race was to be on the "sample commercial vehicle" he had promised Malcomson.

One of Henry's helpers while building the 999 was Charles L. Beebe, who had an avid interest in mechanics and automobiles. His wife is said to have worn out a pair of gloves clapping for Ford during the race. The two couples had much in common and became friends. When Henry and Charles were not working in the little shop on Park Place, they were often working together at the Fords' Hendrie Street residence. According to Faye Beebe, the Beebes' daughter, the families often got together in the evening. While the men worked with auto parts on the kitchen table, Clara and Mrs. Beebe carried on long conversations, and Faye and Edsel, ages five and eight, played together. Henry and Charles would work far into the night, and Faye would shout, "When are you going to quit? Let's go home!"

By all accounts, Edsel was a well-mannered child with a gentle disposition; Faye Beebe, however, was quite a tomboy. Faye taught Edsel to slide down the banister and almost land in the cut-glass punchbowl Henry had won. Every time the Beebes visited, Clara had to move the punchbowl away from the stairs. On one occasion, when the Fords were visiting at the home of the Beebes, Faye decided that Edsel should know how to climb a tree. She managed to get him up an apple tree in the orchard. He fell and broke his arm and had to be rushed to the doctor.

On Sundays, the Beebes and the Fords would often go riding in one of their automobiles. Usually, it was the Beebe vehicle, which had a

Clara Ford and Edsel at the Bryant farm, 1902. Guns were a normal part of life for people who lived in the country. After Ford had achieved fame and wealth, both Henry and Clara possessed guns for protection. (P.0.3065)

back door and could accommodate all six members of the two families. According to Faye, the car was a "mongrel, having been assembled from parts that had fallen off other cars."

Clara's parents were getting older, and the issue of caring for them became a topic of discussion in the Bryant family. Kate wrote to Milton in Louisville on November 7, 1902:

You heard of course that Ma and Clara & son were out to visit us for a few days. We had a very nice visit. Ma seemed in very good spirits while Clara always seems happy. Edsel is a fine boy he enjoys himself immensely while out here, he says there is always something going on with the horses, and he does love to drive. Have done very well on the farm this year.

Clara said in her last letter that Eva is going to work in Heyns Bazaar, and Roy and she are going to stay in the city altogether. It seems very hard to think after Ma & Pa have raised ten children, that there isn't one left to comfort them as they are growing older. I think it is too bad to think they have to spend the long winter in that great big house all alone. I just feel like going back home to stay with them. We must write real often to them.

Henry's machine did fine work in the races, didn't it?

Eva wrote to Milton on December 12, 1902, giving the other side of the "Ma & Pa" issue:

You, no doubt, have heard that Roy and I are located in the city at last. Roy attends high school and I am teaching embroidery and doing sample work for Heyns Bazaar, we have a very nice suite of rooms on Second Ave. corner of Pitcher, the finest locality in town and are very contented and happy, we are within walking distance of the store and also the school and you never could believe how much good the exercise is doing me. Of course it isn't very nice for the folks to be left alone but I think we owe ourselves a certain duty as well as them—and they never gave us any advantages, so I don't feel the least bit sorry for them. We always go home Sat. night. Roy works for Mr. Blessed on Sat. you know it helps out some. Now about the Xmas presents—We are thinking of getting the folks two pairs of lace curtains and a couch if we can raise money enough, there will be only Kate, Clara, and you and I to put in this time so every cent you can give will be welcome. I can't do so very much as I have to help Roy a great deal and my wages are not enormous. Will you send it right away as I will not have any time to spare the last week. You had better send the money to Clara.

Eva left Detroit for California on her own later that winter, where she stayed with a girlfriend in boarding houses; Clara did not approve of her move. Roy, Clara's youngest brother, then moved in with Henry and Clara in order to finish school at Detroit's Central High School, which was seven miles from the Bryant farm in Greenfield Township. Clara's parents continued to live on the farm, and the children began to visit more often; an electric streetcar now served Grand River Avenue. Henry and Clara, of course, drove out by automobile. The large number of photographs taken by Henry at the Bryant farm are proof that the Fords were frequent visitors.

In December 1902, the "sample commercial vehicle" designed by Ford and Wills was completed. The Ford & Malcomson Partnership, with operations at 81 Park Place, took the name of Ford & Malcomson Company, Ltd. To keep abreast of automotive developments, Henry and

Clara attended the auto show in New York. Edsel stayed home and wrote to them as follows:

Detroit Mich
Jan. 16, 1903

Dear Papa and Mama

I received your telegram This P.M. We went to the temple theatre the show was good but I have seen better ones. There was a train wreck last night. Miss Gould of Taylor-Wolfendon was killed in it. The car was crossing the track when a grand trunk freight train came and shot the car a rod down the track. Aunt Jane came and stayed with me untill Roy came home from school. Eva was out with Frisky. We made fudge last night. We have had the music box going ever since.

Annie Meclaclan went down town with us this P.M. How does Papa like Fattered Tom. The train Wreck was on the corner of Gratiot Ave. and Dquindor. Eva knows a girl that was in the wreck. Eva gits mad sometimes at me. She told me to do this.

Askins moved their store 3 days ago. they opend their store today. The furnace has not gone out once yet. We have had the telephone wire hot every since, Frisky is coming to-morrow night. One of the girls is coming up from Heynze Bazzarr tomorrow afternoon.

I guess I will close for to-night. Write monday

Your little son ("of a gun")
Edsel

The following April, the Ford & Malcomson automotive operations moved from 81 Park Place to a larger building at 697 Mack Avenue. Malcomson leased the building from Albert Strelow, a prosperous building contractor, for seventy-five dollars a month. Strelow restored and enlarged the building for his new tenants.

The Ford & Malcomson Company could not raise funds to capitalize adequately. It was not until John S. Gray, Malcomson's wealthy uncle, came to the rescue with $10,500 in cash and a proviso that he be made president, that incorporation was feasible. The new company—Ford Motor Company—was incorporated on June 16, 1903, with a total of $28,000 cash invested by twelve stockholders. Gray was duly appointed president; Ford was made vice president and chief engineer with a salary of three hundred dollars a month.

At last, Ford had solid backing for the car of his dreams. In November, he purchased a dress suit for sixty-five dollars, a tuxedo coat for thirty dollars, a business suit for twenty-five dollars, and extra pants for another six dollars.

On May 27, 1903, two warranty deeds were signed. The first reads as follows: "William Ford a widower to Henry Ford and Clara Ford, for $1.00, 39 acres, plus 10 acres, plus 1 acre lying in Springwells and Dearborn Townships." This described the Ford homestead property that had been purchased in Henry's name alone a year earlier for four thousand dollars. The second deed, also for one dollar, again conveyed to both Henry and Clara property describing the eighty acres in Dearborn Township known as the Moir farm.

Edsel turned ten in 1903. On November 5, Clara sent invitations to his friends, including Marion Smith, a former neighbor on West Grand Boulevard:

Dear Marion:

I am giving a little theatre party at the Temple Sat. afternoon for Edsel's birthday and would like to have you come.

Be at 332 Hendrie Ave. at 1:15 P.M.

Dress warm for if the weather is fair we will take you in the auto.

Sincerely,
Mrs. H. Ford

Later, Marion sent a note to Clara, saying she remembered the party, that is was quite an event, and that it was the first time she had ridden in an automobile.

In her reminiscences, Clara's friend Ester Davis noted the following from this period: "Clara wasn't certain Edsel liked the name of Edsel, and wondered sometimes if Edsel liked his name. Clara thought perhaps children should choose their own name after reaching the age of perhaps sixteen or eighteen." Edsel was beginning to grow up.

Chapter 4
Ford Motor Company
Takes Off

*F*ord Motor Company's first car was the Model A. Little machinery was needed at Mack Avenue, because the parts were manufactured elsewhere according to the drawings of Ford and Wills and then assembled at the Mack Avenue plant. What machinery was needed for assembly was installed at the plant in June 1903. Plans were to sell the car as a runabout for $750 or with a tonneau for $850. About a dozen workmen, each receiving $1.50 a day, were expected to assemble fifteen cars a day.

Although well financed at the start, by mid-July, the company was down to a balance of $225.60 after paying for parts and wages. The day was saved by Dr. E. Pfennig in Chicago on July 15, who purchased a Ford for $850. An additional infusion of $5,000 from a new stockholder, the company's Mack Avenue landlord Mr. Strelow, brought an end to this first crisis. Business was brisk from then on. Within seven weeks, Ford Motor Company had $23,000 in the bank.

The company stockholders were probably extremely nervous in May and June of 1903, but Clara remained unperturbed. Henry's "Believer" purchased an ivory iron bed with Ideal springs for their apartment at 332 Hendrie and had a hair mattress and laundrying tick made over. A new Wilton rug from the William H. Elliot Company cost her $27. She also bought a gold locket ($8.50) and a clothes wringer ($3.50). There is no record that Clara had help with her housekeeping during this period; the clothes wringer is a pointed reminder of how backbreaking housework was in those days. In preparation for the coming fall, Henry purchased a lawn rake ($0.50) and an overcoat ($40). Clara subscribed to *Ladies Home Journal* ($1).

Ford Motor Company soon outgrew the Mack Avenue plant; at the end of 1903, the company moved to a well-planned building at Piquette and Beaubien streets that was ten times larger.

July 15, 1903
Ford Motor Company
sells its first car

March 8, 1905
William Ford,
Henry's father, dies

October 22, 1906
Henry Ford becomes
president of Ford Motor
Company

November 26, 1906
Jane Ford, Henry's sister, dies

October 1, 1908
First Model T is available

The Mack Avenue Plant, circa 1904. Ford Motor Company's first factory was located at Mack Avenue and Bellevue in Detroit; Malcomson paid seventy-five dollars a month in rent. By July 1903, fifteen workmen were on the payroll. A group of about a dozen workers could assemble at most fifteen cars a day. The second floor and ramp were constructed by the building's owner, Albert Strelow, to accommodate the paint shop. By that time, Strelow had become a stockholder. (P.188.8315)

Not all business developments were positive. A major threat to the company appeared on October 22, 1903, when the Electric Vehicle Company and George B. Selden sued Ford Motor Company for infringement of Selden's patent. Selden claimed his patent covered all automotive vehicles developed after 1879. This lawsuit would be an annoyance to the company for the next eight years. While trying to expand production and working capital, Ford Motor Company was forced to keep extra cash reserves on hand in the event of a judgment against it.

Racing was a popular form of advertising among early automobile manufacturers. Henry had vowed that he would not race on an oval track again after his defeat of Winton in 1901, and he never did. But on January 9, 1904, Henry took another hair-raising ride, this time racing a four-cylinder Ford on a straight course over the ice of Lake St. Clair at New Baltimore. Snow had been cleared, and the ice was covered with cinders. The track looked smooth, but it was not; often, Henry would hit a rift in the ice, and his vehicle would become airborne, sometimes landing askew.

Clara, Edsel, and Henry's crew (Spider Huff, C. H. Wills, and John Wandersee) were all on hand for the two p.m. race. Henry set an unofficial record of thirty-six seconds for the mile. The race had been advertised by Hotel Chesterfield, which treated Henry and his guests to a muskrat dinner. There was another run on January 12; the official speed for the same mile was posted as thirty-nine seconds. In either case, the world record had been broken.

In 1901, Clara had written glowingly of Henry's defeat of Winton; there is no written record of her reaction to this race. Watching Henry, who was now forty, flying through the air in a vehicle that was out of control must have been frightening. Henry decided to turn the racing

Ford Model A, 1903. This was the first car made by Ford Motor Company. Designed primarily by Ford and C. H. Wills, Model A's were assembled from purchased parts at the Mack Avenue plant at the rate of about fifteen per day. The car had a two-cylinder engine developing eight horsepower and weighing 1,250 pounds. It sold for $750 in 1903. (188.10193)

Hotel Chesterfield, C. A. Marantette, Prop.

AUTOMOBILE RACES

At New Baltimore,
SATURDAY, JANUARY 9th, 1904.

Henry Ford of the Ford Motor Works of Detroic will attempt to lower
the Worlds Record.

The Race will be over a four mile straight track on the ice opposite the Hotel Chesterfield.   The
snow will be cleared from the ice and the track will be sanded.   The races will start at 2
o'clock and continue until Mr. Ford lowers the worlds record.   He proposes to
make a mile in 36 seconds.

Starting points 2 miles below and 2 miles above New Baltimore.

There will also be ice boat racing for a valuable prize.

Come and see the fun.

Poster for January 9, 1904, race. (D.4)

Lake St. Clair, January 12, 1904. Henry sits on his racer, ready to better the world's speed record. From left to right: John Dodge, A. Y. Malcomson, John Anderson, Henry, James Couzens, and an unidentified man. "Spider" Huff, who rode with Ford in the race, may have taken this picture. The record-breaking race brought Ford tremendous publicity; Huff received a fifty-dollar bonus. (P.0.188.4747)

Atlantic City, 1905. Clara, Henry, and Edsel are easy to recognize. The gentleman with his arm around Edsel may be Clara's unmarried younger brother, Milton. Edsel and Milton seem to have been close friends; there are many photographs of them together at the Bryant farm during this period. (0.504)

over to young Frank Kulick, who had many of the daredevil attributes of Barney Oldfield. No doubt, Clara influenced Henry's decision.

In January 1904, Henry and Clara attended the auto show in New York, where Ford Motor Company had a display for the first time. John Wanamaker was one of Ford's retailers in New York City. Wanamaker's company sent Ford the following letter on July 15, 1904, regarding promotional racing arrangements:

> *We beg to thank you for your kindness in having Mr. Kulick here for the races. We have a few apologies to make for our stupidity in not making an entry several days ago. We found this morning when we wanted to enter the "Ford" that everything had been closed up and*

they would not accept our entry. It is a serious disappointment to us since we had expected to have the "Ford" run away with the "Cadillac" and its competitors. We had a fine engine and Mr. Kulick worked very hard to get the car ready.

Very truly yours.
John Wanamaker

P.S. Have arranged with the Cadillac people to race them after the meet at Empire Track. The car runs like a breeze. Kulick says with wire wheels he will do the mile in one flat.

At that time, Wanamaker's sold horseless carriages in the toy department.

During 1905, a workforce of three hundred was building twenty-five Fords a day. Two new models were introduced: the B, which sold for $2,000, and the C, at $950. Profits for 1905 were $200,000, and the first branch assembly plant was established in St. Louis. On April 1, 1906, the company purchased a fifty-seven-acre tract in Highland Park for $81,225, where the company would later build a larger plant. By July 1906, production at the recently built Piquette plant had reached one hundred cars a day.

Although Henry's company was producing a steady stream of automobiles, Clara was still boarding a horse at the North End Livery & Boarding Stable during the spring of 1906; the cost was fifteen dollars a month. She also purchased two whips and harness parts for $95.95, and on April 15, she rented a coach from the stable for six dollars. Clara disliked having to crank a gasoline engine, and she never drove one alone. During the Edison Avenue years, she drove an electric car, which required no cranking.

During 1906, Ford Motor Company purchased two thousand sets of tires from Firestone Tire & Rubber Company; at that time, it was the largest order for tires ever placed. Harvey Firestone, who became Henry's lifelong friend, responded by sending him an elegant firearm on January 30, 1907:

> One model 1907, .351 caliber high power Winchester Rifle, 20" Round Barrel, fancy English Stock, Pistol Grip and Fore-arm checked, Engraved on left side of Receiver "Henry Ford." No charge, Compliments Firestone Tire & Rubber Company.

The Model N, designed by Ford and Wills, was very popular; it sold for $500. Ford Motor Company was now manufacturing its own engines for the Model N at a separate location, and it was looking for a larger factory site. The Model N's success was an annoyance to

The Piquette Avenue Plant of Ford Motor Company in 1906. In this photograph, Clara is leaving the plant driving a Model N Ford car with her friend Myrle Clarkson beside her. Henry's office was on the ground floor to the left of the front entrance. This building, designed by Ford officials, was extremely appropriate for automotive production and is where the Model T was developed. At this date, the building still stands, and there is hope that it can be restored as Detroit's automotive history museum. (P.O. 3511)

Malcomson, who preferred larger and much more expensive cars such as the 1905 Model B and the 1906 Model K. While still treasurer of Ford Motor Company, Malcomson organized and became president of the Aerocar Company. Henry was not pleased.

On July 6, 1906, John S. Gray died, and the stockholders elected Henry Ford president. Ford wanted full control of the company. He and Couzens were doing the work of managing the company, and they were irritated by Malcomson's antics. On July 12, 1906, Ford borrowed money from Dime Savings Bank; Couzens endorsed his notes. Ford bought out Malcomson for $175,000, and Couzens became treasurer of the company. Ford now owned 58 percent of the shares but was considerably in debt. Three other stockholders who were friends of Malcomson also sold out to Ford and Couzens by September 1907.

Henry had been investing a good share of his own dividends in a separate corporation called Ford Manufacturing Company, which sup-

Henry and Edsel, 1906. This formal portrait was produced by Hartsock
Studio, Broadway Mercantile Place, Los Angeles. The original photograph
has a brown tone and was touched up to look like a drawing. (P.0.188.4783)

Clara driving a 1906 Model N on Grand Boulevard in Detroit. It was rare for Clara to drive a gasoline automobile; she did not agree with Henry that the engine was easy to crank. Alongside Clara is Myrle Clarkson, secretary at the Piquette plant. If the car stalled, it was likely Miss Clarkson who would do the cranking to restart it. (0.3344)

plied parts for Ford Motor Company. On July 5, 1907, Ford Motor Company decided to purchase Henry's new company for $450,000. Henry, the major stockholder, received $261,000 as his share of the selling price. This more than covered his debt from buying out Malcomson in June of the previous year.

With the retirement of that debt in 1907, Henry and Clara probably realized for the first time that they were becoming quite wealthy.

Things began to change at home. That summer, Clara started buying some prepared foods from catering firms; chicken sandwiches were $0.10 each, lobster salad $1.50 a quart, and tutti-frutti ice cream $0.75 a quart. A case of ginger ale from James Vernor was $0.70.

Although Ford Motor Company was doing well, 1907 was a year of panic for the automotive industry. Five companies in Detroit—including Malcomson's Aerocar—ceased production. Ford's idea of a small, inexpensive car had been a tremendous success; with Models N, R, S, and K, the company sales amounted to $4,701,298. Dividends, however, were low, because profits were used for expanded production facilities.

As befitted his company's growing stature, Henry took on increasing professional responsibilities during this period. He was a member of the Automobile Club of America and the Automobile Club of Detroit. As an officer of the Goods Roads Committee of the Department of Commerce, he contributed an extra one hundred dollars for the improvement of Woodward Avenue. In March 1907, he published an article in *Harper's Weekly* on vanadium steel, an alloy he was touting for its unusual strength.

Throughout 1904 and 1905, Henry and Clara also worked on fixing up the old Ford homestead in Dearborn. In March 1904, nursery stock was ordered, and in April, a pony harness cost them $23.90. These two purchases mark the beginning of major renovations. In September, Henry bought sixteen rolls of fence wire, and Clara bought inexpensive furniture from H. B. Barker & Sons—a table, four chairs, one bed, one spring, and two mattresses—for $29.25. Barker & Son were again called upon in December to supply one bed, one spring, and one mattress for $14.50. Six golden oak chairs cost $24, and a golden oak chiffonier was $17.50.

From Theo. Neuendorff, a Dearborn blacksmith, two pumps were purchased, one for a 35-foot well and one for a 26-foot well. In January 1905, a three-beam bobsled was bought for twenty dollars. Two stable blankets and a brush and comb were purchased from C. L. Livingston; a roller and fertilizer from J. W. Theison; and lumber, cement, and coal from J. D. Wallace—all totaling about six hundred dollars. Henry was also involved in the purchase of twenty hogs for $111.82 from Charles Roe Commission Co. of Detroit. Not all purchases were for the farm; Clara paid Mrs. A. V. Shephard, a dressmaker, $11.88 for a dress, of which $9.00 was for labor.

In the spring of 1906, there is another order for nursery stock: four catalpa trees, two flowering peach, one Althea, one white lilac, one early Crawford peach, and one crimson rambler. After so many rented apartments, Clara no doubt was yearning to have her own garden again. She and Henry would soon begin planning to build a house in Voight's Park.

As a young man, Henry had disliked farm labor; now, he was a gentleman farmer with hired hands doing the work under his personal guidance. He was farming both the Ford homestead and the Moir farm; taxes were $70.55, and fire insurance was $5.50. Although Henry had a lifelong aversion to horses, he was buying harnesses, blankets, collar pads, bridles, halters, a two-horse cultivator, a handy wagon, buggy net, lap robe, and whips.

For dairy production, Henry bought a milk separator and churn for $160. Soon, he was ordering clover and mixed baled hay in carload lots at thirteen dollars a ton and oat straw at nine dollars a ton. One bill for ten tons of hay (three carloads) was $138.51. A carload of yellow corn was purchased at 61.5 cents a bushel. The corn must have been fed to the hogs, for in 1908, Henry sold 4,890 pounds of pork to Parker-Webber & Company in Detroit at 6.65 cents a pound, totaling $325.

Henry bought a gasoline engine from his friend Charles Strelinger. Clara purchased a refrigerator for the homestead from Stone Brothers, and later a washboard, kettle, and three pans from J. L. Hudson Co.

At home, Clara was sending suits, skirts, and pants to the American Garment Cleaning Co. She subscribed to *St. Nicolas, Good Housekeeping,* and *Munsey. St. Nicolas* was a children's story magazine, and *Munsey* was a sophisticated adult magazine devoted to art, literature, and the stage. Henry and Clara often went to the theater. As for newspapers, they subscribed to the *Detroit Tribune* and the *Detroit News.*

Henry and Clara always found time to socialize with their brothers and sisters. The Bryant and Ford families, however, did not maintain close relationships. Clara's younger brother William, who lived in Detroit, wrote to Milton Bryant on July 11, 1904: "I haven't seen Henry's folks for about two months, so you can see how we visit back and forth."

It was during this period that Henry underwent a conversion of sorts. On occasion, he went hunting with Clara's brother Marvin on the Bryant farm. William Finzel, who lived nearby, went hunting with Marvin and Henry:

> Marvin was quite a hunter. When we were out at the farm he was always hunting and there was always a deer hanging in the barn. We practically always had venison there through the winter.

> One time Marvin, Mr. Ford, and myself went out hunting meadow larks. We went out one morning, and a meadow lark flew up. Mr. Ford and myself, in fact, all three of us, shot at it. I know that I wasn't within ten feet of it and Mr. Ford said he wasn't. Marv hit the bird pretty squarely and when he picked it

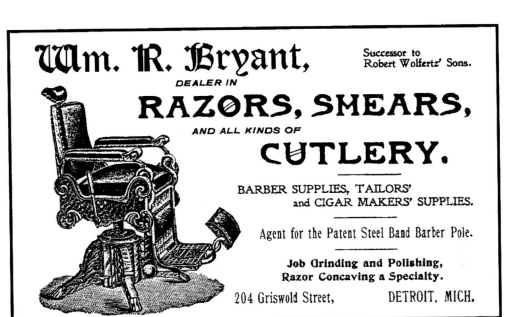

Clara's younger brother William was in business at 204 Griswold Street, Detroit, as "Manufacturer and Dealer in Cutlery and Barbers' Supplies." Among the wares advertised were tailors' shears and cigar makers' tools.

up, we all looked at that bird and Mr. Ford said, "Well, I'm through. When three big able-bodied men with guns will pick on a little bird like this, I've fired my last shot."

I said, "Well, I have too." Mr. Ford and I went back to the farm and Marv kept on hunting.

Henry continued to hunt and collect guns for several years after this. During the winter of 1906-07, he purchased several guns from Fletcher Hardware. Hunting was not just a sport but a necessity for survival on the Michigan frontier. As he and Clara grew older, they became active birdwatchers and conservationists, but they possessed firearms for personal protection throughout their lives.

Henry and Clara were still living almost next door to Henry's father, William, and sister Jane at 338 Hendrie when William died on March 8, 1905. William was seventy-eight years old and had suffered from paralysis for some time. The funeral took place at the farmhouse of his daughter Margaret Ruddiman on Emerson (Southfield) Road. Reverend Stephen W. Frisbie of Detroit provided the eulogy. William was buried in the Ford Cemetery on Joy Road near Greenfield, next to his wife, Mary.

It is not clear where Jane Ford, Henry's spinster sister, lived after her father's death. Jane had always been sickly and overweight; in September of the following year, there was a large medical bill from

Henry and Clara Ford and Martha Bryant at the Grand Canyon, 1906. Edsel took this photograph. They were traveling to Pasadena, California, where Clara's sister Eva lived, and to Seattle, where her brother Harry was at that time. It was a wonderful trip, especially for Clara's mother, Martha. (P.0.35287)

Christopher Campbell, M.D., of 318 West Grand Boulevard in Detroit. The bill had been sent to "Miss Jane Ford, 177 Joseph Campau Avenue" and was presumably paid by Henry on October 10, 1906. Jane died on November 26, 1906, of hemiplegia at the age of thirty-seven; she was buried in the Ford Cemetery. A receipt from B. Schroeter, florist, indicates that Henry purchased a "Pillow to Geisto" and a "Flat Bouquet of Lilies with ribbon" for the funeral.

After the death of his father in 1905, Henry and Clara had no reason to stay at 332 Hendrie. The new company was doing well, and their personal finances were improving. That fall, they moved to 145 Harper. A bill from Central Storage Company for moving two loads of furniture for six dollars (including a piano for an extra fifty cents) suggests that

the moving date was September 30, 1905. The new apartment was about three blocks closer to the Piquette plant; the rent was sixty dollars a month, substantially more than the sixteen-dollar rent for the Hendrie apartment.

On September 21, 1905, Edsel reported to Detroit University School; Henry paid his seventy-dollar tuition for the semester ending in January 1906. Edsel was now eleven; this was his fifth year in school.

Clara bought furnishings for the new apartment: linens from D. J. Healy, a set of new dishes from L. B. King & Co., two new chairs from Keenan & Jahn, and a "Bagdad Rug" ($177) and a Brussels rug ($40) from Newcomb-Endicott. She received $8.50 credit for her old Wilton rug. In preparation for the winter, two tons of "Egg & Stove" coal were purchased at $7.50 per ton plus $0.60 for "stowing." The family burned six tons of coal that season.

Percival L. D. Perry and his wife came to visit while the Fords were living at 145 Harper. Perry sold Ford cars in England and wanted Ford to establish a branch in Great Britain. The Perrys found the Ford home

145 Harper Avenue. The Fords entertained the Percival Perrys of England and the Gaston Plantiffs of New York here in 1906. Both gentlemen were important sales representatives for Ford Motor Company; their wives, Catherine Perry and Ellen Plantiff, became very good friends of Clara. This photograph was taken in 1939. (P.0.188.26468)

surprisingly simple, and Perry had to compete with Edsel for use of the bathroom. One conversation they had regarded a quote from the Bible; the Fords could not find their copy. Perry eventually played a major role in Ford's international operations; he is quoted as saying, "Ford is a man to whom you would give your last penny."

Gaston and Ellen Plantiff also stayed with the Fords at 145 Harper. Plantiff was manager of the New York branch of Ford Motor Company.

Throughout this period, Clara's unmarried sister, Eva, gave the Bryant family much cause for concern. Eva had moved to California, where she enjoyed an active social life as well as the climate. In 1903, Eva wrote to Clara about the beach parties at Poppy Cottage: "I did not think it possible to live so much in so short a time." She returned to Detroit in late 1903 but moved back to California a year or two later. The following excerpts, which trace her social life, are from letters written between 1903 and 1906.

Edsel wrote his parents when they attended the 1903 automobile show in New York:

> We are going into Pulfords this evening to-morrow eve, Eva is going to have Mary Gearheart and her fellow, "Chester," Wednesday eve, Eva is going to Mr. Risk here.

> Thursday night Eva is going to have some girls from Heyn's come up. Friday night we are (Roy, Eva, and I) going skating.

> Saturday night we are going to be all alone going to make fudge and eat nuts. Yesterday we had Miss Gearheart up to tea. Roy brought his skates in. he is going to stay with us all the week.

While on a trip to Cincinnati in February 1904, Henry received the following letter from Clara:

> I went out skating yesterday and again last night with Edsel and Eva. This morning with Miss Ward. I put Evas skates on her, but she was afraid so we will try again tomorrow with a chair, she is very anxious to learn.

In 1906, a letter from Eva in California probably gave Clara cause to regret teaching Eva how to skate:

> Having hilarious time for last three weeks, lost 18 lbs. so you will know I have been going some. I am either dancing or roller skating every night.

Another letter was even more disturbing:

George R. Brubaker, circa 1902. When George married Clara's sister Eva in 1907, Clara was not too happy about it. In 1915, George, Eva, and their two daughters, Grace and Bernice, moved to Dearborn, where George worked for Henry Ford & Son, and later for the D.T.& I. Railroad as secretary-treasurer. (0.15725)

Eva Grace Bryant, 1907. Clara's sister at about the time of her marriage to George Brubaker in California. (B.32026)

I am "dead broke" can you send $25.00. I'm going to a swell ball and I had to buy a dress. I borrowed the money from one of the girls. Dress is white point de spirit. Going with a swell fellow. P.S. Will you send it right soon.

Eva's letter in November 1906 probably caused both relief and consternation:

I am engaged to the dearest boy in the world—I suppose you will think this is rather sudden, but you know when you meet the right one it does not take long to make up your mind. He is not rich though. I used to just hate the idea of keeping house, but now I just can't wait until I have a nice little house of my own. Pa gave you and Kate a nice wedding but it is hard telling what he will do for me. It is awfully hard to be away out here from everybody.

She wrote again in December:

Clara hasn't Pa said anything about sending me some money—I'll worry my old head off if things keep up this way. The 25 from Ma was thankfully rec'd but that is only a drop in the bucket—barely enough for a taylor suit—I thought Pa would embrace the last opportunity to do a generous act.

Eva Grace Bryant was married to George R. Brubaker on February 7, 1907, in Los Angeles. George had his office in the Pacific Electric Building in Santa Anita. The newlyweds immediately started looking for a house in Altadena, but Eva would not have the nice home she wanted until five years later, in December 1912. Henry and Clara visited the Brubakers in California and bought Eva and her husband a house at the corner of Santa Rosa Avenue and Alameda Street in Altadena (then 2218 Santa Rosa, now 600 East Alameda). The location had been chosen by George Brubaker, with help from Louis J. Hampton, the local Ford agent.

George Brubaker later played a significant role in Ford Motor Company. Henry and Clara were quick to hire close relatives over outsiders. In particular, several members of the Bryant family received lucrative Ford dealerships.

The fall of 1907 brought the family medical problems. Edsel required dental work costing $166 by Dr. Milton T. Watson, an orthodontist. Clara had a more serious problem that resulted in major surgery. During October and November, she was examined by three doctors, including an anesthesiologist; the bills totaled $244. On November 26, Harper Hospital (considered the best in Detroit at that time) issued a bill for services rendered to Mrs. Ford:

Model T Touring Car, 1908. Henry's crowning achievement; 15 million would be sold over the next twenty years. Henry's chassis design remained basically the same, but some cosmetic and styling changes were later developed as a result of Edsel's influence. With lights and horn, this Touring Car sold for $850 in 1908. It had a speed of 40 miles per hour, carried 10 gallons of gas (enough for 225 miles), and weighed 1,200 pounds. The tires were 30 by 3.5 inches, and the wheelbase was 100 inches. A Roadster, Coupe, and Town Car were introduced the same year. (B.4449)

Room 4 wks @ 21.00: $84
Operating room: 5
Nurses Board—Miss Bruce: $1.50
Miss Bauer: 10.50
Miss Robertson: 14.00
Ambulance: 2.00
Extras—Champagne: 1.55
Total: $118.55

The hospital bill was paid on December 2, 1907, by the treasurer of Ford Motor Company, F. L. Klingensmith. Another receipt, dated

January 7, 1908, credits full payment of $2,700 by Mrs. Henry Ford to Dr. William F. Metcalf, whose business card read: "Physician, Practice Limited to Abdominal & Pelvic Surgery." Clara was forty-one at the time; the surgery may have been a hysterectomy.

Henry and Clara must have been pleased with Dr. Metcalf. A prominent surgeon on the staff of Harper Hospital, Metcalf resigned in 1909 to spend time organizing and raising money for Detroit General Hospital, to which Henry and Clara became major contributors and which Henry took over in 1912. Dr. Metcalf was responsible for bringing Dr. Frank Sladen to Detroit from Johns Hopkins University in January 1913; Sladen became chief of medicine at the new Henry Ford Hospital.

Another unfortunate event occurred that fall. The company's racing driver, Frank Kulick, was gravely injured in a race at the Michigan State Fairgrounds. Henry took an active part in getting Kulick out of the wreck and to a hospital. Kulick survived, but he never raced again. Henry had little enthusiasm for speed racing after that, even though he did not reform his own reckless driving habits.

On March 9, 1908, Ford Motor Company announced the Model T at a base price of $825; orders began to pour in. The Model T was designed principally by Ford, Wills, and Joe Galamb and was much better than the Model S or any other car in that price range. Deliveries began on October 1, 1908. At the Piquette plant, fourteen hundred men worked on a two-shift basis in late 1908; by 1910, the company employed three thousand workers to keep up with orders. Sales nearly doubled each year for the next six years, income rose by a factor of 23, and profits were enormous.

The Model T was an especially capable car for its time, thanks to a powerful motor in relation to its weight. It proved itself in many competitive events that involved negotiating muddy roads, climbing hills, and speeding on straightaways. Its ability to perform on rugged terrain was critical to its success, because of the lack of roads in America at that time.

Henry and Clara had begun to plan a house of their own. They bought two lots (440 and 441) in Voight's Park subdivision on Edison Avenue near the corner of Second Avenue on August 19, 1905. On November 7, two more lots (439 and 442) were purchased. A fifth lot (438) was added on June 14, 1907, giving them four adjoining lots and the corner of Edison and Second. Their land was only three blocks south of Alexander Malcomson's home at 63 Boston Boulevard. The neighborhood was about five miles out Woodward Avenue, nearly to Highland Park, about halfway between the Ford Piquette Plant and the future Ford Highland Park plant.

Chapter 5
The Edison Avenue Years

hings would never be the same for Henry and Clara. With the success of Ford Motor Company and the stunning popularity of the Model T, they had achieved wealth and prominence. On his fiftieth birthday, Henry quipped that the downside of their success was that "Mrs. Ford stopped cooking." Of course, there were many other downsides as well.

Clara had certainly earned the right to a more leisurely life. Charles E. Sorensen, who began working for Henry in 1905 and was one of his top lieutenants for decades, had the following to say about Clara during her early days in Detroit:

> Women's influence in business has ever been a controversial matter. I can follow Mrs. Ford and her part in the Ford Motor Company from the grandstand seat that I had. My first impression of her was gained when I was going for rides with Henry Ford on trips to see suppliers or checking on some work on a new car. He liked to stop for a few minutes at the home on John R Street. My first impression was that she was not too well. I believe she was delicate and sickly, but she was always bright and cheerful. My wife and I would go on Sundays to their country home and sit around the lawn and visit. We enjoyed these visits. Henry Ford and I would talk shop and she would perk up and inject a little sarcasm at some of our efforts. I learned that she was Henry Ford's real critic. . . . It was evident that Henry Ford shared his troubles with her.

> She had the courage to express her views on these problems when I was around. It convinced me that she was lending encouragement and urging Henry on in his work. She was

May–June 1908
Henry, Clara, and Edsel move to Edison Avenue

January 10, 1911
Ford wins the Selden patent suit

October 13, 1911
Martha Bench Bryant, Clara's mother, dies

June 1912
Edsel graduates from Detroit University School

July–August 1912
Henry, Clara, and Edsel tour England, Ireland, and France

The rear of the Edison Avenue home. Clara's flower garden is in the foreground; the garage is at the left. Note the flower boxes at some of the upstairs windows. The Fords loved this estate, but the publicity from Henry's five-dollar day forced them to move in 1914. (P.188.4776)

eternally loyal. She was what Henry Ford needed. She was very ambitious, there is no doubt about that. I saw more of this as time went on.

To begin with, her life with Henry Ford was not easy. They were just getting along with their small income. There was the shifting from one home to another. Every penny they had to spare Henry Ford used for his experimental work. That was before I knew her. She told my wife how hard she struggled to make ends meet. They had no time for a social life. They loved their farm and spent their weekends there. Edsel was seldom with them.

They had no servants. Everything was work to them. Their home they built later on Edison and Second Avenue was the result of her planning. It was far below what she could have had. She furnished it herself and it was not overdone.

It is not surprising that Clara confided in Mrs. Sorensen about her first twenty years of marriage to Henry at this point. Henry and his

The Edison Avenue home of the Fords on the northeast corner of Edison and Second Avenue in Detroit. The house was built during 1907 and early 1908 on several adjoining lots. Clara had the grounds plus a lot across the street professionally landscaped. The Model T was introduced in the fall of 1908, after this house was completed, so the house was built from profits on the Models N, R, and S. After a recent restoration, it was placed on the list of State Historic Sites. It is a fine example of the homes in the historic Boston-Edison district of Detroit. (188.9283)

"Believer" had turned the corner. Clara no longer had to worry about moving on a regular basis while trying to rear a small child and balance a tight household budget. She probably never complained to Henry, but those two decades must have taken a heavy toll on her. Looking back, she surely wondered how she had survived.

Henry and Clara had more time to spend together. There were pleasant weekend activities on their farm in Dearborn and plans for a new house on their Edison Avenue lots in Detroit. After leaving the Square House for Detroit almost two decades earlier, Clara was about to get her own home again.

The Edison Avenue house (the address is said to have been chosen by Henry in deference to his hero) was designed by Malcomson,

Clara's 1908 Detroit Electric automobile looked very much like the one pictured here. This model is the second Detroit Electric Henry bought for her, in 1914, and is now on display in the Henry Ford Museum. The passengers faced one another in parlor fashion, with the driver sitting in the rear of the car and steering with a lever. Flower vases were standard equipment; the vehicle's silent operation allowed for pleasant conversation. (B.41737)

Higginbotham & Clement (William G. Malcomson was a distant cousin to Alexander V. Malcomson). The primary architect was probably Hugh B. Clement. The house was built in Italian Renaissance Revival style and constructed of red brick with stone trim; there was a porch with stone columns. Inside were living and dining rooms, a den, three bedrooms, a kitchen, servants' quarters, and a butler's pantry. Except for the servants' quarters, the floor plan was simpler than one might expect from an up-and-coming industrialist and his wife. Henry and Clara had not yet fully understood all the demands of their new status.

Frank Goddard was in charge of construction (in 1911, he built his own house three blocks north of Edison on Boston Boulevard). Louis C. Scott, who was married to Clara's cousin and had been a driver for Ford in the New York-to-Seattle race, oversaw the work. Clara was more comfortable when a Bryant family member was involved in deals requiring trust and large sums of money.

Henry provided a well-equipped shop for Edsel and himself over the garage. Next to the garage, Edsel had a house for his dog, a Boston terrier Henry had bought for fifty dollars. (The dog was not very healthy and spent a good part of 1909 at the Strathearn Boarding Kennels; it was treated by a veterinarian on several occasions.) For his gasoline vehicles, Henry installed an above-ground gasoline tank that held about three hundred gallons. Edsel, at age fourteen, was already driving his own Model N.

Gasoline vehicles were responsible for the Fords' wealth, but Clara never liked the cranking needed to start them. Henry insisted cranking a Ford was easy and an electric starter was not a necessity on his cars, just a convenience. Every Model T from 1908 through 1927 was fitted with a permanent crank, but Clara won the battle at home. On July 20, 1908, Henry bought her a Model C Detroit Electric car for $2,600 from Anderson Carriage Company. It was a quiet, genteel vehicle that required no cranking and could run for several hours on one charge, making it suitable for running errands and attending social affairs around Detroit.

Clara took charge of furnishing the house. The following letter, dated January 21, 1908, came from Harry J. Dean Company at 167-171 Griswold Street in Detroit:

> *We propose to do the decorating, furnishing draperies, rugs, carpets, etc. for the interior of your new residence on Edison Ave., in accordance with the accompanying specifications, and sketches and fabrics submitted. The above work to be done in a first class manner, for the sum of Six Thousand Five Hundred Dollars, ($6,500).*

In May, Clara purchased a mahogany dresser, mahogany bed, box spring, and hair mattress from A. A. Gray Company. That same month, she also purchased an oak bed, box spring, hair mattress, oak desk, oak bureau, two chairs, a table, and a stand from the same company. In July, picture frames totaling $325.15 were purchased from James E. Hanna. By August 15, expenses charged by Harry J. Dean Company had accumulated to $10,588, considerably more than their January estimate of $6,500.

The bulk of the Fords' furniture — including the piano — seems to have been moved to 66 Edison Avenue from 145 Harper on May 29,

1908; there is a Riverside Storage & Cartage Company bill for twelve dollars on that date. According to tax and utility bills, the Fords completely vacated 145 Harper on June 30, 1908.

The move to Edison Avenue marked the beginning of Clara's library. She had always loved to read, and now she had both the money and the space to indulge her passion for books. For the next four years, Clara collected nearly a thousand volumes of English literary masterpieces; most came from the large New York publishing houses such as Charles Scribner's Sons and Houghton Mifflin, which sent her long lists of available first and special editions of noted titles. Nearly every well-known classic work was represented. Receipts, all credited to Clara, amounted to at least twenty thousand dollars. As Clara gained experience over the years, her acquisitions increased in quality.

Clara's other great love was gardening, and a greenhouse and gardens were planned. The greenhouse contract went to Lord & Burnam Company of Irvington-on-Hudson, New York; bills for its construction amounted to $6,361.32 in 1910. Clara supervised construction of the greenhouse as well as a summer house and pergola. After years of rented residences, Clara was going to indulge her green thumb on a grand scale.

Clara chose T. Glen Phillips, the well-known Detroit landscape architect, to design the grounds around the house and also the lot across the street. Phillips started work on September 5, 1908; his list of nursery stock included twenty-four shrubs, two hedgings, nineteen trees, and fifty-seven perennials. Clara participated in choosing both big and small plantings. By the end of the year, Phillips's bill was $1,193.41.

In August 1908, Henry, Clara, and Edsel took a break from the process of settling in at 66 Edison and spent a week at Hotel Cape May in Cape May, New Jersey. The Gaston Plantiffs of New York joined them for three days. The Fords' suite cost seventeen dollars a day, and the adjoining room for the Plantiffs was an additional five dollars a day. Laundry, telephone, carriage, and newsstand expenses added another $6.24. Henry paid for everything.

Henry did some business while in New Jersey. Local real estate agents guessed that he was going to build a large manufacturing plant nearby, and letters started arriving at 66 Edison offering luxurious vacation homes on the Jersey shore. On October 28, 1908, Henry and James Couzens did indeed invest twenty thousand dollars each in 357 acres of farmland and marsh on Cape May Harbor west of the inland waterway. The site could provide a seawater loading and unloading port, but it was never developed. (In July 1938, the property was sold for $4,500; Henry's loss after having paid property taxes of $26,800 was reported as $44,871.)

Of course, the new Ford home at 66 Edison would not be complete

Clara and her brother Roy relax on the back porch at 66 Edison Avenue about 1910. Clara, in the sun and bundled up, seems pensive. She is wearing heavy dark shoes and perhaps has been working in her garden. Edsel may have taken this snapshot. (B.33835)

without music. In March 1909, their friend Charles Beebe took a trip to New York to buy a variety of musical instruments from Grinnell Brothers for the Fords. The bill of sale lists a Steinway mahogany grand piano for $1,675 and a Themodist Metrostyle. On the same bill but dated one day later is a $2.50 charge for moving a piano from 66 Edison to W. Bryant of 938 Vinewood, Detroit (it was probably the piano that took Henry and Clara so many years to pay off). Also purchased were one Victrola for $200 with a dozen or so records and a Pianola player piano and music.

Clara also purchased subscriptions from her friend Mr. Beebe. Perennial choices were *Garden Magazine, Good Housekeeping, St. Nicolas,*

Detroit University High
School Track Team,
1909. Edsel stands at
the far right. (P.0.524)

Ladies Home Journal, and *Vogue.* Clara provided three gift subscriptions to her sister Eva, who lived in Los Angeles, and to Kate Raymond's children, Russell and Milton, when they lived at 80 Glynn Court in Detroit. Henry subscribed to *Scientific American.*

Edsel was getting interested in sports. In March 1909, Henry gave him a portable punching bag; the bag was mounted on a vertical stand and could be moved from room to room, depending on where Clara would allow it. At the end of April, Edsel rented canoe space No. 133 at the Belle Isle Boat Livery; the fee was ten dollars for the season.

In June 1909, a Model T "Special" was purchased for Edsel; the list price was $825, but a discount brought the price down to $701.25. Edsel had finished public school and was to attend Detroit University School, a private college preparatory institution. On September 1, 1909, Henry paid tuition of one hundred dollars a semester per student for both Edsel and Edsel's cousin Frederick Flaherty of Detroit. He was the grandson of Henry's aunt, Rebecca Ford Flaherty, who had taken Henry in when he left the farm in 1879.

Henry's friend and mentor William Cotter Maybury, former mayor of Detroit, died on May 7, 1909; Henry was invited to join members of the Detroit Board of Commerce in an official delegation to honor Maybury. A note on the invitation suggested that "the conventional costume, including frock coat, silk hat, and black gloves be worn."

Detroit society had taken notice of Henry's success. He was being invited into the city's top social circles. That same May, Henry accept-

ed membership in the Bankers Club of Detroit and joined the Country Club of Detroit located at Grosse Pointe Farms; the latter cost him $200 for initiation and $65 for annual membership. Then he joined the Detroit Golf Club ($125 for initiation and dues) and the next day purchased one share of stock for $250 in the Bloomfield Hills Golf Club.

Little or nothing is recorded of Clara's experiences during this time, but she was certainly being approached by the social elite and asked to join their activities. In the coming years, Clara would become a force to be reckoned with in the highest gardening circles.

Clothing was Clara's responsibility. According to Ester Davis, an old family friend:

> His [Henry's] clothes were always very well made. Mrs. Ford must have seen to it that he had very good tailors. He never wore any of those two-toned affair. . . . He always wanted to look nice. I'm sure Mrs. Ford was the one who looked after his clothes. It was her interest, more, in clothes that kept him interested.

> Mrs. Ford was dressed very daintily. From the first time I saw her, her clothes were always perfect. Her color combinations

Edsel takes his uncle Roy Bryant for a ride in his own Model T roadster in 1909. Edsel is fifteen years old, and his Uncle Roy is twenty-four. Roy stayed with Henry and Clara that year. This car is a standard Model T; the next year, Edsel had a custom-built open sports car built for him. (P.0.2570)

Clara in her garden at
66 Edison Avenue about
1912. (P.0.482)

were very nice, not noisy or loud. Her hats were always about the same type. . . . She had lovely clothes. She was rather a petite woman.

Clara was indeed petite and "pleasingly plump." As she and Henry moved into the social limelight, she became image-conscious.

A large number of archival photos of Clara show her penchant for extremely tall—almost overpowering—formal hats. Now that she and Henry were public figures and Edsel was fully grown, Clara donned hats tall enough to make her as tall as her male family members. The formal photographs of Clara in her tall hats speak eloquently of her rise in stature as the matriarch of the Ford family and Henry's mainstay, as well as how overwhelming it could be for a pioneer farm girl to become an international public figure.

After joining four clubs in one month, Henry declined applications to the Old Club at St. Clair Flats and the Au Sable Trout and Game Club. Henry replied that he did not have an interest in those forms of recreation, but the truth is that he had far more experience as a hunter than as a golfer. Although Henry had been heard to swear off hunting, in September 1908, he bought three guns for $211.56 from Fletcher Hardware Company in Detroit (two 35-caliber Remington rifles and one Winchester 12-gauge shotgun). Henry occasionally joined his friends on hunting trips along the Au Sable River in Lower Michigan and to the Upper Peninsula. As his sixteenth birthday approached, Edsel was initiated into the male rites of hunting; on November 9, 1909, Edsel was issued a deer-hunting license at Iron Mountain, County of Dickinson, Michigan.

The social elite of Detroit were not the only ones who took note of Henry's increasing wealth and status. He received the following neatly written letter from Greenfield dated November 2, 1908:

The young ladies of St. Mary's Church Redford, are preparing for a bazaar to be held in Witmantis Hall, Mar. 9-10-11.
One of the means used for making it a financial success is a voting contest. The candidates being three young ladies, one German, French, and Irish. I being the Irish girl, and the one most likely to fall far short, presume to appeal to some of the kind hearted business men of Detroit for votes, the price is ten cents a vote. The money is to be used for the interior decoration of the church.

Trusting you will consider my cause a worthy one I am

Sincerely Yours
Sadie Blanchfield

Ford Motor Company's treasurer answered on November 5:

In reply to your letter of Nov. 2nd, addressed to Mr. Henry Ford, beg to hand you herewith his check for $5.00 for 50 votes in your beauty contest.

With most earnest wishes for the success of the Irish girl, I remain,

Yours very truly, Frank Klingensmith

Requests for charitable donations from the Fords and their company would increase dramatically from this point on. Charity became an ongoing interest for Henry and Clara. Their charitable activities were characterized by involvement in determining how their gifts were utilized and an emphasis on education. Gulley Farm in Dearborn may have been their first major enterprise.

Henry gave Gulley Farm to Clara in November 1908. Clara's brother Fred Bryant was hired to manage it, and during October and November 1908, Henry paid twelve workers $1.50 a day at various jobs. Joseph Troster and William Hambly must have held managerial positions of some sort; Troster received three dollars a day and board, and Hambly got two dollars and board.

Gulley Farm was to raise something more than just crops and livestock. Henry had accepted membership on the Board of Council for the Protestant Orphan Asylum of Detroit in January 1909. In December of that same year, twenty iron beds and twenty kapok mattresses were delivered to the farm from A. A. Gray in Detroit. The Fords had offered to house, feed, and clothe a group of fifteen or so boys from the Protestant Orphan Asylum. Clara's landscape designer, T. G. Phillips, handled the necessary property alterations to accommodate the boys.

During the summer of 1909, Henry responded to monetary appeals from the Anti-Cigarette League of the United States and Canada, headquartered in Chicago. Their motto was "Save the Boy." Henry was strongly opposed to the use of tobacco and alcohol throughout his life.

In April 1910, J. F. Spence, director of Lincoln Memorial University with schools in Cumberland Gap and Knoxville, Tennessee, wrote the Fords asking for financial aid. The school's objective was:

> to educate the mountain whites, of the class from whence Lincoln came, having good brain and brawn, and each filled with the patriotic spirit. In this property there is six hundred acres of beautiful blue grass land, ten splendid buildings, and a number of cottages, six hundred and fifty students in roll, twenty teachers on the faculty, the school is industrial, agricultural, horticultural, mechanical. Many of the students work for their board, walk one hundred and fifty miles or more, and pull through on fifty dollars a year.

Henry replied that he "may consider later," and he did provide help sporadically. Gifts over the years included use of the two-hundred-acre Lon Overton Farm purchased in 1927 and donated to the school in 1933. Gifts of tractors, farm equipment, fertilizer, a schoolbus, an automobile, an Estey organ, and phonographs were valued at $47,679.

In June 1910, Henry sent his first donation (one hundred dollars for the scholarship fund) to the Tuskegee Institute in Alabama. This was the beginning of his acquaintanceship with Booker T. Washington and Dr. George Washington Carver.

Not all requests came from charities. In May 1910, Henry received

The Gulley farmhouse, where boys from the Protestant Orphan Asylum were given housing, food, and clothing in return for helping raise crops and livestock on the farm. These same boys became the nucleus of the Henry Ford Trade School, which over the years graduated eight thousand students. (Photo courtesy of the Dearborn Historical Museum)

a letter from his old friend J. M. Colquhoun, who ran the Owl Night Lunch Wagon, asking for help in finding a used automobile. That same month, Henry also learned that his former neighbor at 58 Bagley, Felix Julien, was in such poor physical condition in Los Angeles that he was not able to work. Mr. Julien had let Henry use his half of the shed behind Bagley to build the Quadricyle. Henry now helped him by sending the old carpenter money from time to time through a Ford dealer in

Los Angeles. Henry also offered to pay off the mortgage on Julien's house "if he would stop 'boozing.'" A few months later, the Ford dealer reported Julien was back at work.

Success made the Fords vulnerable in other areas as well. On Saturday afternoon, December 19, 1909, between five and six o'clock, a boy named Romp was running and collided with Henry's automobile on Michigan Avenue in Dearborn. Henry's insurance company wrote him the following:

> *We note that apparently there is no injury to this boy, but we would like to make absolutely sure about this, and believe the better way to secure the information would be through Mr. Ford himself . . . because if we start to investigate, it might make the boy's parents suspicious and result in their bringing a claim. If it is possible for you to get in touch with the boy's family to secure the desired information, we will thank you very much for doing so.*

Henry's secretary, Frank Klingensmith, replied: "Mr. Ford has seen this boy and made a liberal Christmas present and paid his doctor bill and he thinks there is no danger of anything further developing."

The architects presented their final statement of charges for 66 Edison Avenue in November 1909: $940 of the total $2,440, which was 5 percent of the $48,000 value assigned to the house. This covered "Complete Services, Drawings, Specifications & Superintendence of Buildings etc, Edison Ave."

Two other houses were being built near 66 Edison Avenue; their construction was under the direction of Clara's brother Marvin. One, at 80 Glynn Court, was for Kate and Sam Raymond, Clara's sister and brother-in-law. Sam was listed in the Detroit City Directory as a salesman. In 1910, the Raymonds moved in and lived there until Sam established a Ford dealership in Adrian, Michigan, in December 1911.

The other house, at 102 Glynn Court, was built for Henry's sister Margaret Ruddiman and her daughter Mary Catherine. Margaret's husband, James, had become too ill to work their farm on Southfield Road; they moved into Henry and Clara's Square House, where James died on August 5, 1909. During the winter of 1909-10, Margaret and Catherine were invited to stay at 66 Edison with Henry, Clara, and Edsel. Roy Bryant also stayed with the Fords that winter.

Catherine learned much from Aunt Clara about botany during that stay:

> I was seven years old the Fall Mother and I lived with Mr. and Mrs. Ford on Edison Avenue, Detroit. Mrs. Ford enjoyed her garden and greenhouse. This was a sunken garden, with a brick

and wooden wall around two sides, a pergola on the third side, the fourth side opened onto the driveway. Wide borders of perennial phlox banked the brick wall. The pungent fragrance of the phlox lingers in my memory. There was a pool with water lilies, and also many roses. Another flower that I remember was the "red hot poker." Mrs. Ford knew the botanical names of flowers but usually called them by their common or familiar name.

There were flowers in the house at all times. I remember one plant Mrs. Ford called "sensitive fern." When it was touched the fern folded up. I am afraid I made that fern do a lot of unnecessary work, as I liked to watch it fold up and so, touched it whenever I passed by. Mrs. Ford was very tolerant of a little seven-year-old with an inquisitive mind.

Mrs. Ford liked unusual plants as well as the old familiar ones: roses, phlox, and heliotrope. She was very fond of the tree plants which were taken up and wintered in the greenhouse. Another favorite was a very special pink geranium which she had slipped each year.

Catherine's reminiscences give us a peek into Ford family life during this period:

The work shop over the garage on Edison Avenue was an interesting place. One Sunday afternoon Edsel and I caught some very large crickets. Probably Edsel was collecting them for a science class and I was a willing helper and fascinated with their actions. We had them in a large glass jar, but thought they would be better in a cage. The cage was built. It was a family project. What would we give the crickets to eat? Mrs. Ford came to the rescue of the poor crickets with some red flannel material.

I learned to roller skate in the basement that winter. It was a family project, even Edsel, the high school student, was happy when I could stand up and finally skate by myself. We all stood on the front lawn and watched Halley's comet make its way across the heavens.

The Highland Park plant was completed and Model T cars were rolling off the assembly line. Sometimes Mr. Ford returned to the office in the evening, often the whole family went with him.

It was noisy but it was fun to see the wheels go round.

Margaret and Catherine moved into their new house in 1910 and lived there until 1921.

Despite the upscale comfort that Henry and Clara enjoyed in their new Edison Avenue house, they continued to spend considerable time on the old Ford homestead in the Dearborn area. They were also investing a sizable amount of their dividends in farmland, livestock, and equipment. Farming was in their blood, and good farmland and breeding stock must have been the first investment opportunities these children of pioneer farmers thought of once the money started pouring in.

Between October 18, 1907, and October 10, 1918, records show purchases of 5,053 acres in the township at a cost of $2,222,609. During the summer of 1909, Henry hired Fred Gregory as a special agent to buy farms in Dearborn Township. While Henry and Clara lived at the Edison address, Henry completed approximately 125 land transactions in the Dearborn area.

Henry's increasing land purchases drew the attention of a real estate agent in Detroit, who tried to interest Henry in large tracts on the Rouge River bordering Dearborn and Ecorse townships. In February 1910, Henry was offered about five hundred acres with the river dredged to within two miles of the property at a price of less than a thousand dollars an acre. At that time, Henry was promising to put a farm tractor on the market early the next year. No doubt, he was also considering the future location for the mammoth plant he would build on the Rouge River to produce tractors.

In 1908, Henry bought thirty-seven head of cattle from John I. Mason, a livestock broker at Union Stockyards in Chicago, for $661.06 (these may have been the Jersey cattle with which Henry stocked his dairy farm on the Moir property in Dearborn). He also bought a herd of Jersey cattle from T. F. Marsten of Bay City, Michigan, in March 1909. That same month, he bought a giant Avery steam tractor plowing outfit that pulled eight sixteen-inch plows and cost $3,798.25. Earlier that year, in January, Henry had purchased ninety tons of shredded cattle manure (shipped in hundred-pound bags) from the Pulverized Manure Company at Union Stock Yards in Chicago to sweeten the soil at Gulley Farm.

The dairy farm on the Moir property had cows, pigs, and chickens and supplied milk, eggs, and dressed chickens for use on Edison Avenue. Mr. and Mrs. Jerry Wolfe managed the farm, and Samuel Raymond, Clara's brother-in-law, for a while managed the dairy herd. Clara could make the trip to the farm on one battery charge in her electric car, and occasionally Henry would walk the entire eight miles to the farm and arrive in time to have breakfast with the Wolfes. The farm was a model operation. Men in white overalls milked the cows, donning a clean pair before each milking. Buildings were clean and neat, the grounds were well groomed, and hired helpers were plentiful. Mr. Wolfe had a team of heavy farm horses at his disposal (Henry had yet to develop a workable tractor). To Mr. Wolfe's relief, he was not expected to make a profit.

Henry and Clara's private investments also went to more traditional (and more lucrative) outlets. In February 1909, Henry wrote a nine-hundred-dollar check "for first call of 10% on your stock subscription in the Highland Park State Bank." The bank officers were James Couzens, president, and Ernest G. Liebold (an experienced banker), cashier. Henry had an account at this new bank in Highland Park, from which Klingensmith paid his bills. Henry and Clara also had a joint account at Detroit's National Bank of Commerce.

In April 1911, Henry purchased the D. P. Lapham Bank in Dearborn. It was renamed the Dearborn State Bank, and Ernest Liebold was appointed manager. Henry and Clara established a personal account with this bank, and henceforth Liebold paid nearly all of the bills charged to either Henry or Clara.

The bank takeover revealed a debt to the bank that Henry could not tolerate. A loan was outstanding to the Detroit-Dearborn Automobile Company, a firm that built a fine car but could not pay back the loan. The company was forced into bankruptcy.

Clara enjoyed farm life as much as Henry did, but for her there was an added bonus: it helped to keep her extended family employed. Her brother Fred Bryant was already running Gulley Farm. On July 12, 1909, Henry and Clara bought the Black Farm of two hundred acres on the Rouge River for forty thousand dollars. This became the center of the farming operations (later known collectively as Ford Farms), and Clara's brothers Marvin and Roy, both unmarried, lived at the Black Farm during this period. Marvin was the manager and Roy the bookkeeper. Their wages and bills were handled through Frank Klingensmith, Ford Motor Company's treasurer.

Edward Bryant, a married brother of Clara's who had his own house, was also hired. He worked as game warden on the Black Farm. At first, Edward paddled up and down the river in a canoe to ward off trespassers, but Henry was planning a game preserve on that land.

Among the stock Henry purchased were two pairs of Hungarian partridges and several pairs of bobwhite quail for breeding purposes. Henry searched for gray or black squirrels and bought two pairs of black squirrels from Edwards' Bird Store in Detroit. He turned down an offer of several bear cubs (offered by Hudson's Bay Company of Tanagami Park, Canada, at thirty-five dollars each and a "cross cub" for only twenty dollars) and two pairs of foxes. Late in 1909, Henry purchased seven head of cattle raised by the Eastern Michigan Asylum at Pontiac. Clara's

The "Bungalow" under construction about 1910 on the west bank of the Rouge River in the village of Dearborn. The location was across the river from the Black Farm house, headquarters of Ford Farms. Serving as a summer retreat, this clapboard structure was furnished less elegantly than was the home on Edison. Clara once was very upset to find Henry had been using some of her fine china for entertaining his friends at the Bungalow. (Photo courtesy of Dearborn Historical Museum.)

brother Milton helped Henry locate deer in Michigan's Upper Peninsula. R. C. Bradley, steward of the Hospital for the Insane at Newberry, shipped a buck to Dearborn in June 1909, but it died of heat prostration two days after arriving. Another buck was shipped during cooler weather.

More deer were to follow. In November, Charles S. Pierce, a state game, fish, and forestry warden, directed C. J. Phelps of West Branch, Michigan, to ship Henry "three nice fawns, one buck and two does," which had been taken from poachers. "I have given each [fawn] a quart of milk daily and with the clover heads in the hay, they have done fine— the two in the one crate are 'Teddy' and 'Lady'—the other 'Dolly.' They are quite tame when they want to be." The bill to Henry listed sixty- seven quarts of milk and one bale of clover hay as part of the shipping costs of $5.20.

A particularly private spot Henry and Clara liked very much was on a high bank of the Rouge River almost opposite the Black Farm. It was at the north end of Brady Street, which bordered the eastern edge of the Village of Dearborn. There they built a bungalow where they could stay overnight. In February 1910, architects Malcomson & Higginbotham provided Henry and Clara "Drawings of Bungalow (not erected)" for $88 and "Drawings of Bungalow as built" for $140. This small house was used considerably between 1910 and 1915 as a retreat and as a guest house, where close friends such as the Perrys, the Plantiffs, the Edisons, and naturalist John Burroughs were informally entertained.

During the quiet time Henry and Clara spent at the bungalow on the Rouge River, Henry got the idea of building a water-power plant for his Black Farm. On August 11, 1910, Gardner S. Williams, a professor of hydraulic engineering at the University of Michigan, visited the property at Henry's request and reported:

> After an examination of the grounds, I became convinced from the smallness of the fall and the character of the fall and the character of the location in general that the development of a water power plant would be an extremely expensive proposition for what the output would be. The development would run to $15,000 or $20,000.

As usual, Henry went his own way; he had little faith in college professors. On October 7, 1910, he ordered the following from James Leffel & Company of Springfield, Ohio: two thirty-five-inch Samson Leffel's water wheels, running left hand, together with shafts, couplings and bearings, to be shipped to Dearborn. Shipment was to be made in two weeks; the cost was $787. The power plant ran successfully for a number of years. It was replaced with a larger plant that powered the entire estate at Fair Lane. Henry and Clara were firm believers in self-sufficiency.

Edsel started his second year (tenth grade) at Detroit University School in the fall of 1910; Henry sent a check on September 28 to cover tuition and sundry expenses. Textbooks included *Wells Geometry Essentials*, $1.25; *Bacon's German Grammar*, $1.25; *History of Western Europe*, $1.60; and Cheyney's *A Short History of England*, $1.40. The school athletic fee was three dollars, and one pair of athletic shoes was seventy-five cents. (There is also a bill from Dr. Metcalf: "For Edsel Broken Arm, Sept. 1910, $35.") Two pencils and a tablet were twenty-five cents; the balance due the school on December 1910 was $14.55. At home, Edsel enjoyed reading the Horatio Alger books and was showing considerable artistic talent, particularly in sketching still lifes, including automobiles. Clara saved many of his drawings. Some of Edsel's early photographs also exhibit an artistic flair.

Edsel had developed another interest that caused Henry and Clara some concern: aviation. When Henry was invited to the Hotel Pontchartrain on December 16, 1908, to attend a meeting of the Aero Club of Michigan, he had asked permission for Edsel to attend. In 1910, Edsel and his friend Charles Van Auken built a plane with a Model T engine. After a few flights several feet off the ground, Van Auken struck a tree, damaged the plane, and was slightly injured. Henry canceled the project, and Edsel was forbidden to pilot a plane. Despite this, Edsel never lost his interest in flying.

Clara was most certainly in charge of the household staff at Edison

The dam and powerhouse built by Henry at the Black Farm in 1910. At the far side of the dam is a fish ladder aiding fish swimming upstream. The water was relatively pure, and fish were abundant. (Photo courtesy of Dearborn Historical Museum)

Avenue. On December 1, 1910, she asked Henry to pay a bill for seventy-five dollars from George R. Andrews, M.D., for treatment of her gardener, William Roberts. On January 17, 1911, Clara received a letter from Mr. Roberts:

> *Hoping you will pardon me for taking the liberty of writing you. The plants in plant house I promised to label for you. I shall be delighted to label if you wish me. Your past kindnes I shall not forget. I feel ashamed of myself to have come down so weak so as to be treated by a doctor. Last week a person sent for me who had taken the treatment twice, and advised me to throw the medicine away. He also was the means of finding me pleasant employment until I had gained my strength. I shall follow his advice and be through with drink and doctors. If there is anything about the heating system you would like to know, I shall be glad to furnish you with all the information on request to do so.*

Clara employed Roberts twice again. In 1913, he worked two to seven hours a day (at fifty cents an hour) preparing a mushroom bed at the Edison residence. Clara also employed a maid from the Women's Exchange at a rate of $2.50 per day, and for a time she had a Japanese couple—Kiku the maid and Kovel the houseman—in her employ.

The year 1911 started with a bang for Ford Motor Company. The suit against Selden's patent, which allowed the Association of Automobile Manufacturers to collect royalties on all automobiles manufactured since 1879, was settled on January 10. Eight long years of litigation (and millions of dollars in attorney fees) came to an end, and large amounts of money that had been set aside to pay for back royalties in case the company lost were now released for better uses. Henry and his allies were triumphant, and his reputation was again raised to new heights.

Edsel, now eighteen, was old enough to appreciate the magnitude of this event. He wrote in his diary on January 10 in capital letters: "HEARD THE GOOD NEWS, WON THE SELDEN SUIT." A banquet was held on January 13 at Rector's in New York for about fifty of the participants in the suit; Edsel skipped school and attended the affair.

Edsel and Clara — "self & son" — took dance lessons at the Strasburg School of Dancing during February and March of that year. They took five dance lessons together at three dollars each; and "son" took six music lessons at fifty cents each. These are the first documented music lessons for Edsel, although as a child he must have learned much from his mother at the family piano. Edsel's musical appreciation lasted a lifetime; in later years, he financed the Detroit Symphony Orchestra. His appreciation of a fellow student—Eleanor Clay—would also last a lifetime. He would marry her in 1916.

The farms Henry and Clara owned provided more than just fresh dairy, produce, and chickens for their table at Edison Avenue. About every two weeks during the summer of 1911, a load of about 250 gallons of gasoline was delivered to the Black Farm. This fuel was presumably used to test tractors. The previous winter, Henry had rented a barn at 1302 Woodward Avenue in Detroit at forty dollars a month; he hired six men to build "traction motors" from Model T parts together with special castings and wheels brought from Russell Wheel & Foundry Company at a cost of $515.41.

Ford Farms were a testing ground for tractors, but horses still did most of the heavy farm work. The following item appeared in the *Dearborn Independent* on April 11, 1911:

Roy Bryant, a brother-in-law of Henry Ford, the automobile manufacturer, and John Dunning, age 50, an employee of the Ford Farm, were badly injured Friday morning when the wagon in which they were driving was struck by a Detroit,

Jackson & Kalamazoo interurban car near the city limits. They had just driven out of the gateway at the Gray farm, when the car approached. The horses shied and then ran directly over the tracks. The wagon was dragged fully 200 feet before the car was brought to a stop. The injured men were taken to the hospital at Eloise, where it was found that Dunning had sustained a fractured arm and several fractured ribs. Bryant was able to leave the institution a short time later.

A later statement read:

John Dunning, who was badly injured in a street car accident near the city limits last week, died Monday at Harper Hospital as a result of his injuries. Dunning was 54 years of age. Roy Bryant is still at Harper Hospital. His injuries are not considered serious.

This was not the last accident on the Ford Farms.

As Ford Motor Company burgeoned, many firms and organizations were eager to become Ford's suppliers. Some were quite clever in their approach. One enterprising subscription agent, a Miss McDonald of Greenfield, inquired of Clara if Mr. Ford would like to give his employees magazines at Christmastime and offered to handle the orders. But surely one of the most unusual came from W. S. Adams, an agent at the Riverton, Wyoming, office of the Department of the Interior:

I have had inquiry in regard to taking Game Heads in payment for cars, both mounted and unmounted heads, consisting of ELK, DEER, and ANTELOPE. I can secure as fine a selection as can be found anywhere in exchange for cars, if you can use them.

If you care to do so, you can fix up one of the finest displays of Game Heads in your State, at a very small cost. I live in the heart of the Big Game country, and can secure the finest specimens that are to be had in the country. If your office is of sufficient size to hold eight or ten large Elk head, with Deer and Antelope mixed in, it would be a good advertisement and a pleasure to yourselves.

All of the fine saloons, Hotel lobbies and offices are using them, and sometimes the selections are very costly.

If you are interested in any thing of this kind I will be pleased to hear from you at once. If you will state what you could use, I will be in a position to trade one or two cars for a fine collection.

No game heads from Wyoming appeared in Henry's office. Instead, in late March 1911, seven large and elaborate birdhouses were delivered to the Black Farm. In addition, there were six bluebird nest boxes, six house wren and tree swallow boxes, and six chickadee boxes, all from Jacobs Bird House Company of Waynesburg, Pennsylvania.

Henry and Clara were getting seriously involved in birding. During the next few years, Henry would erect hundreds of birdhouses on all his farms. The lumber was purchased from C. R. Wilson Body Company, from which he had earlier bought automobile bodies. Thousands of "whitewood" pieces were used. Henry also bought dozens of leather-covered bird guides at a time for one dollar each and gave them to his friends, particularly to children.

Jefferson Butler, a Detroit attorney, wrote to Mr. Liebold in August 1911 that he had noted ninety species of birds on the Ford Farm in Dearborn. He felt that the number of species could be increased:

> There should be a place where wild rice could grow. An acre of sun-flowers should be grown yearly and the seed left for the birds. Mulberry trees should be planted on all parts of the farm. Two or three drinking fountains back from the river would attract many birds as numerous small birds could bathe that dare not try the river. I would add a greater variety of bird boxes. I think I could make Ford Farm famous as a nature farm but it would take time and money. I have a plan to submit later by which we could get large numbers of wild ducks and wild geese. . . . I am waiting to get a key to the gates before taking a delegation of School Teachers for a tramp. The Boy Scouts are also coming. If there is any more I can do kindly let me know.

It is not clear how many of these suggestions Henry implemented at that time, but his interest in birds only grew stronger over the years.

The French automaker Louis Renault toured the Highland Park plant with Henry as his guide on May 11, 1911. Renault praised Henry's work and invited him to visit the Renault plant in Paris. Henry must have had an equally high opinion of the Frenchman, for he had already placed an order for a Renault car. The Renault selling branch in New York had written him on April 19:

> I take this opportunity of enclosing a regular contract covering your order for an 18-24 six cylinder chassis for your son, and I desire in the meantime, to thank you very much for this order and assure you that I appreciate it particularly, coming from you.

On October 23, nearly six months later, Henry paid $4,045.60, the

Clara's parents, Melvin and Martha Bryant, with their granddaughter
Florence at the Bryant farm about 1908. Clara's brother William was
Florence's father. Pictures of Melvin are scarce; he is usually wearing a hat,
and there is some indication that at times he wore a toupee. This is perhaps
the best photograph of Melvin in the Ford Archives collection. (P.0.14954)

"balance due on 24 h.p. car, No. A3540," to Renault's New York branch. Contrary to the order confirmation from Renault, Edsel did not get this car. On December 7, Henry's secretary sent a check for eighteen dollars to the Michigan Secretary of State to cover 1912 registration fees for the following six automobiles: Henry Ford, Renault; Mrs. Henry Ford, Detroit Electric; Edsel B. Ford, Ford; Marvin Bryant, Ford; Roy Bryant, Ford; S. W. Raymond, Ford.

The Fords liked to slip away for a vacation during the month of August, and Niagara Falls was one of their favorite destinations. On August 26, 1911, E. G. Liebold wired for reservations at the Clifton Hotel in Niagara Falls for two connecting rooms in Clara Ford's name. Clara took her mother, Martha Bench Bryant, and Arvilla Bryant Turner, Martha's sister-in-law. They used cabs for local transportation; the four-day hotel cost was $79.75, which was paid on August 29.

This was probably the last trip that Clara's mother took. On October 13, 1911, Clara lost her beloved mother, and Henry lost a staunch supporter. Her obituary was highly complimentary:

> Mrs. Bryant was well known as a worker in the church and for charitable causes. She was a woman of unusual attainments and concerning her, Henry Ford, the automobile manufacturer says: "She was one of the greatest factors in my success." Surviving Mrs. Bryant, besides her husband and Mrs. Ford, are Mrs. S. W. Raymond, Edward L. Bryant, Marvin R. Bryant and Roy Bryant, all of Detroit; Mrs. George Brubaker, Los Angeles; Frederick Bryant, Pearl Beach, Mich.; Harry H. Bryant, Seattle; Milton D. Bryant, Traverse City.

Martha was buried in Woodmere Cemetery in the same Bryant lot as her sister Mary Anne.

Henry later said of his mother-in-law:

> There were three women in my life, my mother, my wife, and my mother-in-law. When all others lost faith in me when I was a young man, my mother-in-law didn't. She said, "You leave that young man alone. He will make out all right. I believe in him." She always had faith that I would succeed.

The Bryant family had lost its matriarch, but Clara had been groomed to take over the role and was already watching out for her brothers and sisters. The Bryant clan gathered on January 15, 1912, to form the Bryant Land Company; the incorporation document was signed by a majority of the children of Martha and Melvin Bryant, including Clara. Fred H. Bryant was chosen president, Marvin R.

Bryant vice president, and Roy Bryant secretary-treasurer. All male stockholders were directors. On January 31, 1912, letters were sent to those who could not attend the January 15 meeting (including Harry in Seattle and Milton in Traverse City):

> Shortly after the death of mother, the majority of us decided that it would be to the best interests of all concerned to have father deed the Greenfield property to the children, subject to a life lease, (which has been retained by him) to the children in the name of the Bryant Land Company, which has been regularly incorporated, and the property it now owns leased to Fred on a five year lease.
>
> The capital stock was fixed at $10,000, and comprises 100 shares at $100.00 each, and there being ten of us leaves 10 shares equally divided among us.
>
> To cover our expenses, an assessment of $5.00 has been levied upon each of us, and I trust you can send this amount to me by return mail.
>
> In am enclosing herein your certificate of stock standing in your name for ten shares, and would also ask that you sign and return the enclosed receipt.
>
> Trusting that this is agreeable to you, and with kindest regards, I am,
>
> Sincerely yours,
> Roy Bryant
> Secretary-Treasurer

A separate arrangement was made between Henry Ford and Clara's oldest brother, Fred H. Bryant. In this agreement, dated February 19, 1912, Henry offered twenty shares of Bryant Land Company stock, consisting of Clara's ten shares and Fred's ten shares or their value in cash, for the following commitment on the part of Fred:

> The said Fred H. Bryant, shall, will, and by these payments does agree to abide with, board, comfort and care for Melvin S. Bryant, father of the said Fred H. Bryant, during the period of the natural life of the aforesaid Melvin S. Bryant, to the satisfaction of all concerned.

The document was signed in the presence of E. G. Liebold, which suggests that the formation of the Bryant Land Company was the idea

Bryant Land Company
stock certificate for
Clara Ford.

of Henry and Clara. Certainly, of all the Bryant clan, Clara had the
most knowledge of such business matters, thanks to her life with Henry.
(The two original stock certificates still reside with the papers of Henry
and Clara Ford.)

In January 1912, Clara had started a diary and kept it up for three
months. Among the entries are frequent references to visits with close
friends and family (Rose and Dutee Flint, Margaret and Catherine
Ruddiman, Roy and Marvin Bryant), visits to the Garrick Theater
(almost always including Edsel), and walks in the country with Henry.
The entries on walks mention the birds and wildlife she saw. Henry may
have been paying for stocking their farms with birds and wildlife, but
Clara obviously enjoyed the results. She was just as involved as Henry
in creating wildlife preserves on their farms.

Jan 3 — Henry, Edsel & I went to N. Y. Arrived OK next morning.

Jan 5 — Rose Flint came over to spend a few days with me.

Jan 6 — Dutee Flint came to spend Sunday with us.

Jan 7 — Mr. Plantiff took us out to Country Club for dinner.

Jan 9 — Henry and Edsel visited Edison's laboratory.

Jan 11 — Arrived home 10:30, cold, Edsel went to school.

Feb 8 — Henry and I went to see "Little Women" played at Garrick.

Feb 10 — Maggie and Catherine [Ruddiman] stayed for dinner.

Feb 16 — Helped with church luncheon for Bishop Loyd & other clergymen.

Feb 22 — Stayed at home fearful of blizzard.

Feb 24 — Edsel & I went to see Fritzie Scheff in "Night Birds."

Feb 25 — Henry, Edsel & I went to farm. I put on rubber boots & tramped four miles.

Mar 2 — Took Kate to see the "Gamblers" at the Garrick.

Mar 3 — Henry & I walked to the bungalow on ice, saw rabbits, one cardinal, 12 quail and a number of muskrat houses.

Mar 1 — Edsel, Roy, Henry & I went to Grosse Pointe, walked on ice.

Mar 18 — Henry, Edsel, Marve & I went to hear McCormick sing.

Mar 23 — Henry, Marve, Roy, Kate & I went to hear Kubelik — very fine.

Mar 24 — Henry & I went to NY, Roy stayed nights with Edsel.

Mar 25 — Shopped all day, went to see "Bought & Paid For" in evening.

Mar 31 — Went to farm for breakfast. Made maple syrup, saw lots of birds.

April 1 — Henry has bad neuralgia, pains in shoulder.

Edsel's final report card from Detroit University School, dated June 1912, listed English, Geometry, German, Physics, and Mechanical Drawing. His grades were excellent; Clara had signed almost all of his report cards. William H. Murphy, president of the school, was Henry's friend, and Henry was on the board of trustees. Most of the graduates had prepared for colleges such as Harvard, Yale, and Princeton, although many enrolled at the University of Michigan. Edsel is said to have wanted to attend Cornell, but Henry had other plans for him.

Tuition that year at Detroit University School was $110 for primary instruction, $160 for intermediate, and $220 for secondary. During 1911-12, Henry had also been paying expenses for Wesley Ives of Dearborn at the University of Michigan, Ann Arbor. Wesley was the son of Mr. and Mrs. Louis Ives, longtime friends of Henry and Clara (see Appendix 2).

Edsel (left) and his uncle Roy Bryant in 1912. Edsel had graduated from Detroit University School and Roy from the Bryant and Stratten Business College. Both were living at 66 Edison Avenue with Henry and Clara. (B.32029)

During the summer of 1912, Henry and Clara took their first trip abroad. No doubt, the relief from settling the Selden lawsuit played a part, but the loss of Clara's mother probably also stirred a desire to search for family roots. Martha Bryant had emigrated from England in 1847; Henry's father had emigrated from Ireland in 1846. Whatever the impetus may have been, this journey was the beginning of a long effort by both Henry and Clara to trace their ancestors.

The Fords took Edsel and Marvin Bryant with them on this extended business and pleasure trip. Marvin was thirteen years younger than Clara and recently divorced from his first wife. Their ship, the *George Washington*, landed at Plymouth on July 20. Percival Perry of the London branch of Ford Motor Company met them and drove them in a Rolls-Royce to Exeter Cathedral, Windsor Park and Castle, and a variety of other castles, gardens, and factories in England. Perry and his wife, Catherine, had stayed with the Fords in 1906 during their visit to Detroit; now the Perrys returned the hospitality. (The diaries of both Clara and Edsel from this time are in Appendix 2.)

Clara's mother was originally from Warwick, England. In her diary, Clara describes the visit to her mother's home.

On board the *George Washington* during the summer 1912 trip to Europe. From left: Clara (in one of her signature tall hats), Henry, Edsel holding camera, Marvin Bryant, and their host, Percival Perry. The photographer is unknown. (P.0.747)

Arrived 7 P.M. Inquired about Grandma's home. Had supper at 9:30. All of us walked about town. Retired at 12. After breakfast we strolled into book stores and afterwards went into the church which grandmother attended, from the sexton we secured a copy of her certificate of baptism. We then went to Linen Street where we found her old home. Took pictures of it.

Ireland was next. They spent time in Cork, Clonakilty, Killarney, and Dublin. Near Clonakilty, Henry found and photographed the stone cottage where his father, William, had been born and where his grandparents, John and Thomasine, had lived. Edsel recorded the visit in a rather uninterested fashion:

We arrived in Cork at 9:30 had breakfast at Metropole Hotel. Walked around town. Father walked off alone—waited for him until 11, then drove to Blarney Castle saw some girls kiss the stone enough for me. Had lunch there, went on to Bandon then to Clonakilty found Aunt Ann's house took pictures saw church and school. Drove through rain to Bantry Bay stayed at Vickery's Hotel—rather poor. Saw much bog, lots of peat.

Edsel may have been bored, but Henry was eager for information regarding his family. On his walk in Cork that morning (August 10), he consulted with Reverend O'Connor of St. Mary's Cathedral and left a gift for the Sisters of the Assumption. Henry asked Reverend O'Connor to search for information regarding Henry's foster grandfather, Patrick Ahern. In a follow-up letter, Henry explained:

My grandfather, Patrick Ahern, lived here in Dearborn, Mich. in 1841, but sometime prior to that resided at Fair Lane, and it would appear to me that if your clerk would institute a search among the Ahern families who reside there during earlier years, some trace of them might be found.

The reverend replied as follows:

I shall certainly endeavor to do all I can to trace any members of the Ahern family that may still be living in or about Cork. Fair Lane is quite near this Cathedral, so there will be no difficulty in finding out if any of them are there or in the district around it.

Then it was on to France, where their escort was Mr. H. B. White of the Paris branch of Ford Motor Company. On August 25, they again boarded the *George Washington* at Cherbourg for the trip home.

Shortly after Henry's visit to Cork, the following advertisement appeared in Cork newspapers:

INFORMATION WANTED

Of the relatives of PATRICK AHERN, who resided at Fair Lane, Cork, about the years 1820-1840. He emigrated to America about the latter date, and lived at Dearborn, Michigan, in 1841. Any information which succeeds in locating them will be liberally rewarded. Apply to

HENRY FORD, Ford Motor Company
Detroit, Michigan, U.S.A.

A flood of letters arrived in Detroit. Mr. Liebold, Ford's secretary, screened them and found most respondents provided little useful information but were in expectation of a large reward or an inheritance or were asking a favor of some kind. One lady, Mrs. Anne Barry, who described herself as the "oldest inhabitant living in Fair Lane," was rewarded with five pounds at Reverend O'Connor's suggestion.

Chapter 6
Back to Dearborn

During the trip to England, Clara and Lady Catherine Perry had become close friends, and Henry and Sir Percival had a lengthy discussion on wages and the plight of the working man. Perry felt strongly that workers deserved a wage sufficient to allow them to support their families in a decent manner.

Back home in Michigan, the Fords would turn their energies to business and family life, with their horizons having been expanded by their European travels.

Beginning on August 1, 1911, nine separate transactions are recorded for property purchased by the Fords lying between Lake St. Clair and Jefferson Avenue. Included were five parcels from Josephine Gaukler costing $300,000, including what is known as the "Pointe." Another large property facing Lake St. Clair was purchased from William A. Dwyer for $188,690. Other purchases through March 1913 included such names as Trombley, Wacker, Piquette, and the Detroit and St. Clair Railway Company. Total costs added up to $677, 640. Almost immediately, a spate of publicity appeared in Detroit newspapers congratulating Henry Ford on his purchase of Grosse Pointe property and his intention of building a two-million-dollar residence facing Lake St. Clair.

Henry and Clara purchased a piece of property known as Gaukler's or Milk River Point from Jessica M. Brady on November 14, 1912. The price was $53,000. Although the Gaukler property had been purchased presumably as a residential site, it was never used by the Henry Fords for a residence. It was quite likely considered by Henry as an alternative site for his landlocked Highland Park factory. But on December 10, 1926, the property was sold to Edsel for the original purchase price, as the Edsel Fords by this time were planning a palatial home for themselves on the Gaukler site.

1912–1913
A deer and bird preserve is established on the Black Farm

Spring 1913
Building plans are under way for the Fair Lane residence

January 1, 1914
Five-dollar-a-day wages are started at Ford Motor Company

Spring 1915
The Fords move from Edison Avenue in Detroit to the Ten Eyck farmhouse in Dearborn

September 20, 1915
Henry and Clara establish Henry Ford Hospital in Detroit

December 4, 1915
Henry departs on the *Oscar II* for his peace mission to Europe

Spring 1916
Fair Lane is ready for the Fords

May 31, 1916
Henry and Clara purchase a home next to Thomas Edison's home in Fort Myers, Florida

November 1, 1916
Edsel Ford marries Eleanor Clay

Relatives of Henry and Clara had been eager to join in the profits of the Model T by applying for Ford dealerships. One of the earliest and most prolific dealerships in Michigan was that of E. G. Kingsford in Iron Mountain. His business included nearly twenty subdealerships across the Upper Peninsula. From a beginning in December 1908, he estimated his sales to be 200 cars per year by 1913. Kingsford was a son-in-law of Henry's aunt Nancy Flaherty, who was living in the Upper Peninsula at that time. Kingsford also later managed the more than 400,000 acres of timberland owned by Ford in the Upper Peninsula and founded the town of Kingsford, Michigan.

Henry's cousin Addison Ford was also among the first Ford dealers when he began selling Model T's at his farm in Dearborn Township in 1909. Clara's sister Kate's husband, Samuel Raymond, acquired a dealership in Adrian, Michigan, in November 1911. He added subdealerships in the smaller surrounding towns of Tecumseh, Blissfield, Morenci, Onsted, and Tipton. Henry had promised his brother-in-law all of Lenawee County, but Henry was soon adding other dealerships as well. In Adrian, Raymond received the standard 25 percent discount on his cars, while the subdealers received 20 percent with Raymond collecting the 5 percent difference. Milton Bryant, listed in 1912 as salesman for Ford Motor Company in Detroit, was associated that same year with a Ford dealership in Traverse City, Michigan.

Harry Bryant, Clara's brother, was given a dealership in 1913 in Boise, Idaho; Milton Bryant opened his own dealership in Traverse City in 1917; Roy Bryant purchased a Ford dealership in Xenia, Ohio, in May 1921, another in Detroit in 1925; Henry's brother Will was given the Fordson Tractor distributorship for Michigan and northern Ohio in 1920; Will Ford's son Burnham purchased a dealership in Flat Rock, Michigan, in 1924; and Robert Ford, son of Henry's brother John, obtained one in Dearborn in 1927.

By 1912, "Ford Farms," with operating headquarters still at the Black Farm, managed by Marvin Bryant with Roy as bookkeeper, was now getting increasing attention from Henry and Clara. Photographs show Henry and Clara in their Renault automobile with Henry's Aunt Nancy and Henry's cousins the Gardners all visiting the farm.

Edward L. Bryant also was working on the farm, but his outside work and overexposure to cold resulted in pneumonia, and he died on April 29, 1913, at age fifty. From Los Angeles, Eva sent this handwritten letter to Roy in Dearborn: "Am shocked at brother Ed's sudden death. The sorrow is hard to bear. I grieve with you all. Give Laura and family my heartfelt sympathy and condolence. Regret I cannot be there at this time. Will you kindly buy flowers for me. Will send five dollars."

Following Edward's death, and no doubt feeling somewhat responsible, Henry paid Edward's wife, Laura, the sum of $6,000, followed by

$100 per month as long as he lived. Clara then continued the payments for the rest of her life.

With war raging in Europe, Clara became aware of the plight of Belgian refugees who had fled their country and were homeless in England. With the help of their friend Percival Perry, the Fords leased Oughtrington Hall and its thirty acres of land. This estate was near Warrington, between Liverpool and Manchester, not a great distance from Clara's mother's birthplace. The mansion was renovated, furnished, and opened in fall 1914 to accommodate ninety refugees including families with children. Among them was a Catholic priest, a doctor, a pharmacist, a tailor, a dressmaker, and a shoemaker. Farm implements and livestock, supplied by Henry, allowed production of considerable food for the group. For the children, a teacher, a schoolroom, and playground equipment were provided. Trades were taught to adult refugees, and many of them eventually were able to find work and living quarters with relatives and friends in Britain. The Fords gave about ten thousand dollars a year to Oughtrington Hall for operating expenses, spending a total of more than one hundred thousand dollars for rent of the estate, food, shelter, clothing, and schooling for nearly four years before the home was closed near the end of the war in 1918. Final assets of several thousand dollars were turned over to the Manchester Belgian Refugee Committee.

Following Edward's death in 1913, Clara's father, Melvin, who was then traveling quite a bit, began sending letters to Laura, Edward's wife. In August 1913, he wrote from his son Harry's place in Seattle; in 1915 from Harry's Ford dealership in Boise. On January 3, 1916, he wrote a long letter to Laura from Eva's place in Los Angeles. Excerpts from these letters follow:

Seattle, August 16, 1913

Well Laura how are you all. Hope you are well. Neglected writing to you, have been very busy going around from one place to another. Got a letter from Fred saying they had a very bad storm out home. Up here very cool nites and mornings, very dry here. We were all out in the country last Sunday 45 miles, had a little picnic of our own, all but Harry. Sunday is his best day for business. He bought a new Ford car and Melvin drives it. He sold one of his cars the other day for two thousand cash. We are all going down to the Sound tonite to see the Admiral Samson *off to Alaska. Went out on the Sewamish river. Had a little picnic, two of the neighbors went with us. We took our cooking outfit along, cooked our chicken in the woods, took a beer along of course, got home eleven o'clock. . . . Harry and family are coming East next month to make you all a visit. We*

This photograph of Melvin Bryant, Clara's father, was taken by Melvin's grandson Edward Bryant shortly after the death of Clara's mother, Martha, in 1911. The street is said to be West Milwaukee Avenue in Detroit. (B.32320)

are going down through California to see Eva. I am going to stay at Los Angeles this winter if nothing happens. Laura do me a little favor. Please write a note to all of the boys and Kate not to write me letters after the 25th of next month, for I would not get them. Will write you all after I am there. They say its very warm in Frisco. Well this is all for this time so good by, love to all

Grand Paw

Boise, Idaho, July 30, 1915

Dear Laura and all. How are you all getting along, I am feeling well after my long trip from Detroit—twenty four hundred and 8 miles from Detroit. Well I think of you all. This is wonderful mountainous country. We went up in the mountains to the summit last Sunday 9 miles high, a very high altitude. Took our dinners with us, one of the ladies from the grand hotel. Had a fine time.

In the Boise ranges some great canyons some great sights. Very hot today 96 in the shade. Boise is a nice city but everything is very high. Plenty of fruit. Harry is very busy don't know which way to go first. Harry junior broke his left arm about 3 months ago. Fell from his wheel. We are all going to Frisco in August overland with a Ford car. Will start from Portland. Well good bye, love to all. Write soon.

M S Bryant

Los Angeles, California, January 3, 1916

Dear Laura and all. How are you all. We are all better now, have all been sick with grip and pneumonia I was very very sick did not get walking for 8 days. Eva was very sick. How did you enjoy Christmas. Rather lonsome I supose. Well it rained all day. Mount Wilson was covered with snow, looked very pretty only 8 miles away. First rain since last March, very warm in the middle of the day and cold nites. How is Wallace coming with his work in the factory. Los Angeles, Sacramento and Santa Monica are fine cities. We had a lovely Christmas tree all to ourselves Eva says she will answer Margarets letter as soon as she can. Guess Clara had a lonesome Christmas. I am planning to go both to San Diego and to Mexico in the Spring—might as well die for an old sheep as a lamb. A merry Christmas and a happy new year. Goodby to all. Write soon. My addres is 1239 Fedora Street Los Angeles California

Grand Paw

Henry and Clara spent considerable time at the Black Farm establishing the deer and bird reserve. About twenty acres were allotted to the "Deer Patch" and "Deer Park." Hundreds of birdhouses were erected to feed and protect Henry's favorite avian species. Henry had been taught to imitate bird calls by his grandfather Patrick. He would give bird identification books to children, hoping they, too, would take an interest in birds. In addition to sponsoring a project with the Michigan Audubon Society, building 500 birdhouses, and supplying special foods for the winter months, Henry, with help from his friend Thomas Edison, was promoting the Weeks-McLean Migratory Bird Bill which was passed by Congress in 1913. This bill gave the U.S. Department of Agriculture power to protect migratory and insectivorous birds in their flights from one habitat to another.

When the Fords had visited England, they were convinced that English songbirds possessed a more delightful melody than their American counterparts. In early 1913, Henry made arrangements with

Clara and Henry
birdwatching. This
photograph may have been
taken by Edsel at the
Bungalow in 1914. (P.0.701)

the Shackleton Apiary in London for the importation of 600 pairs of English songbirds, including finches, skylarks, linnets, blackbirds, nuthatches, grosbeaks, warblers, thrushes, cardinals, jays, bluebirds, and many more. Ornithologist A. Shackleton accompanied the birds on the long trip across the ocean, attending the cages with food and water. Quite a few birds died on the trip. The survivors were released on the grounds of the Black Farm (later Fair Lane) before dawn on April 16, 1913. Several hundred expensive birdhouses had been placed over hundreds of acres. Feeding stations — suet cages with millet, sunflower seeds, and cracked grain — were hung in a multitude of places. Newspapers described the Ford development as a "3000-acre Bird Paradise." It was disappointing, however, that the great majority of these birds soon vanished from sight.

In the fall of 1912, when Henry was creating his bird reservation on the Black Farm, he was reading books by naturalist John Burroughs and became fascinated with the philosophy of the elderly gentleman. The fol-

John Burroughs in the
Model T given to him
in 1913 by Henry.

lowing June, Burroughs visited the Fords in Detroit. At that time, Henry was also well aware of Jack Miner of Kingsville, Ontario, who had been tagging ducks and geese to determine their migration habits. Later, Henry would lend Miner a motion-picture crew to document migrations of Canada geese at Miner's bird sanctuary, and the Miners were invited to the old-fashioned dances later hosted by the Fords.

The Black Farm, which the Fords had purchased in 1909, managed in 1912 by Marvin Bryant, was being equipped as a dairy farm to accommodate 156 head of Ayrshire cattle. Henry intended to go into the retail milk business. A mammoth barn, 300 feet long, constructed with glazed tile to the roofline, and with attached twin silos, was dedicated on March 20, 1913. The very next day, a terrific windstorm destroyed the barn, and it was never rebuilt. No stock had yet been put into the barn, so there were no casualties. Henry blamed Marvin for the debacle.

Henry had been seeking a Dearborn location along the Michigan Central Railroad main line from Detroit to Chicago for his first tractor manufacturing plant. On February 8, 1913, he purchased an abandoned brickyard with railroad siding alongside the old brick-making buildings and three large water-filled clay pits. The eighty-five acres cost $15,000. At this same location, barely one mile from the Black Farm house, the Ford Engineering Laboratory was built in 1923.

Henry was also well into collecting farm machinery from his boyhood days. In 1913, he had found and restored the little steam engine he had used for threshing work for farmer Gleason in 1881. Having gathered other old threshing equipment, he was making the rounds of Dearborn farmers, offering to do their harvesting. With Ford Farms personnel, Henry would often put in a personal appearance at these summer and fall harvesting events and again operate the little engine. A. G. Wolfe, son of Jerry Wolfe, states in his reminiscences, "I think it's a well-known fact that Mr. Ford would create an extensive interest in a farm or a piece of machinery while he was learning about it; then after he'd learned about it, he'd start on something else."

Henry's nostalgia led him in many directions. In May 1913, he was inquiring into the availability of school seats from the period when he and Clara were in school. A letter addressed to Henry by C. J. Linendell of Adrian, Michigan, read as follows:

Dear Sir:

I find your school seats were bought from the Superior people of Muskegon, am enclosing an old price list and I think it will be the best thing for your board to direct to them for the repairs.

A turn-of-the-century list issued by the "Superior Manufacturing Company, Manufacturers of School and Church Furniture and Opera Chairs," provides prices for single and double maple seats ($1.80–$2.40, depending on size); adjustable desks ($2.20–$2.60); recitation seats with and without tablet arm ($.50–$.80 per running foot); oak teacher's desks ($4.75–$11.75).

While Henry was looking backward, Clara was looking forward. During the final quarter of 1913, at Detroit jewelers Grainger-Hannan-Kay, Clara spent $2,967.25 on items such as a "flexible diamond bracelet," a "diamond lavaliere," and a "gold bag."

When John Burroughs visited Detroit during July 1913, Henry showed him around the Ford Plant in Highland Park, and Henry and Clara entertained him for two days at the Bungalow in Dearborn. Burroughs, like Henry, was fond of birds, but he held a grudge against modern progress. To interest the elderly Burroughs in a Ford car, Henry shipped a Model T to his home so he could "get around more easily to witness nature." After more than his share of mishaps, Burroughs wrote about his Model T, "How ready it is to take to the ditch, or a tree, or a fence."

On September 30, 1913, Henry wrote a check for $272 to the Union Pacific Railroad for three fares, one drawing room, and one compartment to Pasadena for Clara, Edsel, and Roy Bryant. On October 15, in Pasadena, near the home of his sister Eva, Roy married Katharine Hayes Wright, a native of Circleville, Ohio, and daughter of Dr. and Mrs. Thompson-Barrett Wright. Katharine had been attending Stanford University. The newlyweds came back to Dearborn, where they made their home on Morley Avenue in a large house known as the "Honeymoon House," which had been built expressly for them. Roy was soon working for Henry Ford & Son.

Ford Motor Company, with its gigantic Highland Park plant and its twelve new American assembly facilities, was profiting to the extent that Henry and Clara were becoming embarrassed. The new federal income tax records would show Henry's 1913 income to be $6,359,133, taxed in steps from one to six percent, resulting in Henry's having to pay $372,287.02 at a tax rate averaging 5.8 percent. His salary being around $10,000 per month meant the bulk of the income was derived from Ford Motor Company dividends.

It was Henry's decision that some of the excess profits should be given to customers and employees. For customers, a rebate of fifty dollars per car was offered providing the number of cars sold reached 100,000 per year—a customer dividend of five million dollars. For employees, a startling plan was envisioned. Whether it was Ford's idea or James Couzens's is not clear, but on January 5, 1914, at a directors meeting at which only Ford, Couzens, and H. H. Rackham participated, a minimum wage of five dollars for an eight-hour day was established for all men age twenty-two and older, and for those ages eighteen to twenty-two providing they led an exemplary life—sober, saving, steady, and industrious. This involved about 25,000 employees. Clara was instrumental in having the raise apply also to office help. The concept was not new to Henry. In 1912, Perry had described a similar plan put into effect at Trafford Park in England, where a raise in minimum wage had resulted in better production as well as a better standard of living for workers.

Across the nation, Ford was hailed by the general public as the greatest and most generous American industrialist. Other manufacturers were aghast at such foolishness and predicted the Ford Motor Company surely would collapse after paying twice the wages others could afford to pay. Although Henry and Edsel were in New York the day of the public announcement, and the press clamored for an explanation, Henry insisted on telling only about the electric automobile Edsel was going to manufacture in Detroit using batteries supplied by Thomas Edison.

To help implement the wage plan, Dr. Samuel S. Marquis was engaged. Both Clara and Henry were well acquainted with Marquis and his wife, Marquis having been dean of St. Paul's Cathedral in Detroit since 1906. Clara, in particular, was a loyal follower of the Episcopal

The home at Harbor Beach, on Lake Huron about sixty miles north of Port Huron. The *Sialia* sometimes docked nearby, or the town could be reached by automobile or train from Detroit in a few hours. This was the Fords' summer home before they purchased the Huron Mountain property in 1929. (B.35283)

faith. The two couples often carried on lengthy discussions regarding family economics and factory working conditions. Ford was elated when Marquis joined the company and proclaimed, "I want you, Mark, to put Jesus Christ in my factory." Henry's sister Margaret states in her memoirs:

> My brother, even at an early age, had a very unprejudiced attitude toward religion. We were all unprejudiced because I think our home influence was there. We were taught that there was no difference. It was the way you live, and how you use it. That was instilled in me, and with my brother it was the same. We felt that one church wasn't the real answer. It was the way you lived and used your training.

On the corner of Cass Avenue and Ledyard Street in Detroit was the Priscilla Inn, occupying a five-story brick and stone building devoted to accommodating more than a hundred self-supporting young women. Clara was greatly interested in the welfare of these single ladies, and on April 2 she purchased 602 shares of Priscilla Inn Company stock valued at $6,020. Bills in Clara's files indicate she also had donated several sewing machines for the use of occupants. Although she owned only five percent of the stock, Clara was soon appointed treasurer. With property valued well over $100,000 and an annual profit of about $5,000, the company was able to pay an annual dividend of 2 percent. However, in later years, much higher city taxes together with social security taxes made operation of such a facility difficult. In 1943, Clara donated her stock back to the company, by then legally a nonprofit corporation.

Life was not easy at 66 Edison during 1914. The house, close to the street and not far from the factory, was besieged by men seeking five-dollar-a-day jobs. Henry and Clara found it necessary to get away as much as possible. The rustic Bungalow they had built in 1910 served admirably for entertaining guests during the summer months. Clara's guest book for the seasons in 1913 and 1914 lists perhaps a hundred visitors. The families of William, Milton, Edward, Kate, and Roy were listed, as were the E. G. Kingsfords of Iron Mountain. On July 30, 1913, George Cato and James Bishop attended Henry's fiftieth birthday party at the Bungalow. During the summer of 1914, the Flints of Providence, Rhode Island, were guests, as was Gaston Plantiff of New York. Sir Percival Perry of Manchester, England, and H. B. White of Paris, France, likewise were entertained in 1914. John Burroughs listed his address as "Slabsides." Thomas, Mina, and Charles Edison all signed in on October 25, 1914. The last entry was "S. W. Raymond and family, Adrian, Michigan."

In addition to the Bungalow in Dearborn, Henry, Clara, and Edsel spent some time at Harbor Beach on Lake Huron. This was about 150 miles from Detroit; one could reach the small town by rail, lake steamer, or automobile. At that location the Fords owned one of a group of cottages on the lakeshore governed by the Harbor Beach Association. The clubhouse opened in June. Bills show the Henry Fords shipped one auto from there to Detroit via the Detroit & Cleveland Navigation Company at the end of July 1914 and received a laundry bill from the Association that October. "Speed bumps" in the road in front of the cottages are said to have been necessary because of Edsel's fast driving. Later, both Henry and Edsel Ford's families occasionally used these Harbor Beach facilities.

The Louis Iveses of Dearborn were very good friends of Henry and Clara. On June 14, 1914, Mina Ives entertained eleven of her friends at luncheon, and among them were Clara Ford and her sister-in-law, Katharine Bryant. At this meeting, the Dearborn Garden Club was formed with Clara elected president. Clara later became president of the Woman's National Farm and Garden Association.

At the Edison Avenue residence for the 1914 season, William Ellis & Son charged sixty-five dollars for lawn work. As a Christmas gift to Eva, now Mrs. George Brubaker of Los Angeles, California, Clara ordered linens sent from Wm. Coulson & Sons of Antrim, Ireland.

Although a good many of Henry's friends had located their new homes in Grosse Pointe on the east side of Detroit, and Henry and Clara had been thinking of building their main residence there, as they began to observe the social life of Grosse Pointe there was considerable indecision. It was Clara who chose Dearborn over Grosse Pointe, feeling that the Fords' associates in Dearborn were more like themselves.

Henry had been in touch with Frank Lloyd Wright regarding a new residence, but the flamboyant avant-garde architect had just created a serious marital problem for himself and was not in a position to take on such a project. He offered the lucrative Henry Ford contract to a colleague, Marion Mahony Griffin, who would be assisted by the Chicago architectural firm of Von Holst and Fyfe.

By early spring 1913, there had apparently been an agreement between Henry Ford and Frank Goddard of Detroit concerning the hiring of Von Holst and Fyfe to provide sketches and an estimate of costs for a new home in Dearborn not to exceed $250,000. The Detroit contractors Goddard and Piggins began foundations for a residence to be called Fair Lane on the Black Farm site in Dearborn. The name *Fair Lane* undoubtedly came from Henry. His beloved foster grandfather, Patrick Ahern, had grown up in the Fair Lane district of Cork, Ireland, and during Henry's childhood, Patrick had depicted his homeland as a setting of beauty and birds.

Fair Lane would require a new and much larger powerhouse than had been operating at the Black Farm, both for the residence and to power the pumping station supplying water from the Rouge River to the village of Dearborn, population 1,200. Henry had committed himself to this arrangement on October 15, 1913. This larger powerhouse, a four-story structure costing $244,000, was dedicated by Henry's friend Thomas Edison on August 26, 1914. While the Edisons were in Dearborn, they were entertained at the Bungalow.

The new powerhouse would be equipped with two water-driven turbines on vertical shafts. Two electric generators produced 110 kilowatts of direct current. The turbines were supplied by James Leffel & Company in December 1913. Neither Edison nor Ford accepted alternating electric current as practical at that time. A paper entitled "Unique Hydraulic Power Plant at Henry Ford Farms" was delivered by designer Mark A. Replogie at the December 1915 meeting of the American Society of Mechanical Engineers. Also in the powerhouse were a twelve-car garage at ground level and Henry's private workshop on the top floor. A hydraulic-powered elevator moved heavy items from one floor to another. For his automobiles, Henry purchased two fuel tanks from S. F. Bowser Company, one for 240 gallons of lubricating oil and one to hold 1,000 gallons of gasoline. From the powerhouse, private systems of electricity, telephone, steam, compressed air, vacuum, and hot, cold, and refrigerated water were carried through a 300-foot pedestrian-size tunnel to the residence.

By early September 1913, a bid for a sewage disposal system for the Fair Lane residence had been offered by H. V. Von Holst. And somehow about that time, word got out that Ford planned to build a two-million-dollar marble mansion. This upset both Henry and Clara. A few months later, when Henry saw the bill of $115,920 for 2,200 tons of rough stones and 750 tons of cut stones, he said, "This is too much." A large amount of money was being spent with little evidence of work done. To settle, the Fords paid $142,300 and dismissed architects Von Holst and Fyfe on February 18, 1914. Later that year, the Fords' lawyer, Alfred Lucking, filed for damages against Goddard and Piggins, a case that seems to have extended until February 1922.

Searching for a new architect, Clara is said to have heard of W. H. Van Tine of Pittsburgh while she was shopping for furnature in New York and apparently recommended him to Henry. Van Tine was contacted by Henry in January, and on February 18, 1914, Van Tine was given the following written statement by Henry Ford: "To whom it may concern: This will testify that Mr. W. H. Van Tine is my architect and has authority to act in connection with the building of my residence at Dearborn, Michigan."

But there was also trouble with Van Tine, whose reputation was in question. On March 7, 1914, Liebold wrote Henry a long letter predicting that Van Tine could not be trusted to stay within an allotted budget and would take on responsibilities that had not been assigned to him. Van Tine was already using new unauthorized stationery with a Henry Ford letterhead. He immediately announced to the press that he would be hiring 1,000 men to build a one-million-dollar house for Henry Ford, that he would be general manager and consulting architect in laying out an estate of 5,875 acres along the river for twelve miles, and that he would have charge of design and construction of buildings, landscape architecture, furnishings, decorations, silverware, and so on. Just who drew in the reins on Van Tine is not known for certain, but it was likely Clara.

Clara's brother Marvin was still managing Ford Farms, receiving $200 a month. Roy helped him with accounting. Model T tractors were being tested on the farm. Marvin took it upon himself to provide a picture of a Ford Model T tractor to the Jarecki Chemical Company which was published in color on a Jarecki calendar advertising their "Fish and Bone Fertilizer." At the bottom of the calendar was printed: "Henry Ford Farm, Marvin Bryant, Manager." Henry did not like this one bit and told Marvin never to do it again. A "Henry Ford Farms" financial report for the year 1914, prepared by Roy Bryant and dated February 20, 1915, was addressed to E. G. Liebold. On it are listed expenses of

The Scandinavian-American liner *Oscar II* leaving the Hoboken, New Jersey, dock for Oslo, Norway, on its peace mission, December 5, 1915. An estimated fifteen thousand people, including Clara, Edsel, and Thomas Edison, crowded the dock to see them off. (P.0.636)

$138,634.70 and receipts of $12,566.41. Over the years, Ford Farms was to grow in size and grow in losses, to the point where year after year, the thousands of acres in Michigan, Massachusetts, and Georgia were losing from $800,000 to $1 million annually. At that point, the Internal Revenue Service refused to believe a viable business could lose so much and limited Ford's annual farm deductions to $25,000.

At this time, Henry, Clara, and Edsel were officially residing at 66 Edison and anxious to get away from the pressure surrounding them there. On February 13, 1915, Clara ordered a load of cartage moved from 66 Edison to Dearborn by Leonard's Reliable Storage Co. for twelve dollars. Then, on March 31, two more loads were moved by the same movers. On April 14, the same company put six roll rugs into storage for Clara. The moves of household goods are thought to have been to the Ten Eyck house located close to the Black Farm. That home, owned by the Fords, had been modernized in 1912 and was considered suitable as a temporary residence while Fair Lane was being constructed. Clara was quite insistent that the current occupants, the William Gregories, get out quickly.

On March 20, 1915, Clara paid five dollars to T. M. Fujimori, proprietor of the Japanese Reliable Employment Agency of New York City, for providing a butler. Sato not only worked as butler but was the cook and ran the laundry at the Ten Eyck residence for the Fords. He would later be the cook on the annual vacation trips enjoyed by Ford, Edison, and Firestone.

On April 23, Clara had a $400 phonograph sent to Marvin Bryant at Ford Farms in Dearborn. Through May 1915, tableware, china, and a desk set amounting to $965 were billed to Clara at 66 Edison. The last invoice to the Edison address seems to be the electric light bill dated June 7, 1915. On June 26, sixteen pounds of back bacon delivered to 66 Edison were forwarded to Dearborn. In August, Clara approved a contract for windows and door screens for the Fair Lane residence and powerhouse amounting to $9,155. The Fords may have spent the late summer on Lake Huron; J. L. Hudson, on September 4, sent four blankets to Harbor Beach addressed to Clara. Sent to Dearborn on September 8 were twelve copies of "Cause of War," a fifty-cent pamphlet and harbinger of trouble.

Henry had once told a reporter he would give all he possessed to stop the war in Europe, and he offered $1 million to inaugurate a worldwide campaign for peace. Henry's strong antipatriotic stance induced James Couzens to leave Ford Motor Company on October 12, 1915. When peace advocates Rosika Schwimmer and Louis Lodhner came to Detroit in November 1915 to get support from Ford for a peace conference with President Wilson in Washington, they were invited to the Ten Eyck residence to discuss the matter. Clara was quite impressed by Schwimmer's belief in the concept of "continuous mediation." Instead of meeting in Washington, however, Henry thought New York would offer added publicity. At a luncheon there on November 21, his speech was short and to the point. The *New York Times* quoted him as saying that "he had never made a speech and that this was the first time he had ever faced a public audience": "I simply want you to remember the slogan, 'Out of the trenches before Christmas, never to go back,' and I thank you for your attention."

Clara did her part for the cause. The *New York Tribune* on November 25 reported: "It will take the Women's Peace Party about two days to run through the $10,000 gift of Mrs. Henry Ford. Five thousand letters to the Pacific Coast went out yesterday urging women to send return telegrams to President Wilson asking him to call a peace conference." The appeal read, "For the sake of all the anxious mothers, dreading that their sons may be added to the ten millions already killed or crippled in the war, will you strengthen the appeal to be made next Friday to President Wilson by telegraphing him immediately as follows: 'We urge a conference of neutral nations dedicated to finding a just settlement of this war.'" Clara was invited to Washington to watch them "wire away" her $10,000, but she replied that she was too busy preparing Thanksgiving dinner.

Meanwhile, in New York, Henry asked Gaston Plantiff, manager of the New York branch of Ford Motor Company, to handle arrangements for a chartered ship, and the *Oscar II*, a Danish ship, was quickly obtained for the sail to Europe. It was scheduled to leave on December 4, allowing only nine days for organizing the trip. Clara recognized the venture as foolhardy, and President Wilson thought the same. Of Henry's close friends—Edison, Burroughs, Firestone, and Wanamaker—none agreed to go. Clara begged Reverend Marquis, Ernest Liebold, and Raymond Dahlinger to go with Henry, and they did. Clara and Edsel were in New York to see them off, trying up to the last minute to persuade Henry to change his mind, but he did not. Edison, a big smile on his face, was in the crowd with Clara and Edsel when the ship left the dock, and Henry, hatless, was smiling from the deck.

The *Oscar II* was filled with newsmen and photographers. By the time the group arrived in Oslo, Henry had caught a nasty cold and was advised by Marquis to return to America. What little Henry had to say to the press had nothing to do with peace but instead was about the wonderful tractor he was going to produce in Dearborn. Liebold was able to arrange a secret getaway for Henry and Marquis on the liner *S.S. Bergensjord* returning to New York on January 1, 1916. Liebold had agreed to stay on with the peace advocates for several more days in Europe.

While Henry was away during December 1915, Clara received this letter from Milton:

> *I have watched the press very carefully and am thoroughly disgusted with the criticism the papers have heaped upon Henry. I cannot understand why this should be so because if he could only save one human life his undertaking would be wonderfully successful and I surely admire his work and I have confidence in his success.*
>
> *I notice that he is slightly indisposed but trust that it is nothing serious. I also notice that sentiment is changing in his favor. He will make them take off their hats to him yet. I am too nervous to write you an intelligent letter tonight. We will be down to the Auto Show if nothing unforeseen prevents. Trusting you will all have as cheerful Xmas as possible and that Henry will return in the near future. I am with lots of love—Milton*

Henry received plenty of publicity both as a hero and as a nitwit. One American newspaper described him as "God's Fool." Henry's friend Burroughs remarked, "Henry's heart is bigger than his head. He might just as well try to hasten spring than try to hasten peace now." Ford's peace group, however, continued to the Hague and helped to form the Neutral Conference for Continuous Mediation, which stayed in session until February 1917. The venture cost Ford $465,000, which Henry viewed as inexpensive advertising.

At a 1915 Christmas party before Henry returned from Norway, Clara served a buffet luncheon with soft drinks and sandwiches to all the men employed on Fair Lane construction. During the 1914–15 construction of Fair Lane, between 500 and 800 artisans and craftsmen were employed. The house itself, according to Charles Voorhess, Ford's powerhouse engineer, is situated where the noisy Black Farm pigsty had been. The stonework exterior of both residence and powerhouse is of Marblehead-Buff limestone obtained from the Kelly Island Lime & Transport Company of Cleveland, Ohio. The house was to contain 31,770 square feet of floor space divided into fifty-six rooms. Included were a swimming pool, a bowling alley, a recreation room, a kitchen, service and storage rooms, seven bedrooms, and fifteen baths. The swimming pool (now a restaurant), bowling alley, billiard room, and golf fairway on the grounds were amenities for the benefit of Edsel, then twenty-one. The building's gray outer walls, eighteen to twenty-four inches thick, and inner partitions averaging fourteen inches thick, together with heavy carved oak and walnut interior trim and many massive fireplaces, presented to some a rather oppressive atmosphere. Clara would later have some of the darker interior paneling painted in light

A view of the Fair Lane residence showing the front entrance and curved driveway at the time of the building's completion in early 1916. The wing to the left is the swimming pool. (P.0.7170)

Henry Ford Hospital
as it appeared in 1927.
(P.189.4851)

colors, and both Henry and Clara were inclined to favor rooms well lighted by outside windows. The sun parlor facing the river was a favorite.

Between October 1915 and February 1916, carpeting for Fair Lane was ordered from B. Altman & Company of New York. On one list are fifty-four rugs, eight floor mats, two jardiniers, and several pillows. The rugs ranged in cost from $130.90 to $6,375.00, the former being for a brown rush basement porch carpet. Total cost of rugs amounted to $57,105.81. The rugs were all approved by Clara before Altman's received their payment. Clara turned down only one item, a $104.64 piece of linoleum. Yards and yards of linens, brocades, tapestries, silks, and velvets were supplied by stores such as John Wanamaker, Gimbel Brothers, and Arnold Constable of New York and Carson Pirie Scott, Marshall Field, and Mandel Brothers of Chicago.

Building the greenhouses was Clara's responsibility. She dealt with the Willens Construction Company, which bid $6,850 for three greenhouses, each eighty-three feet long and twenty feet wide, which were attached to the south side of the powerhouse. Nine hundred dollars was charged for disposing of a previously constructed conservatory on the site. In March 1915, Clara was also dealing with Jens Jensen of Chicago. The renowned Danish horticulturist and landscape artist was employed by Clara to convert the Black Farm yard and adjoining fields, meadows, and woodlands into a beautiful natural setting for the residence. Many visitors to Fair Lane are convinced that Jensen's contribution was more significant than the architecture of the residence itself. Added to the premises over time were the gatehouse, cottages, pony barns, peacock and chicken houses, boathouse, and grandchildren's playhouse. Altogether, the cost of Fair Lane is estimated to have been in the neighborhood of $3 million. At about the time of its completion, Henry asked his resident engineer, Voorhess, "Don't you think a fellow is a darn fool for building a place like this?"

Since 1909, Henry had been a member of the Detroit General Hospital Association. Henry was a major donor and was made chairman of the board of trustees. In 1911, work had begun on the hospital building. Progress was slow, however, because of insufficient financing, and members were proposing to turn the project over to the city of Detroit. In June 1914, Henry made the following offer:

Gentlemen:

Learning that it is proposed to turn the assets of the Detroit General Hospital over to the City of Detroit, and believing that this would be a serious mistake, both for the city and from every other point of view, I hereby make you the following proposition:

If you will make a good and sufficient deed to me or my assigns of the land and buildings now owned by you at the corner of West Grand Boulevard and Hamilton Boulevard, Detroit, Michigan, I will pay a sufficient sum of money on delivery of the deed to repay to each subscriber the moneys paid in by him or her to the hospital association, and I will assume the outstanding debts and contracts for buildings of the Detroit General Hospital, but you are to relieve me of all other obligations, such as continuing obligations to employ particular individuals and everything of that nature.

In conclusion I will state that it is my intention, if this proposition is accepted, to go forward with plans for a complete and creditable hospital for the benefit of Detroit.

As I am planning an absence from the City in a short time, please favor me with a prompt reply and greatly oblige.

Yours sincerely,
Henry Ford

The site and unfinished buildings of Detroit General Hospital were transferred on June 26, 1914, to Henry and Clara Ford, who, in turn,

The Clara Ford Nurses
Home was added to the
hospital in 1925.

deeded the property to the not-for-profit Henry Ford Hospital on
September 20, 1915. Completion of the buildings and staffing of the
hospital became the responsibility of E. G. Liebold. The Clara Ford
Nursing Home was added to the hospital in 1925. Clara paid particular
attention to the children's facilities and saw that every possible convenience was available to young patients. The Henry Ford Health System
now serves southeastern Michigan as an affiliate of the University of
Michigan Medical School and operates thirty-three outpatient clinics
throughout the area. Many view the Henry Ford Hospital as the greatest philanthropic accomplishment of the Fords.

The 1915 Panama-Pacific Exposition in San Francisco celebrated
the opening of the Panama Canal. Ford Motor Company was present-
ing a magnificent three-theme exhibit. The first part included a demonstration of the moving automobile assembly line building twenty-five
Model T cars a day; the second part showed the remarkable improvement in worker living conditions brought about by the five-dollar day
introduced by Ford; and the third part presented motion pictures show-

Clara and Rose Flint
enjoying themselves at the
Panama-Pacific Exposition
in early November 1915.
(P.0.4015)

ing classes in English and citizenship for foreign-born workers and the
Highland Park factory operations where 1,000 cars a day were produced.

On October 13, Henry had reserved the private railroad car
Washington to accommodate twenty-five people on a round trip to
California, starting October 14 in Detroit and returning to Detroit on
November 13. Payment to the Pullman Company was $1,715 for the
car rental and $750 for commissary supplies. The trip included
stopovers of one day at Lake Tahoe, ten days at the Exposition in San
Francisco, one week at Los Angeles, two days at the Grand Canyon, two
days at Colorado Springs, and one day in Denver. On October 14, the
Detroit passenger agent of New York Central Lines notified the manager of the Inside Inn, on the Exposition Grounds, that "Mr. Ford's

The 1915 visit to the home of Luther Burbank at Santa Rosa, California. The photograph was taken on the front steps of the twelve-room house built in 1906. From left to right are: Dutee Flint, Mrs. Kellogg (local society writer), Edsel Ford, Emma Burbank Beeson (Luther's sister), William G. Bee (Edison's secretary), unknown lady, Harvey Firestone, Elizabeth Waters (Burbank's secretary, and later Burbank's second wife), Mrs. Edison, the Edisons' son Charles, Thomas Edison, unknown lady (partially visible), Luther Burbank, Henry Ford, Clara Ford, Dutee Flint's father-in-law, a Burbank servant, Mrs. Dutee Flint, Roy Bryant, and an unidentified gentleman. (P.188.16057)

room should of course be the best of those reserved. Also please see that Mr. Edsel Ford, Mr. Henry Ford's son, has a good room adjoining those occupied by his father and mother."

On October 18, "Mr. Henry Ford and Party" registered with the Inside Inn in San Francisco for ten days, paying a bill of $375.10 when they left. Frank Vivian of the Ford Motor Company office in San Francisco handled local arrangements. Edison and Firestone had planned to be in San Francisco at the same time. Together, Edison, Ford, and Firestone, with their families, took a private car up to Santa Rosa, where they were entertained by Luther Burbank, along with Burbank's sister Emma and Burbank's secretary, Elizabeth Waters. Henry was so impressed by Burbank's botanical accomplishments that in 1928 he would have the California Garden Office of Burbank moved to Greenfield Village and would place Burbank's spade at the entrance to Henry Ford Museum. In 1936, Henry would arrange to purchase, dismantle, and move the 1800 birthplace of Burbank from Lancaster, Massachusetts, to Greenfield Village. Henry's attempt to move the remains of Burbank's dog from California to Michigan, however, failed. Mrs. Burbank would not allow it.

A few days after the Santa Rosa visit, Ford, Edison, and Firestone traveled together down to San Diego. These short trips in 1915 inspired the three men to plan similar summer vacation trips together in future years.

Because Clara's brother Edward had died in 1913 while employed by the Fords, Clara felt obligated to help his children. From Dearborn, on 66 Edison stationery, Clara wrote a letter postmarked December 15, 1915, to her brother Edward's seventeen-year-old son:

Master Edward Bryant
Interlaken School
Rolling Prairie, Ind.

Dear Edward:

I rec'd your letter yesterday and am glad you are getting along so well. You may draw money enough for your R.R. fare and return, but not any for clothes.

We are having very cold weather for the first time, and we feel it. Uncle Henry and I have just returned from New York and Washington. And both cities were especially nice at this time of year. Will see when you return home.

With best wishes
From Aunt Clara

On Fair Lane stationery, following the holidays, Clara again wrote:

Dear Edward:

Enclosed please find bill, for which I would like an account from you. When you asked if you could have a new suit, as the one you had was a little shabby, I said you might, and knowing what you had paid before, cannot understand how you could pay $24.00 for a suit, and five dollars for a hat, also how did it cost you $11.60 R.R. fare to Detroit? And I bought you all the shoes you could possibly wear for a year or more. How did all this happen! Please do not come out to see me, as I will be too busy this week, but write and explain, and send me back the bill.

Sincerely
Aunt Clara

The bride, Eleanor Clay, daughter of Mrs. Elizabeth Clay of Grosse Pointe. (P.0.5965)

From the Estey Organ Company of Battleboro, Vermont, in late 1915, Henry had ordered a pipe organ for Fair Lane. It was a 125-note player rather than the standard 100-note player. Henry had visited Battleboro and asked Jacob Estey to provide him with a confidential list of employees and their salaries. To the 273 employees Henry sent individual bonus checks based on a percentage of their regular pay. These checks totaled $3,154 in addition to a final payment of $3,503.50 for the organ. The organ arrived at Fair Lane on February 5, 1917, having been delayed not only by the war but also by installation of a similar organ for Ransom E. Olds at his home on Grosse Ile. Also delivered to Fair Lane were 127 player rolls. Clara would decide which selections she wanted by listening to them. This, of course, took some time, and it wasn't until September that $464 was paid for music. A screen separated the pipes from the parlor, and as the years passed the organ became used less and less until Clara decided the space occupied by the organ pipes should be converted into a private study for Henry. It is said the Estey organ was removed and given to a local church.

Edsel never spent much time at Fair Lane. He apparently paid little attention to the features that were designed just for him. While Henry and Clara were getting settled during the spring of 1916, Edsel was golfing in Hot Springs, Virginia, and spending time with the Clays

The groom, Edsel Bryant Ford, only child of Henry and Clara Ford of Dearborn. (P.833.5463)

and Kanzlers in New York City. From New York, Edsel wrote: "We had a slick time . . . with Eleanor and Josephine. We were shopping with them two afternoons. Were in Lucille's—saw some beautiful gowns. Eleanor is buying a trousseau, fancy that." Edsel was engaged to Eleanor Clay, an intelligent and wholesome girl with whom he had attended dancing classes years earlier. Eleanor was a niece of J. L. Hudson, founder of Detroit's most prestigious department store. Both Henry and Clara liked Eleanor very much. After a honeymoon trip to California and Hawaii, the couple made their home at 439 Iroquois Avenue, in a fashionable district east of downtown Detroit. Edsel and Eleanor would have four children: Henry II (born in 1917), Benson (1919), Josephine (1923), and William (1925).

From Detroit newspaper clippings:

The marriage took place the evening of November 1, 1916, at the home of Eleanor's uncle at 63 Boston Boulevard. Attendance was limited to close friends and relatives, and although millions of dollars were represented, the wedding was simple, having the air of a quiet family affair with no attempt at display. The bride had not yet entered Detroit society. Few jewels were evident and the wedding was quite similar to that of any bride of middle class. A Russian motif was prominent among the gowns, as well as Russian head-dresses of pearls and rhinestones. Mrs. William Clay wore a gown of taupe velvet, and Clara Ford was dressed in apricot-yellow and tulle of the same shade. Among the bride's attendants was Eleanor's sister Josephine Clay, and the best man attending Edsel was Thomas Whitehead, a close friend and Harbor Beach neighbor. Dominating the guests were those of the younger generation; whereas those of the age of Henry and Clara as well as Eleanor's widowed mother, Elizabeth Clay, remained in the background. A simple ceremony was conducted by Reverend H. Smith of Central M.E. Church. The orchestra played the wedding march by Lohengrin, the service was short and ended with a prayer. A group of a hundred or so friends were outside the door to greet the bride and groom as they left the house.

The Ford home at 66 Edison Avenue (now 140 Edison) was sold by Henry and Clara in March 1916 to Annie D. Murphy, sister of the William Murphy who had backed Henry in his early automobile ventures. The home now belongs to Jerald and Marilyn Mitchell and family. The Mitchells have restored the home, and a historic marker designates it as a State Historic Site.

In June 1916, a bird fountain was being built at Fair Lane in honor of John Burroughs, who was to lay the cornerstone. Thomas Edison would give a short speech and place a written copy of the speech in the cornerstone. Clara wrote the speech for Edison. In her own handwriting, it reads as follows:

June 6, 1916

Mr. Ford has asked me to write something to be placed in the cornerstone of his new bird fountain which cornerstone is to be laid by that lover of nature, John Burroughs.

I am greatly pleased to do so, because while mankind appears to have been gradually drifting into an artificial life of merciless commercialism there are still a few who have not been caught in the meshes of this frenzy and who are still human, and enjoy the wonderful panorama of the mountains, the valley, and the plain with their wonderful content of living things, and among these persons I am proud to know my two friends, John Burroughs and Henry Ford.

Thomas A. Edison

Next to the campfire in the Everglades of Florida in February 1914 are the Edisons, the Fords, and John Burroughs. In the back row of the photograph are the three native guides. In the middle row is an unusually jovial Thomas Edison, then Mina Edison, then Lucy Bogue (longtime friend of the Edisons), then the bearded John Burroughs. The front row shows "Bessie," a friend of Madeleine Edison, daughter of Thomas and Mina. Next is Madeleine leaning against her brother Charles Edison in laced boots, who is whittling on a stick. Next to Charles is Henry Ford with eyes closed, knife in hand, but not whittling at that moment. Clara Ford is at far right. Clara is said to have been especially afraid of the snakes, while Henry, it is said, shot several snakes in the head with his .22-caliber revolver. (P.0.755)

At Fort Myers about 1920, the Fords are entertaining Thomas Edison on the enclosed veranda of the Mangoes. Clara has in her lap a copy of *The Spur*, which was a magazine of arts and decoration. (0.1346)

During February 1914, when living at 66 Edison was an ordeal, Henry and Clara had visited the Edisons at their winter home in Fort Myers, Florida. The Fords, the Edisons, and John Burroughs had explored and camped in the Everglades. They were very impressed with the climate and the luxuriant foliage of the region. Soon after Fair Lane was finished, the Fords heard that the house next to the Edisons' was for sale, and they purchased it on May 31, 1916, paying $20,000. The place was called the Mangoes.

The house, guest cottage, and garage had a total area of about 8,000 square feet. The house was a fourteen-room gray shingled bungalow on a lot of about four acres, with 177 feet of frontage on McGregor Avenue and land stretching back 450 feet to the Caloosahatchee River. Most appealing were the exotic trees. The landscape was described by an anonymous writer: "There is a giant Mallaluca Lucadendron, probably one of the largest in the area. Beside it is the Fiscus Exotica, with its amazing maze of roots. And then there is the large Banyan tree. There

The restored Fort Myers, Florida, residence once owned by the Fords and known as the Mangoes. The home fronts McGregor Boulevard facing south, and the backyard extends to the Caloosahatchee River where there is a dock. This home, immediately adjacent to the Edison home, was used regularly by the Fords as a winter home from the time of its purchase in 1916 to 1931 when Thomas Edison died. The Fords finally sold the home in 1945. In this 1997 photograph, most of the tropical shrubbery and citrus so appealing to the Fords in the early days no longer appears. The City of Fort Myers now owns the Ford home, and it is maintained as a public museum along with the Edison home. (Photo courtesy Jim Niccum of Fort Myers)

is a magnificent night blooming Cereus, that blooms almost suddenly under an October moon. And the fragrance of the Jasmines and the Cabbage Palms are seasonal delights. In certain seasons there is lush bloom on the Jolia and the Vanilla Orchid." There were also one hundred fifty grapefruit trees, fifty orange trees, mangoes, pawpaws, lemons, limes, guavas, tangerines, bananas, and a large vegetable garden.

Although Thomas Edison was sixteen years older than Henry Ford, the two enjoyed each other's company and spent many happy hours by the fireside during winter evenings, discussing topics of a wide variety. Mina Miller Edison, Edison's second wife, and Clara got along well. The two were nearly the same age. Mina's father, Lewis Miller, had been cofounder of the Chautauqua and a wealthy manufacturer of farm tools in Ohio. One year, Mina and Clara went on a shopping trip to

Atlantic City, where they bought identical white wicker swings for their porches. After Thomas Edison died in 1931, the Fords no longer used the Florida home, but grapefruit, oranges, and mangoes were regularly shipped to Fair Lane. The Mangoes was owned by the Fords until 1945, when it was sold for $21,500. In 1988, the same property was purchased by the city of Fort Myers for $1.5 million to be used along with the Edison home as a tourist attraction.

Chapter 7
Years of Expansion

enry had been experimenting with tractors since 1907, his goal being to rid the farm of horses. His latest design had been demonstrated at the Michigan State Fair in September 1915. Much of the testing had been done on acreage surrounding the Black Farm, and a small factory had been established along the railroad about a mile from the site of Fair Lane. From that same railroad siding, the stone and gravel for Fair Lane was hauled to the building site. In October, newspapers nationwide announced that Ford would "build five hundred thousand of the 'iron horses' the first year and sell them at a price of about two hundred dollars." Henry meant this business to be separate from Ford Motor Company, whose greedy stockholders stifled his expansion plans.

While Henry was building tractors at the Elm Street plant in Dearborn and automobiles in Highland Park, starting May 22, 1915, and until October 10, 1918, he purchased 1,526 acres of Springwells Township land, paying a total of $2,601,758.40. On this new land his intention was to build a much larger tractor plant straddling the Rouge River. It would become the famous Rouge Plant, where, from raw materials out of the earth, could be created cars, tractors, and trucks utilizing Ford's own ships and railroads for transportation.

Henry was trying to get Edsel into the tractor business as well. On August 5, 1916, a certificate of partnership was signed by Henry and Edsel Ford: "name and style of the said firm is Henry Ford and Son and the length of time for which it is to continue is indefinite, the same not being fixed by the partnership contract; that the locality of the place of business of said co-partnership is Dearborn, Michigan." Roy Bryant notarized the document. This partnership also included the "Henry

August 5, 1916
Henry Ford & Son partnership is established

February 1917
The Fords cruise to Cuba on their yacht *Sialia*

December 23, 1917
Melvin Bryant, Clara's father, dies

November 1918
Henry runs for U.S. Senate on the Independent ticket

November 1918
The *Dearborn Independent* newspaper is purchased

January 1, 1919
Edsel becomes president of Ford Motor Company

July 9, 1920
The Detroit, Toledo & Ironton Railroad is purchased

February 4, 1922
The Lincoln Motor Company is purchased

1922–1923
The "Ford for President Club" becomes active nationally

Ford & Son Laboratories" at Fair Lane, where "medical, botanical and chemical research" was carried on for several years on the top floor of the Fair Lane powerhouse.

To help the British produce more food during World War I, on April 17, 1917, Henry Ford & Son, Limited, was organized to build tractors in Cork, Ireland. Shares valued at 100,000 British pounds were divided equally among Henry, Edsel, and Clara. But building a plant in Ireland soon was found to be impractical. On July 27, 1917, Henry Ford & Son was reorganized as a Michigan corporation, issuing 10,000 shares at a par value of $1 million, again divided equally among Henry, Clara, and Edsel, with Henry as president, Clara as vice president, Edsel as secretary and treasurer, and Roy Bryant as assistant treasurer. The corporation was empowered to "manufacture, sell and deal in farm tractors, agricultural implements and appliances, and self-propelled vehicles and mechanisms of every description and character, and all accessories and devices appertaining thereto." This empowerment of Henry Ford & Son is evidence that Henry was looking ahead to the possibility of withdrawing himself from Ford Motor Company in order to expand into manufacturing operations not condoned by other Ford Motor stockholders. John and Horace Dodge were already suing to prevent Ford from using dividends for further plant expansion.

Roy Bryant, with his farm upbringing, was more enthusiastic about tractors than Edsel. He immediately began working as an employee of Henry Ford & Son, with Ray Dahlinger taking over responsibility for Henry Ford Farms. Under the guidance of Liebold, Roy began handling Henry Ford & Son business as well as that of Henry Ford Estate (Fair Lane) and Gulley Farm, of which he was a trustee. During 1917, Henry poured thousands of dollars into the new tractor plant, which was built on the site of the abandoned Wagner brickyard.

On July 6, 1916, Henry Ford deeded Lot 115 of the Detroit Arsenal Grounds for the sum of one dollar to Roy Bryant and his wife, Katharine. This consisted of a 4.16-acre parcel in the village of Dearborn. Roy continued in Dearborn as assistant treasurer, arranged for tractor demonstrations, and was involved with Percival Perry in a million-dollar tractor sale to the British. The tractor business in Dearborn appealed to several other Ford and Bryant relatives. Marvin Bryant lived and worked in Dearborn during the Fordson tractor years of 1916 to 1920. George Brubaker, with Eva and their children, moved from California to work for Henry. Will Ford began working in the tractor employment office, and Edsel's brother-in-law Ernest Kanzler was induced by Henry to join the tractor group.

A bill from New York Central Lines shows that on September 7, 1916, Henry Ford reserved "transportation covering movement of private Pullman car Philadelphia, Detroit to the Coast and return." Cost

Surrounded by a dozen
pretty actresses at
Universal City in
Hollywood, Henry
reenacts proposing to
Clara. This was during
the September 1916
trip around the United
States with the Perrys
of England.

of tickets and fifteen days' car rental to the Pullman Company at sixty
dollars a day came to $3105.95. This trip was organized for Percival and
Catherine Perry and their two nieces, Nancy and Marian. The Perrys
had escorted Henry and Clara around England in 1912; now Henry and
Clara were showing the Perrys around America. "Purely a pleasure trip
and relief from the pressures of business," Henry explained to the press.
Stops were made at Minot, North Dakota, to witness grain harvesting,
and at Seattle, Portland, San Francisco, and Los Angeles for sightsee-
ing. At Altadena, California, the group visited with Eva and her family
and stopped at Universal City, posing with some film stars. Henry was
supporting Wilson for president, predicting he would have a tractor for
sale in a year, and planning to build boats as well as automobiles. The
party returned to Detroit by way of the Grand Canyon.

In 1916, Henry was planning his mammoth tractor plant on the
Rouge River in Dearborn. Because manufacturing operations at
Highland Park had recently been nearly shut down by a strike of railroad workers, Ford vowed from then on his plants would be on water-
ways where raw materials could be obtained from abroad if necessary.
Supplies of iron ore and coal were abundant in Cuba, so he arranged for
his chief engineer, William B. Mayo, to find him a yacht for an
exploratory trip to Cuba. The yacht Mayo found was the *Sialia*, which
belonged to John R. Stewart, a manufacturer of automobile speedome-

At Universal City Zoo, Los Angeles, from the left, the adults are Percival Perry, Catherine Perry, Rose Flint, Henry, Clara, an unidentified woman, and Dutee Flint. The two girls are Nancy and Marian, nieces of the Perrys. The unidentified woman may be a Miss Meals of London, who accompanied the Perry nieces. (P.833.7824)

ters. On January 20, 1917, Henry paid $250,000 for the ship. The *Sialia* was berthed in Brooklyn, New York. Henry and Clara took with them to Cuba as guests Mayo, Eva Bryant Brubaker and her husband, George, and their two children, Grace and Bernice. On their way, they picked up John Burroughs at Roxbury, New York.

They left New York on February 21, 1917, and reached the Edison dock at Fort Myers on February 27, then sailed on to Havana by March 1. The men visited several of Mayo's business friends while the ladies toured the city. They left Havana on March 6, experienced a severe storm on the return voyage, and received an order dated March 5, 1917, from the U.S. Navy to release the *Sialia* immediately for naval coastal defense. The *Sialia* was not returned to Ford until April 20, 1920. After refurbishing at a cost of $150,000, the ship was put back into service. A good deal of the cost was itemized in a November 1920 statement "for decoration and furniture" by Sidney Houghton of London, whose bill

The *Sialia* in open water with pennants flying. The masts supported radio aerial wires rather than sails. Between 1917 and 1929, Henry and Clara used the vessel to cruise the Great Lakes, the Atlantic Coast, and the Caribbean. Clara was the one who wanted the yacht. Henry said, "OK, if you never ask what the thing cost." He knew having a yacht would be very expensive; also, Henry's stomach did not do at all well on the water. (P.0.4980)

came to $99,472.61. In the meantime, there had been an explosion in the *Sialia's* battery compartment. Edison's assistant, William H. Meadowcroft, had warned Liebold that the Edison batteries would give off fumes which could explode, but the warning had been ignored. Apparently, no one was injured in the blast. The *Sialia* is recorded as having docked in Harbor Beach and Traverse City in 1921, in Bar Harbor in 1922 and 1923, in Traverse City again in 1924, at St. Catherine Island in 1925, and in both Traverse City and Harbor Beach again in 1926. After that, the ship was used very little and was sold in 1929.

Ledger figures show Ford spent a total of $1,696,298.67 on the *Sialia* between 1917 and 1926. The big Ford Motor Company ore carriers later furnished Henry and Clara with many delightful vacation trips to Clara's favorite summer retreat in the Huron Mountains of Michigan's Upper Peninsula.

Henry and Clara were helping Milton Bryant, who had married Bernice Robertson of Traverse City on May 15, 1912, to become established there in the automobile business. Henry sent Milton a check for $10,000 in September 1915 and another for $38,000 in May 1917. The latter amount was for the purchase of Marion Island, about 200 acres in Grand Traverse Bay, for a summer home and game preserve. At one time, a steamer carried excursion passengers between the island and Traverse City. A large dance pavilion and recreation spot had made it popular for many years. It was one of the scenic spots of the region; its hills and valleys constituted a natural arboretum, and every type of tree and shrub native to the northern part of the state could be found on the island. It contained some of northern Michigan's finest timber and was a sanctuary for birds and wildlife.

Another check to Milton, for $50,000, signed by Clara on January 8, 1923, was presumably for his dealership, Grand Traverse Auto Company, located at 124 West Front Street. Milton also tried to start a commercial aviation business in Traverse City. In 1926, he arranged a membership in the "We-One-Tong Club" for Henry in case he should want to dock the *Sialia* at Traverse City. Crates of Michigan cherries and sweet white peaches became annual gifts shipped from Traverse City to Henry and Clara in Dearborn. The Henry Fords sold Marion Island in 1944 for $30,000. Henry and Clara never used the island as a summer home.

On December 23, 1917, Melvin Samuel Bryant, Clara's father, died of heart failure at the farm on Monnier Road in Greenfield Township. He had been doing chores, and his body was found in a stall in the horse barn. Melvin was buried alongside Martha in Woodmere Cemetery on West Fort Street in Detroit. In a fiftieth-anniversary issue of the St. Paul's Episcopal Church bulletin, Clara would later write the following about the little church in their neighborhood:

> One evening when I was a little girl some gentlemen came to our house to talk about the necessity of having a church in our vicinity. At that time we had been holding our Sunday School and Church service in the ball room of the "Eight Mile House." Among those gentlemen were my grandfather, William Bench, Mr. James Bossardet, Mr. George Mott, and others whom I cannot remember. Shortly after that they came again with plans of a church, and I remember much talk and arguing about how to get the money to build the church. My father and mother, Mr. and Mrs. Melvin Bryant, were very anxious to have it. We were a family of ten children, and they knew it would help in the training of us. I think Mr. Tuscon was our first clergyman and his son William looked after Sunday School. Later came Mr. Frisbie, and he preached for many years. He married me, baptized our little boy, and buried my father and mother. He died about a year ago. Bishop McCoskry confirmed my two eldest brothers. I remember it very well, as it was our first confirmation class, and the little old church was full to overflowing. Another thing that is

impressed upon my mind is that my grandfather took wood in his buggy each Sunday for many years to make the fire. He really kept the church going. My husband Henry Ford and his family attended the little church also.

In 1918, with encouragement from President Wilson, Henry Ford became a candidate for the U.S. Senate on the Independent ticket. Running against Truman S. Newberry, a Republican, Henry lost in a very close race. The Bryants, who were Republicans, were against his running for office. Possible reasons for his loss may have been his employment of several Germans on key Ford defense contracts and Edsel's wartime deferment. (Henry's explanation was that Edsel was absolutely essential to the war work being done in the factory and that Edsel had turned down several offers of commissions that would have merely placed him behind a desk in Washington.) In 1920, Newberry was found guilty of violating the Federal Corrupt Practices Act in over-spending on the election, and he resigned from the Senate in November 1922.

Henry's gift of Gulley Farm to Clara in 1909 had been used from 1911 to 1916 to accommodate orphan boys. In 1916, it became the nucleus of the Henry Ford Trade School. The boys called the place Valley Farm because of the river valley on the premises. In August 1918, Clara donated use of the buildings and land to the Woman's Hospital and Infants Home of Detroit for a hospital annex, a convalescent home for new mothers who had no family assistance. Most of the women who stayed there did their own laundry, tended gardens, and canned produce.

During Henry's political campaign, he had found big-city newspapers to be very unfavorable to his candidacy. In November 1918, he purchased his own paper, a small local weekly with a good name: the *Dearborn Independent.* To it he added the subtitles "Ford International Weekly" and "Chronicler of the Truth." The Dearborn Publishing Company was formed with Henry as president, Clara as vice president, and Edsel as secretary-treasurer. The first issue of the *Independent* appeared in January 1919. It sold for five cents and, by 1925–26, had reached a circulation of 900,000. Henry allowed many controversial subjects to be presented by guest writers, some very conservative and some quite radical. Also included every week was "Henry Ford's Own Page," written by William Cameron, editor of the *Independent,* and based on Henry's ideas. Within a very few years, the paper was in big trouble for blaming most of the world's problems on the Jews. Clara's and Edsel's names were removed from the masthead in September 1923. In April 1924, Aaron Sapiro, a prominent Chicago attorney, sued Ford for $1 million in a case not settled until April 1927. Ford lost the case, agreed to make a public apology, and paid court costs of $140,000. The *Dearborn Independent* closed down later that year.

Henry's vision of his stupendous new tractor plant on the Rouge River in Dearborn included homes for his employees. He had contracted on August 1, 1918, with Leonard Willeke, a Detroit architect and city planner, to design a 2,600-acre residential area to house 3,707 families and provide for several parks and a community center to be called Fordson Village. But this development was delayed pending the outcome of his control of company dividends. In the meantime, however, Liebold, now with power of attorney for both Henry and Clara, was instructed to form the Dearborn Realty and Construction Company to develop housing for employees of the existing small tractor plant in Dearborn. Stockholders in this housing venture were Clara, Edsel, and Ernest Liebold. Over the next few years, 250 homes were built and either sold or rented to employees. They sold for seven thousand to nine thousand dollars and rented for fifty to sixty dollars a month.

In mid-August 1918, Henry took a two-week camping trip to the Great Smoky Mountain region with his friends Edison, Burroughs, and Firestone. Regarding the Great Smokies, Burroughs quipped, "Mountains and men who do not smoke suit me better." On these trips, Edison enjoyed smoking his big black cigars without his wife, Mina, complaining.

Describing Henry Ford on such a trip, Burroughs wrote: "Mr. Ford is . . . adaptive . . . indifferent to places . . . his interest in the stream is in its potential water power. He races up and down its banks to see its fall, and where power could be developed. He is never tired of talking how much power is going to waste everywhere, and says that if the streams were all harnessed . . . farm labor everywhere could be greatly lessened." As for himself, Burroughs wrote: "It often seemed to me that we were a luxuriously equipped expedition going forth to seek discomfort—dust, rough roads, heat, cold, irregular hours, accidents . . . but discomfort, after all, is what the camper-out is unconsciously seeking . . . we react against our complex civilization and long to get back for a time to first principles."

The Edsel Fords, in 1918, had discovered the coast of Maine, especially Seal Harbor on Mount Desert Island. In a letter to Henry, Eleanor wrote, "I am so crazy to have you come up here that I can hardly stand it. You would just love the forest walks revealing the mountain tops where you are unconscious of the existence of anything human." Henry and Clara did visit Seal Harbor in 1920 on the *Sialia*. Edsel and Eleanor built a home there called Skylands, a sixty-one-acre seaside estate including a summer mansion with a dozen bedrooms where they spent their vacations for many years.

A letter from Clara on November 12, 1918, to her nephew Wallace Bryant, then in the Navy, reviews the situation at the end of the war:

A caravan of this type carried the "Vagabonds," Ford, Edison, Firestone, and Burroughs, on their annual outings. The lead cars carried the lead characters with their chauffeurs. The supply trucks, carrying the cooks, tent erectors, and wood choppers, together with their necessary paraphernalia, followed behind at a respectable distance. This caravan of about eight vehicles including sedans indicates it is the year 1921 when women decided to join the party. The men ordinarily favored the open cars in order to be closer to nature. (B.34342)

Dear Wallace:

I intended answering your letter long before this, but there has been so much to do this last year for all of us that we have all neglected things that we should have done. The war is over, but you may be on the sea for a long time yet. There has been great rejoicing every-where. I have not gone into town to see any of it, but heard the noise, and have read the papers. We have all been very tired of it, having only two weekends in almost two years. I have had no head gardener since last Jan. and have planned and superintended all myself. Also looked after the poultry, in which I have developed a great liking, and have raised several hundred this year. With the help of the "poultry husbandry" professor, I have learned how to cull my flock to know which will lay and which will not. I also have started for winter, quantities of vegetables in greenhouse, have ready for use lima beans which is a new venture, and very successful. Am growing very few flowers this year.

I expect many of our boys will be out of work soon, but hope factories will soon adjust themselves so that men will not be out of work through the winter. What a waste there will be, wonder what they will do with the explosives. I heard that you had an attack of influenza. Hope you have entirely recovered. What a dreadful thing it has been, wiping out whole families. I read where it has reached Alaska, and hundreds of Eskimos are dying. Have had a beautiful fall, and still have nice weather. Aunt Katharine is going to California this winter, Roy is in the ordanance dept. and will have work for a long time he is told. Aunt Kate and family motored to N.Y. this summer and the children would not enjoy anything, would not even go up in the Woolworth Bldg, they wanted to go camping. Have not seen many of the family of late so have not much news. Hoping things will soon clear up, and let you get home soon.

Am sincerely
Aunt Clara

Edward Litogot, nephew of Henry's mother, Mary, died in November 1918. He and his wife, Loine, had been living on a gratuity from Henry. Following Edward's death, Henry asked his secretary to find work for Loine. On January 9, 1919, she was employed in the Magneto Department in the Highland Park plant of Ford Motor Company.

The Dodge brothers' case had been simmering for some time, and Ford suspected they would win. Foreseeing such an outcome, on December 30, 1918, Henry resigned the presidency of Ford Motor Company "to devote my time to building up the other organizations with which I am connected." Edsel Ford was elected president, to take office on January 1, 1919. Edsel, at age twenty-five, was to receive a salary of $150,000 a year. On February 7, 1919, the court ruled, as expected, with special dividends of $19,275,385 to be paid to stockholders of Ford Motor Company. Although Henry would get the bulk of this, the company itself would be short of expansion funds. When

The home of Eva and George Brubaker at Altadena, California, in January 1919. Just visible standing beside the house are Eleanor Clay Ford, Henry Ford II, Mrs. Elizabeth Hudson Clay (Eleanor's mother), and Clara. Henry is busy elsewhere telling the press he is planning a new company to build a $250 automobile to compete with the Model T. (P.O.19733)

minor stockholders such as the Dodge brothers could stifle progress, Henry was in a bind, to say the least.

Even before the court decision was rendered, Henry had taken off by rail for California with Clara, Eleanor, and little Henry II to visit Clara's sister Eva Brubaker and her family in Altadena, outside Los Angeles. Roy Bryant joined them, as did Eleanor's mother, Elizabeth Clay. They vacationed there from January 16 to March 5, 1919. Within a few days of their arrival, Henry announced from Los Angeles that a new vehicle, better than the Model T and much less expensive, would be put on the market by a company other than Ford Motor Company. His announcement made headlines all across the country.

Ford's plans for a new company obviously worried Ford Motor Company minor stockholders—and that was his purpose. To take advantage of their fright, Edsel and William Mayo, who had banker friends in New York and Boston, arranged secretly to obtain options to buy the minority stock. By July 11, 1919, all of the minority shares had been purchased by Ford, at a cost of $105,820,894.57 and involving a credit loan of $60 million. The Ford family now owned all of Ford Motor Company.

At Eva's home in Altadena in January 1919 are Clara, Eleanor (standing behind Henry II smiling in his buggy), and Eleanor's mother, Elizabeth Clay. (P.O.538)

The *Chicago Tribune* trial, a $1 million libel suit initiated by Henry in 1916 because of a statement by the *Tribune* that Ford was an anarchist, was finally settled August 14, 1919, with Henry winning an award of six cents. During the trial in 1916, Henry was castigated in court for being an ignoramus regarding American history. Ford is reported to have stated, "History is more or less bunk." He meant that, as taught in books, history is made up of stories of rulers, wars, political controversies, and extension of territories, with nothing of the ordinary life of the people or of agricultural and industrial progress. Following the trial, Ford told Liebold, "We're going to start something. I'm going to start up a museum and give the people a true picture of the development of the country. That's the only history that is worth observing, that you can preserve in itself. We're going to build a museum that's going to show industrial history, and it won't be bunk! We'll show the people what actually existed in years gone by and we'll show the actual development of American industry from the early days, from the earliest days we can recollect up to the present day." The *Tribune* suit is thought to have been a major motivation for creating the Henry Ford Museum & Greenfield Village.

In mid-August 1919, Henry organized the next vacation trip with Edison, Burroughs, Firestone, and Kingsford. They called themselves the "Vagabonds." With a caravan of autos and trucks, they kept to the back roads and camped overnight in tents, cooking their meals over an open fire. Sato, hired by Clara in 1913, was the cook, driving a truck with the cooking equipment. Ford had his chauffeur, Jimmy Smith, driving a Cadillac. Edison also had a Cadillac on that trip, and Firestone had a Pierce Arrow. Ford's photographer drove another car with his own equipment, and still another truck followed with tents and camp chairs. A special Lincoln refrigeration truck had been added. Edison, Ford, Firestone, and Burroughs usually rode together in one of the large touring cars. This particular trip took them through upstate New York and New England, where they visited the Green Island power site on the Hudson River which Ford had purchased earlier that year. Again, there were no women in the group.

As president of Ford Motor Company and now twenty-five years of age, Edsel was given a portion of Ford Motor Company dividends in July 1919. Then, on October 10, 1919, he was taken by Henry to a downtown Detroit bank and shown $1 million in gold bullion. This was a gift to Edsel, and it is listed as a nondeductible disbursement on Henry's personal 1919 income tax.

Clara's income by this time was considerable. Although she seems not to have filed a federal tax return in 1918, her 1919 taxes were surprisingly high. On a reported 1919 income of $193,307.58, her federal taxes were $75,373.25. She paid the first-quarter installment of $18,935 on April 16, 1920. Of her total income, $166,700 was dividends from Henry Ford & Son, Inc. Interest from accounts in fourteen banks totaled $25,998.21, and interest on bonds contributed $2469.95. The "normal tax" alone, in steps of 4 and 8 percent, was a reasonable amount, but added to it was a "surtax" bringing the total to an average 39 percent of income. For incomes greater than $1 million the 1919 surtax rate was 65 percent.

By June 1920, all Ford Motor Company assets, valued at $300 million, were transferred to Ford Motor Company of Delaware. Included in these assets were Henry Ford & Son, Dearborn Publishing Company, and Dearborn Realty and Construction Company. Of the new stock issued, Henry received 55.212 percent, Edsel 41.652 percent, and Clara 3.136 percent.

With full control of Ford Motor Company and the $60-million debt paid off, Henry launched into a stupendous expansion program lasting throughout the 1920s. His goal was to integrate vertically the manufacture of automobiles and tractors by owning and operating his own iron ore, coal, and silica mines; limestone quarries; hardwood forests; rubber plantations; a railroad; a fleet of ships; an airline; newspaper and radio station; and schools to train his employees. He didn't accomplish all of this immediately, of course.

Henry's first goal was to carry out expansion of the giant Rouge Plant as a tremendous steel smelting complex, plans for which had been obstructed by the Dodge brothers. This plant was located three miles downstream from Fair Lane. Meanwhile, along the Rouge River upstream from Fair Lane, Henry built a series of at least six small, picturesque hydroelectric plants where farmers could work during the winters manufacturing small automotive parts. Henry's respect for watepower led him eventually to utilize almost thirty hydroelectric plants, from one of only 20 horsepower upstream on the Rouge to one of 18,000 horsepower on the Mississippi River at Minneapolis.

To provide his own railroad transportation to the Rouge Plant from his coal mines in Kentucky and West Virginia, on July 9, 1920, Henry purchased the Detroit, Toledo & Ironton Railroad, a 465-mile road, for $5 million. Ownership was assigned to Henry, Clara, and Edsel Ford, not the Ford Motor Company. Henry became president; Liebold was vice president; Eva's husband, George Brubaker, was secretary and treasurer. Clara and Edsel did not become really involved with the railroad's operation. In March 1921, George Brubaker traveled to South America on company business and later that year went to Europe. In 1921, a $15-million improvement program was announced, and over the next few years the railroad became a model of efficiency. By 1927, sick of government regulations hampering further improvements, Henry turned the presidency of the railroad over to a subordinate. In 1928, Edsel contacted the Pennsylvania Railroad, saying, "My father and I have had our fun with the D.T. & I.," and on June 27, 1929, it was sold to Pennroad Corporation for $36 million, with a net profit estimated to be about $9 million. Of the proceeds, Edsel received $11,212,744, Clara received $1,142,079, and Henry took the balance.

Fordson tractor production was moved from the small plant in Dearborn to the Rouge Plant under Charles Sorensen's direction late in 1920. This may have been part of the reason Roy Bryant put his Dearborn home up for sale in June 1921 and was buying a Ford dealership in Xenia, Ohio, a good-sized town near Dayton. By September, the family had moved to Xenia. For the next few years, letters from Katharine to Clara indicated the Bryants missed living near Henry and Clara, with comments such as "I get so homesick for some of my real friends. I notice even Roy misses having any place we can run in any evening uninvited. I miss you more than I do my own family in California."

During the summer of 1920, Clara commissioned Nicholas Longfeather, a plant pathologist and soil analyst from Atlanta, to examine the trees along the driveway leading to Fair Lane. He determined that the chestnuts were in poor condition because of disease and poor soil, the oaks showed signs of hidden decay, and the red maples were in such bad shape that he would not advise trying to save them. Longfeather suggested the soil around the trees be analyzed and treated.

Clara's vegetable garden at Fair Lane in 1921 was planted with "beans, peas, onions, squash, corn, pumpkin, melon, cabbage, celery, brussels sprouts, cauliflower, lettuce, tomatoes, and a few flowers."

A letter from "O S D, 444 Kirby Ave. Det. Mich." to Henry Ford arrived in December 1920. In excellent penmanship it read as follows:

Sir:

I hereby respectfully request of you a sum of $3000, three thousand dollars, because it is very necessary. Send it by post mail, on this upper address. No checks or certificates necessary only money in cash. Warning you if you refuse to mail this problem it will mean you a great danger and there must no be any pur suit after you receive an answer. Then you will know everything where are you giving your money. You will not be sorry for because they will do a great thing as ever before. Warn you must not spread this note unless you get answer if you do it means a danger. Mail as soon as possible.

O S D

After copying it, Liebold immediately sent the letter to E. E. Fraser, Office of Inspector, Post Office Department, Detroit. Then Liebold began corresponding with "O S D" over a period of several weeks concerning the exact manner of transferring the money, including the use of registered mail to the Eliot Station in Detroit. This literary duel ended when the extortionist was identified and arrested. In a letter on April 12, Fraser wrote to Liebold:

Dear Sir:

This will advise you that John Robic, alias O.S. Dean, was arraigned in Court yesterday where he plead guilty to violation of Sec. 215. U.S. Penal Code, and was sentenced to three years imprisonment in the Federal Penitentiary at Leavenworth, Kansas.

Nineteen twenty-one was a depression year in the automobile business. During this difficult period, Henry is said to have had a nervous breakdown which kept him inactive for nearly a month. The move of manufacturing from Highland Park to the Rouge location had been costly to the Ford Motor Company not only in dollars but in personnel. The money shortage gave New York bankers reason to believe they would be taking over the company. And with Sorensen given control of the Rouge Plant, other employees who had had significant responsibilities at Highland Park, such as William Knudsen, Peter Martin, and Samuel Marquis, were either leaving or threatening to leave. About this time, Henry had picked Harry Bennett to be in charge of security at the Rouge.

Charles Sorensen, superintendent of the Rouge Plant, took time off in the summer of 1921 to survey the European vehicle market, and Eva's husband, George Brubaker, who was working for Ford Motor Company, accompanied Sorensen on the trip. Henry gave Eva a new Model T that year to keep her happy while her husband was away.

Clara pledged subscriptions to the Detroit Community Fund, which totaled $50,000 during 1921. In June, Henry gave Clara $1 million in Detroit school bonds, which were given back to Henry in 1934.

Clara liked to shop in New York, and during the last week of April she was staying at the Ritz-Carlton in an "apartment" at $13.25 a day. Her breakfasts at the hotel cost an average of $1.60. With phone bills, she paid a total of $106.90 upon leaving.

In mid-May 1921, Clara was active in the Michigan League of Women Voters, as were her friends Sarah Hodges of Grosse Pointe and Mina Ives of Dearborn. Eleanor Cameron, wife of Henry's spokesman, William J. Cameron, was first vice president, and Clara was appointed "director at large" by the State Executive Committee. Clara held that position for at least ten years. During the depression, both the state and national leagues were in financial trouble. Clara's $3,000 check to the National League in 1931 would draw the following response from the executive secretary in Old Lyme, Connecticut: "About a year ago you came to the aid of us in a way that sent a really electric thrill through the whole organization." There was also a hint that Clara might want to repeat the gesture.

To supplement their personal travel needs, in February 1920 Henry had ordered from the Pullman Company of Chicago a 100-ton, 82-foot-long, all-steel private railroad car with observation platform. The car was named *Fair Lane* and cost $159,000. Elaborate interior wood paneling and furnishings were designed by Sidney Houghton of London. The car was delivered on June 22, 1921, and housed at Dearborn about a mile from the Fair Lane residence. A letter from the Pullman Company read:

> *When considering the cost of this car you must take in full consideration the quality of the material, designs of interior finish, and class of workmanship, demanded by your designer, Mr. Houghton. In*

Henry and Clara's private railroad car, the *Fair Lane*. The 82-foot-long all-steel car weighing one hundred tons was built by the Pullman Company in 1920–21 at a cost of $159,000. The interior was designed by Sidney Houghton of London, who also designed the interior of the *Sialia*. The *Fair Lane* was used by the Fords from 1921 to 1942, when it was given up because of limitations on the use of private railroad cars during World War II. It was sold in 1942 but has found its way back to Dearborn and the Henry Ford Museum. (U.78777)

this respect, this is without doubt, one of the most elegant and expensive designs of car we have ever built, as also were some of the materials, such as Monel roofing, walnut interior finish with specially matched veneering, made to order. Window curtain material with back to match draperies, etc., rather than standard designs of paneling, decoration, etc.

The *Fair Lane* was also perhaps the best-equipped private railroad car in the country. An inventory of equipment included the following:

Crockery:
230 total items including 35 types of dishes, sufficient for 12 place settings.
Grecian glassware:
144 total pieces of 17 types, sufficient for serving 12 people, with 12 types of glasses, including water, beer, claret, champagne, cocktail, and whiskey.

Luxumburg silverware:
169 total pieces of 65 types, sufficient to serve 12 people; 24 corn holders allowed two ears per person.
Pantry equipment:
38 total items of 28 types, including a three-quart ice cream freezer, a coffee mill, an assortment of eight knives and three carving forks, nutmeg and horseradish graters.
Kitchen equipment:
99 total items of 79 types, including 28 pans in sizes up to six quarts, an iron bucket, a shovel, and mop and stick.
Sleeping linen:
80 pillow slips, 80 sheets, 26 blankets, 60 hand towels, and 20 bath towels.
Table linen:
189 pieces, of 13 types, including 10 each of cook's and waiter's aprons, caps, and jackets; 72 napkins, 12 tablecloths, 20 each of dish and glass towels.

Traveling by private railroad car was certainly convenient but also very expensive. The *Fair Lane* was immediately put to use by Edsel as well as Henry and Clara for both business and pleasure. A round trip to New York from Dearborn typically cost $1,364, to Boston $1,649, and to Seal Harbor, Maine, $2,318. One-way fare to Ways, Georgia, was about $850. To move the car to the Pullman shops in Kensington, Illinois, for repairs cost $112. However, to park the car for a day at Mott Haven Yards in New York City cost only $2.40. After twenty-one years, because of advancing age and wartime travel restrictions, the *Fair Lane* was sold in November 1942 to the Southwestern Railway, the "Cotton Belt Route," for $35,000. In 1972, the car was donated to the Cherokee Indian Nation in Talhequah, Oklahoma. Ten years later, it was fully restored, and now, thanks to a donor, it is in the Henry Ford Museum.

The "Vagabonds" ceased to be vagabonds in 1921. The wives thought their husbands were having too much fun and wanted to sample this pinnacle of luxury in the wilds. The summer 1921 journey was through Maryland and Pennsylvania, with President Harding joining them at Hagerstown, Maryland. Invitations were extended to wives and children of the regulars as well as to the president and his wife, which automatically included a number of Secret Service guards and press reporters. Because John Burroughs had died in March that year, an empty chair was constantly displayed in his honor. The excessive publicity accompanying this vacation discouraged Henry from planning similar camping trips in the future.

In the autumn of 1921, the Lincoln Motor Company was in financial trouble. The president of the company was Henry M. Leland, who

Breakfast inside a tent at the campsite near Hagerstown, Maryland. Seated around the table are, from the left, Thomas Edison, Mina Edison, Clara Ford, Bishop William F. Anderson, Henry Ford, and Lulah Anderson. The Andersons were friends of President Harding, who was also with the group on that occasion. Because John Burroughs had died earlier that year, a vacant chair was left to mark his absence. (B.34347)

in March 1902 had taken over Henry's job when the Henry Ford Company became the Cadillac Automobile Company. The vice president was Wilfred Leland, whose wife was a good friend of Clara's. When Henry heard that the Lelands were seeking help, he was not inclined to be supportive. Clara, however, was in favor of Lincoln being helped in some way. And Edsel could see the reason for the Lincoln not selling well: it had very poor styling. So Clara and Edsel together persuaded Henry to offer help. Henry would have it no other way than to buy out the Lincoln Motor Company completely. His only concession was to allow Henry Leland and Wilfred Leland to stay on for a while as executives. On February 4, 1922, the rather generous price of $8 million was paid by the Fords. Edsel found restyling of the Lincoln car to be his most challenging assignment in the automotive business. Henry's gift to Edsel that year was control of the Lincoln Motor Company.

John Burroughs, close friend of both Henry and Clara, had died during 1921. Burroughs and his wife, Blanche, had acquired the 319-acre Burroughs Farm at Roxbury, New York, on November 4, 1913, for

This is Kate Bryant Raymond, about 1920, in her home at 449 State Street, Adrian, Michigan. Kate and Samuel Raymond were married in Detroit in 1898. By this time they had four grown children: Russell, Milton, Harold, and Violet. Kate and Clara were very close throughout their lives. In 1901, before the Raymonds moved to Adrian, Clara and young Edsel stayed with them on their Jasper, Michigan, farm about ten miles south of Adrian when the Raymonds' first child, Russell Bryant Raymond, was born. (P.0.19739)

$1,000 with financial help from Henry and Clara. In Burroughs's will, dated April 10, 1917, he states: "To my friend Henry Ford to whom I owe the possession of the Old Homestead Farm, I give and bequeath my rustic writing table at Woodchuck Lodge." On January 27, 1922, Henry and Clara purchased the farm, including the house called "Slabsides" from Burroughs's heirs. The Fords paid $13,950 for the farm in order to preserve the tract intact for posterity. On July 28, 1947, following Henry's death, Clara would contribute a 3.45-acre portion of the farm to the John Burroughs Memorial Association of New York City to be used as a memorial site. On the very next day, she conveyed the balance of property to heirs Julian and Emily Burroughs for $6,500 after providing twenty-five years of guardianship.

Clara's brother Marvin, eleven years younger than Clara, was stricken with cancer during 1921. Then living in Kalamazoo, Michigan, he was taken to Henry Ford Hospital in Detroit, where he had a special nurse on duty twenty-four hours a day. Later he was taken to Fair Lane, where a Ford Hospital nurse was on duty from seven a.m. to seven p.m. Marvin's room at Fair Lane was on the second floor at the head of the stairway. He died on February 20, 1922, at age fifty-two.

In the spring of 1922, about 140 men met in Dearborn to form the "Ford for President Club." A campaign to create other such clubs was so successful that by June 1923, an estimated thousand such clubs were said to exist, and a third party was planned. Henry's attitude was "Let them go ahead." Clara blamed Liebold for promoting the "Ford for President" push, and she scolded Liebold, saying, "Since you got him into this, you can just get him out of it. I hate the idea of the name Ford being dragged down into the gutters of political filth! My name is Ford, and I'm proud of it! If Mr. Ford wants to go to Washington, he can go, but I'll go to England!" Henry did admit, "I'd just like to be down there about six weeks and throw some monkey wrenches into the machinery." In December 1923, Henry announced he was supporting President Coolidge for another term, a move of great comfort to both Clara and President Coolidge.

Also that spring, Clara received from Mayo Nurseries of Rochester, New York, two dozen twenty-four-inch Golden Queen raspberry plants and two dozen twenty-four-inch blueberry plants. She later complained to the nursery that the blueberry plants didn't do well. Clara also received "tree roses" ($5 each) from Henry A. Dreer in Philadelphia and "doll roses" ($2 each) from the Charles H. Totty Company in Madison, New Jersey. Totty later sent one hundred four-inch "Madame Butterfly" rose plants as a gift to Clara. Shipped to Henry Ford in Dearborn on May 3 was "one freight car lot" of dormant evergreens from the D. Hill Nursery Company of Dundee, Illinois. Ranging in size from one and a half to nine feet, these included 70 "thuya," 57 "tauga," and 129 "juniperus." The cost totaled $3,296.50.

During August 1922, Henry and Clara spent some time in Seal Harbor, Maine, with Edsel and Eleanor. The men came home before Clara, and Henry sent the following wire to her on August 26: "Arrived home OK and feeling fine with plenty of work to do. ECK [Ernest Kanzler], EBF [Edsel Ford] and HF [Henry Ford] all batching it together at Dearborn. Trust you are all well and awaiting letter you mentioned writing. Have tried to call you twice on phone but was unable to get you. Love to all. Henry Ford." Two days later, Clara wired from Seal Harbor: "All well detained by fog will wire when leaving. Mrs. Henry Ford."

After eleven years as a Ford dealer in Boise, Harry Bryant, who had been getting his cars from Seattle, in 1922 requested permission from Ford Motor Company to assemble cars as well. He estimated distribution in his area at 600 cars per year. The company apparently declined the offer, deeming the operation too small to be worthwhile.

Between 1921 and 1924, Clara's sister Kate's husband, Samuel Raymond, was producing in Adrian an inexpensive, lightweight, three-wheel tractor designed to employ a Model T engine and transmission

This is the family home of Kate and Samuel Raymond in Adrian, Michigan. Sam Raymond had been Eva and Roy Bryant's teacher at the Monnier School before marrying Kate. In addition to managing his Ford dealerships in and around Adrian, he was known as the "statesman farmer" because of operating three farms as well as serving as state senator. (P.0.19740)

for its powertrain. The purchaser could, if he preferred, buy the wheel-and-axle kit from Raymond and put them together himself. Sam sold 150 of these machines before selling his patents on the three-wheel tractor to the John Deere and Oliver companies. Sam's son Russell later reported that there was ill feeling at that time between his father and Henry. Henry, it seems, had loaded Sam's dealership with fifty Fordson tractors just before lowering the price, thus causing Sam to lose considerable money. The tractor kit business may have been somewhat retaliatory. Henry is said to have offered to build a Ford Motor Company plant in Adrian, but the townspeople turned him down for fear the factory would change the rural character of the town.

On Valentine's Day, 1923, Henry and Clara departed for Kentucky, where Henry was examining coal mines and camps he had purchased and Clara was assessing living conditions among the people.

On April 9, 1923, a boy was born to Evangeline Dahlinger, wife of Ford Farms manager Raymond Dahlinger. Because Henry immediately paid much personal attention to the boy, named John, there was sus-

The restored Wayside Inn at South Sudbury, Massachusetts, as it appeared about 1926. (P.0.3352)

picion that John was perhaps Henry's son, not Raymond's. And as Henry continued to heap favor after favor on both the boy and his parents over the years, the likelihood of Henry being John's father grew in the minds of associates. Clara may have been perturbed, but she is not known to have made a fuss about it. The love between Henry and Clara seems not to have been disrupted. The Dahlinger boy was welcome at Fair Lane, on many occasions he played with Roy Bryant's children and the Ford grandchildren, and Clara and Evangeline seemed not to be at odds with each other. Later in life, John Dahlinger wrote an autobiography in which he claimed he was indeed Henry Ford's son.

In 1923, Henry and Clara purchased and restored the Botsford Inn on Grand River Avenue, where they had danced in their youth, said to have been the oldest inn in Michigan. In June 1923, Henry heard that the 1686 Wayside Inn, immortalized by Longfellow in his "Tales of a Wayside Inn," was for sale. By September, he had purchased it for $65,000, together with ninety acres of land in Sudbury, Massachusetts. Between 1923 and 1945, after restoring the inn, adding acreage, and developing schools, Henry and Clara are reported to have devoted $2,848,187 to the project. Added property in Framingham, Marlborough, Stow, and Sudbury in Massachusetts consisted of eighty-eight parcels totaling 2667 acres.

It had been forty years since Henry and Clara had enjoyed the old-fashioned dancing of their youth. The horseless carriage had been perfected, and it was time for Mr. and Mrs. Henry Ford to enjoy themselves again. This meant resurrecting old-fashioned music and old-fashioned ballrooms to match.

Near Boston, in October 1923, Henry located a dancing instructor by the name of Benjamin B. Lovett, who specialized in old-fashioned dances. Lovett was asked to conduct a few dances at Wayside to demon-

Clara and Henry sitting by a fireplace in their historic Wayside Inn, built in 1686 near South Sudbury, Massachusetts. The photograph was taken about 1925, when Henry's agents were busy scouring New England for antiques, some of which became furnishings for the restored inn and some of which were sent on to Dearborn, where the Fords were amassing their early American museum. (P.0.1061)

strate his talents. A program of that period, typed on plain pink paper, reads as follows:

Ernest Effort Insures Success
Greetings
Varsovienne   *Orchestra*
Oxford Minuet   *Orchestra*
Plain Quadrille   *Phonograph*

Captain Jenks
Rye Waltz   *Orchestra*
Waltz Minuet   *Orchestra*
Virginia Reel   *Orchestra*
Club Quadrille   *Phonograph*

Life on the Ocean Wave
Sicilian Circle   *Orchestra*
Waltz Quadrille   *Orchestra*

Little Old Log Cabin
Badger Gavotte   *Orchestra*

In Grateful Recognition
Our Honored Guests
"The Climax Number, Yours."
Mr Lovett presides.
Vestigia milla retrorsum.

In restoring the Wayside Inn, both Henry and Clara became serious collectors of early American artifacts. In 1944, a nonprofit corporation would be formed to accept the Wayside Inn as a gift. The Fords would discontinue operation of the inn on November 30, 1945.

Lovett was brought to Dearborn in 1924 to teach dancing steps to friends of the Fords, both adults and children, and to organize dancing parties. Henry searched far and wide for well-qualified musicians, and during 1924 and 1925, he bought nine rare violins costing $103,200. In 1926, the Fords published *Good Morning: After a Sleep of Twenty-five Years Old Fashioned Dancing Is Being Revived by Mr. and Mrs. Henry Ford,* an instruction book complete with music, steps, and dance-floor etiquette. Dances were held in Dearborn at the Engineering Laboratory and later in Lovett Hall, where weekly gatherings hosted by Henry and Clara attracted guests from Dearborn and Grosse Pointe. By means of old-fashioned dancing, Henry and Clara had garnered an enhanced social position.

When the Fords tried to have old-fashioned dances taught in the public schools of Dearborn, there were objections. Some people were convinced old-fashioned dancing had a tendency to inspire immorality among pupils and should be banned. In December 1926, a jury of school officials and parents, after attending an exhibition by schoolchildren, decided the dances were wholesomely dignified and "could be held offensive by no right-minded person." Instruction was begun in Dearborn schools and other schools. Henry is said to have felt that old-fashioned dancing should supplant modern jazz.

Reverend Samuel S. Marquis had guided the "Sociological Department" for Ford Motor Company since he was hired by Henry at

The motor ship *Henry Ford II* at the Soo Locks connecting Lake Huron and Lake Superior. Luxurious passenger quarters were provided in the forward end of the ship, while the noisy engines occupied the stern. This ship became Henry and Clara's "working yacht." (0.4950)

Highland Park in 1914. When the larger plant at the Rouge was put under the management of Charles Sorensen, he decided the Sociological Department was not necessary, that catering to employees was detrimental to productivity. Marquis was very upset when Henry agreed with Sorensen's opinions. In retaliation, Marquis wrote a book published in 1923 entitled *Henry Ford: An Interpretation*, wherein he belittled the tendency of men such as Ford to feel they have undisputable answers to all questions. Clara was so upset with the book that she proposed buying up all copies and destroying them. It is said she never again spoke to Marquis's wife, Gertrude. Henry, on the other hand, being more tough-hided, visited Samuel Marquis at a later date when he was sick and a patient at Henry Ford Hospital.

Vacations in 1924 were not of the camping type. Using their private railroad car, Henry and Clara invited the Edisons, the Firestones, and the Edsel Fords for a late-April train excursion through Michigan's Upper Peninsula, where the Ford-owned lumbering properties had been developed. An overview of the several sawmill sites and lumber camps, of which Henry was very proud, was their objective. Later that year, the same group assembled at Wayside Inn. From Wayside, the men drove up to Plymouth, Vermont, to visit with President Coolidge and his family. The president gave Henry an old sap bucket, and the first lady gave Henry an antique wine bottle for Clara.

In March and April 1924, two huge bulk carriers, ships to bring limestone and iron ore to the Rouge Plant, were put into service. One was christened *Henry Ford II*, the other *Benson Ford*. The *Henry Ford II*, in particular, was fitted with luxurious passenger quarters for the use of Henry and Clara. Each summer, Henry would specify the date they were to board for a cruise of the Great Lakes. Normally, the ship would require only two days to obtain its load of iron ore from Marquette or Duluth on Lake Superior, but with the Fords on board, the trip was extended to perhaps five days in order to circle around into Lake Michigan or other environs. Friends of Henry and Clara, as well as Ford Motor Company executives, were invited as guests on the two ships. At times, employees of Fair Lane and Ford Hospital nurses also were invited to ride the freighters. Boarding the ship was a problem, and, as Henry grew older, an elevator was designed to get him onto the ship. Following Henry's death, Clara is said to have continued using the elevator.

Chapter 8
The Best of Times

I t was in 1922 that both Henry and Clara took a serious interest in the Berry Schools at Rome, Georgia. They had heard of the schools in 1921, when they were visiting the Edisons in West Orange, New Jersey, and Martha Berry was soliciting funds. Berry's schools were designed to provide work together with schooling for farm children who could not afford to go away to study. Berry had invited the Fords to visit her school. Their first visit resulted in Clara's deciding to build a new girls' dormitory at a cost of $1 million. It was named Clara Hall. An impressive dining hall was considered next. The two buildings were completed in 1927, when Berry Schools became Berry College. A new chapel named Henry Ford Chapel would be added, as well as a new recreation hall. Last would come Mary Hall, named for Henry's mother, completing what is known as the Ford Quadrangle. On their annual trips to Ways, Georgia, the Fords regularly visited Martha Berry and the college. Henry and Clara's contributions over the years totaled well over $4 million.

Back in Detroit, on Grand River Avenue, was the old Botsford Tavern, where Henry and Clara often had danced in their youth. They had paid $262,760 for it, and after considerable restoration, they had invested a total of $602,243. For ten years, Henry and Clara operated it as an inn, before its management was turned over to the Oakwood Hotel Company, a subsidiary of Ford Motor Company. It was occasionally used for parties but consistently lost money. In 1937, the new and beautiful ballroom at Lovett Hall in Greenfield Village would begin to serve the dancing needs of Henry and Clara and their friends.

For a convenient summer home on the water, Henry and Clara purchased a twenty-six-acre estate on the Detroit River in Grosse Ile

1922
Henry and Clara become associated with Berry Schools at Rome, Georgia

March 31, 1925
First of the plantations at Ways, Georgia, is purchased to develop a Ford winter homesite

October 30, 1925
Dearborn Country Club opens

Spring and summer 1926
Clara's rose gardens are established at Fair Lane

September 19, 1927
Clara is invited to become president of the Woman's National Farm and Garden Association

September 27, 1928
Greenfield Village and Henry Ford Museum are dedicated by Thomas Edison

October 21, 1929
Light's Golden Jubilee is celebrated at Henry Ford Museum

Early spring 1930
Clara speaks before the National Garden Bureau of Chicago

Township about fifteen miles south of Fair Lane. The large old home was said to be the second oldest on the island. The price was $36,400, and the Fords' investment came to $47,481. It is not established, however, that the Fords ever occupied the home. Another house, closer to the water and with a large enclosed yacht basin, was later built for occupancy by the Harry Bennett family.

Roy Bryant was inquiring about property on Warren Avenue in Detroit in September 1924. Roy was planning to build a garage and gas station for a Ford dealership about ten miles west of downtown Detroit at the corner of Warren Avenue and Patton Street. By January 1925, Roy was in touch with both Henry and Ford Motor Company regarding building designs. Henry paid the architectural costs of $600 for a building with an estimated value of $32,105. At that same time, it was made known to Henry that Roy would want plans for a Dearborn residence about January 1, 1925. The garage was built by the Austin Company, a sales agreement was signed August 28, 1925, and the dealership opened for business in October 1925.

In addition to taking care of Roy's needs, on October 14, 1924, Henry and Clara entertained Edward, Prince of Wales, at Fair Lane, where their guest stayed overnight. The prince had attended the International Polo Matches on Long Island, where Edsel had arranged for Lincoln automobiles to serve the prince and his staff. He was traveling under the name "Mr. Kane." At Fair Lane, Clara made a point of showing the prince her apple peeling and drying equipment in the basement. Apparently, Clara had used this equipment to prepare dried apples for shipment to England during the food shortages of World War I. During the day on October 14, at the Highland Park plant, while Henry, Edsel, and the prince watched, a Ford touring car was assembled. Total assembly time was twenty-three minutes—eight minutes for the motor, two minutes for the axle, and thirteen minutes for final assembly. The car was then offered to the prince as a gift, but he gracefully refused (on the basis of its establishing a precedent).

For entertainment that evening, Edsel had arranged a dinner for some of Detroit's elite at his home on East Jefferson Avenue. The dinner was followed by dancing until two a.m. to the music of Meyer Davis and his six-piece orchestra. Ladies with whom the prince danced were listed in Detroit papers the next day. Following the dance, the prince and guests boarded the yacht *Sialia*, cruised around Belle Isle, and docked across the river near the Canadian National Railways Station, where the prince boarded a train for his tour of Canada.

From the time he was fifteen years old, Edsel was active in aviation, although he never became a pilot. As a member of the Detroit Aviation Society and stockholder in the Aircraft Development Corporation, Edsel convinced Henry in 1923 that an airport should be developed in

Dearborn for the advancement of aviation. During 1924, terrain was flattened by Dahlinger's crew for a 260-acre Ford Airport barely a mile southwest of Fair Lane—cost estimated at $237,254. One Sunday, Clara noticed a large group of aircraft flying overhead and complained to Henry that they should not be flying on Sunday. Henry agreed and closed his airport on Sundays. But this restriction discouraged passenger planes from using the Ford Airport, and it did not become Detroit's major commercial airport as Henry and Edsel had initially expected. And the Dearborn Inn, which Henry built next to his airport to accommodate air travelers, became a severe financial burden.

By 1925, new all-metal airplanes were being built and flown from the field. Edsel's sons, Henry and Benson, sometimes liked to play on the runways near the hangar, which annoyed the pilots. In at least one instance, trying to obtain authority to remove the boys, a pilot buzzed Fair Lane, and Clara complained by phone to airport personnel. When she was told the reason for the buzzing, Clara issued the necessary authority.

Dahlinger and his crew had no sooner finished removing the humps and bumps from the airport acreage in 1924 than Henry asked him to create more humps and bumps on 163 acres of land to be used as a golf course. Henry and Clara had decided that Dearborn should have a fine country club. Although they had no interest in playing the game themselves, they thought their friends and company executives should have the opportunity. Liebold was put in charge. With help from Edsel and a professional golf designer, an eighteen-hole course covering a distance of 66,659 yards was laid out. Clara suggested the clubhouse be built of logs, but others prevailed, and it was of Old English timbered construction. Clara did, however, select furnishings and tapestries billed to her by the Harry J. Dean Company of Detroit in the amount of $9,084. The clubhouse cost the Fords about $250,000.

Golfing began in the spring of 1925, but the clubhouse was not finished until fall. The first meal was served on September 29, 1925, when Henry and Clara entertained Louis and Mina Ives. Dining-room check number one for the party of four amounted to six dollars and was signed with a flourish by Henry. The first official formal function at the club was an invitational dinner for forty couples on October 30, 1925, hosted by Henry and Clara. A wholesome dinner followed by an evening of vigorous old-fashioned dancing clearly demonstrated that the Fords got more pleasure from dancing than from playing golf. Benjamin Lovett had arrived in town, and all of Dearborn was dancing to Henry's musicians.

But Liebold had problems with the club. Financial losses were exorbitant. Henry's rule that there would be no tobacco or liquor on the premises could not be enforced. Members brought their own, producing a club environment quite obnoxious to Clara in particular. The sight of women smoking cigarettes in public was especially intolerable to Clara. Other than financially, Henry and Clara did not continue to patronize the club to any great extent. In 1944, they would transfer the property to Seaboard Properties Company, a Ford family corporation, and in 1952 the club membership purchased the club, land and all, for $300,000.

On January 28, 1925, the Clara Ford Nurses Home was dedicated. It accommodated ninety nurses and was an important part of Henry Ford Hospital School of Nursing and Hygiene. Other 1925 events included a vacation with the Edisons in Fort Myers in February and publication of a book written by Henry in collaboration with Samuel Crowther entitled *My Life and Work*. In explaining his success, Henry states in this book: "It was a very great thing to have my wife even more confident than I was. She has always been that way." Other books with Crowther would be *Today and Tomorrow* in 1926, and *Moving Forward* in 1931.

Both Henry and Clara were interested in property along the Atlantic coast in Georgia. They had been told by Burroughs in 1921 that the timber was magnificent and the birding was excellent. The first bit of property, known as Rabbit Hill and consisting of 100 acres, was bought on March 31, 1925, for $2,100. This was the first of more than

The Dearborn home desigend by Albert Kahn and built in 1926 for the family of Roy and Katharine Bryant. (0-14342)

500 purchases that within ten years would total 70,000 acres, more than 100 square miles of land. The property was centered at the town of Ways Station on the Atlantic Coast Line and Seaboard railways about twenty miles south of Savannah. A dozen or more antebellum plantations were purchased, some of them rice plantations with acres and acres of marshes. Henry's object was to establish a sawmill to harvest the lumber and give the people of the area more honest employment than producing moonshine. Clara was thinking in terms of a winter home with gracious Southern charm—less humid than Fort Myers and less accessible to crowds of people. In fact, she had a particular house in mind, the Hermitage near Savannah. On a bluff where the Richmond plantation once stood overlooking the Ogeechee River would be the site of Clara's Southern mansion, to be called Richmond Hill. The Hermitage was in ruins, but the unique brick from which it had been built was available, so Henry had the brick brought to the Richmond location to be used later in Clara's house. Between 1925 and 1950, the Fords would invest an estimated $4,267,020 in land, buildings, and operational losses.

On July 25, 1925, Katharine Bryant had written a letter to Clara saying she was coming to Dearborn to close the house contract. The house had been designed by Albert Kahn. Invoices for materials began to arrive in September 1925 and through June of 1926 had accumulated to $65,750, all of which was paid by Henry. With an added garage and a host of modifications, another total of $91,906.26 is reported. The Roy Bryant home was located a few hundred feet east of Brady Street as an

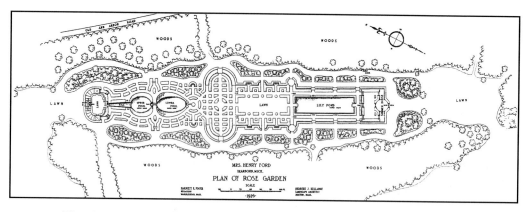

The plans for Clara's rose garden at Fair Lane, 1926.

extension of Northview (now Cherry Hill). Although it was in the village of Dearborn, the location was beyond certain existing utilities. Ford Motor Company installed those as needed. The Roy Bryant home was very close to Fair Lane, although the Rouge River separated the two. The family moved into the new home in about October 1926. A private railroad car was used to bring the Bryants from Zenia to Dearborn, with an extra baggage car to move their belongings. The family was added to the Ford Farm dairy list to receive monthly allotments of 155 quarts of milk, 17 quarts of cream, and 26 pounds of butter.

Clara, in July 1925, invested $500 in the preferred stock of Walton-Pierce Company in the Women's City Club Building in Detroit. The dividend rate for the preferred stock was 7 percent. This clothing store specialized in "gowns," and for the year of 1925–26 had sales of $123,158 with an after-tax profit of $20,055. Clara purchased many of her clothes from this establishment, as did Eleanor Ford. Some of Clara's dividend checks remain uncashed in the Ford Archives files. During the depression years, Clara did not attend stockholder meetings but sent Liebold with instructions to help in the business. The last meeting Liebold attended was in January 1944.

From February 17 until March 13, 1926, the Fords traveled south with their Dearborn friends, Mina and Louis Ives, utilizing both the *Fair Lane* and the *Sialia*. The itinerary covered the full length of the D T & I Railroad and the cities of Charleston, South Carolina; Savannah, Georgia; St. Augustine, Palm Beach, Fort Myers, and Pensacola, Florida; Havana, Cuba; and Rome, Georgia. (A copy of the diary kept by Louis Ives is in Appendix 2 of this book.)

Clara that spring was dealing with the Agassiz Association, which was offering wildflower plants of a wide variety at prices from as high as $1 each to as low as $35 per thousand. A memo in Clara's handwriting states, "Started rose garden in 1926." She was indeed in touch during February 1926 with Harriett R. Foote, "rosarian," of Marblehead, Massachusetts, who became consultant and designer of the spectacular

Aerial view of Clara's rose garden (circa 1950). (U-99210)

rose garden for which Clara would become so famous. In 1924, Foote had suggested Clara visit the Tothingham's garden at Easton, Massachusetts, for a good example. Collaborating with Foote was Herbert J. Kellaway, a landscape architect from Boston. Foote was also a supplier of rose bushes and sent 650 climbers to Clara at $1.25 each.

Clara's rose garden was about 500 feet long and 100 feet wide, located almost a third of a mile north of the Fair Lane residence, and surrounded by large shrubs backed by woods. Several mowed entrances led from the woods into the gardens. At the end farthest from the residence is a pergola on relatively high ground from which water flowed in rill-like fashion into a series of oval ponds in the garden area. Mowed lawns separating the multitude of garden plots led to a large rectangular lily pond. At the end of the garden nearest to the residence is a summer house. There are said to have been 10,000 rose bushes in the garden. The garden occupied a great deal of Clara's personal attention, and that of an army of garden laborers, for the next twenty years. As late as October 1945, Harriett Foote was offering Clara advice on the care of the gardens, and they were in a reasonable state of maintenance when Clara died in 1950.

On early Sunday evening, March 27, 1927, Henry had driven his coupe to the Engineering Building by himself. While returning along Michigan Avenue at about eight-thirty near Fair Lane, Henry was sideswiped by another car, sending Henry's car down a steep embankment and into a tree. Stunned and bloody, he made his way to the Fair Lane

gatehouse and was put to bed. Clara was concerned that the perpetra-
tors might be kidnappers or members of one of the gangs that ruled the
Detroit underworld during those Prohibition days. Two days later,
Henry was moved to Ford Hospital on doctor's orders. Minor surgery
was performed, but no serious complications were expected. Later, one
of the hospital doctors revealed that Henry may have had a temporary
blackout: "He did not seem to remember what had happened." The
FBI, together with Harry Bennett's Ford security men, worked on the
case and are said to have apprehended two boys who said Henry had
been "hogging" the road. It was decided there was no criminal intent on
the part of the boys. Henry did have a reputation for driving recklessly
on public roads, so much so that some people refused to ride with him.
Bennett, Ford's security chief, assured Clara that it could not have been
gang members who caused the accident, because he would have known
of any such plans in advance. Bennett took credit for protecting the
Ford families from harm at both Fair Lane and Grosse Pointe.

That summer, Charles Lindbergh landed his *Spirit of St. Louis* at
Ford Airport on August 11, 1927. He offered Henry a ride in his plane,
and Henry accepted; it was his very first airplane flight. Edsel also had
his first flight with Lindbergh. (Clara herself may never have flown in a

A view of Clara's five-
acre Rose Garden
with approximately
ten thousand plants.
This photograph is
taken from in front of
the pergola looking
toward the summer
house to the south.
Some distance
beyond the summer
house is the Fair
Lane residence.
(0-5967)

plane.) While at the airport, Lindbergh flew the little single-place Flivver plane developed by Ford Motor Company and tried his hand as copilot in a Ford Trimotor. Lindbergh had no license to pilot a multi-engined aircraft at that time. He became one of the few notables who were invited to stay at Fair Lane. For a short period during World War II, Lindbergh would be hired by Ford to test B-24 bombers.

At about this time, Clara met the mother of the princess of Siam at Ford Airport when her party visited Detroit. In a note, Clara describes her as "a dear little lady who had ten children and looked about forty years old." Clara was offered two Siamese cigars; she took about three puffs of one.

On May 26, 1927, recognizing that the Model T was obsolete, Henry stopped all production of the car after more than 15 million of them had been made. He closed his assembly plants completely until October 20, 1927, when he offered the redesigned Model A with a much-improved four-cylinder engine and styling similar to the Lincolns that Edsel had designed. Both Edsel and Clara had known the Model T was obsolete long before Henry would admit it.

Henry's friend Harvey Firestone had alerted the Fords in February 1923 to the British monopoly on Far Eastern rubber which caused the price of automotive tires to skyrocket. Firestone and Ford searched for other areas where they could produce rubber independently of the monopoly. Firestone began developing a plantation in Liberia, West Africa, and in 1926, Ford sent a team of botanists to explore the Amazon valley in Brazil. In July 1927, a "free" land concession of 2.5 million acres along the Tapajos River was negotiated for Ford. The $125,000 in bribes to Brazilian officials paid by his land agent, however, was upsetting to Henry. Ford, Firestone, and Edison together also organized experimental work in Florida to find a domestic plant from which rubber could be extracted. After testing 2,300 plants, Edison found goldenrod to be the best, but it was not as good as *Hevea brasiliensis*, the Brazilian source of rubber.

An enthusiastic Henry announced in October 1927 that he would fly with Lindbergh on a South American tour, but Henry did not go. The Brazilian settlements of Fordlandia and Belterra never came into full rubber production before synthetic rubber was developed during World War II. In 1945, after an investment estimated at $20 million, Ford Motor Company disposed of its rubber interests to the Brazilian government for $250,000.

Henry had been collecting antiques since at least 1913, when he found and restored the old Westinghouse steam engine he had operated for James Gleason in 1881. Henry hated seeing anything that interested him being allowed to deteriorate. If an old piece of machinery was standing out in a farmer's field, and it was something he was interested

in, he would buy it and have it restored; likewise any old house, old mill, or old schoolhouse.

By 1924, Henry and Clara were inviting friends to visit their "museum" in a portion of the old Fordson tractor plant, where they had quite a collection of clocks, antique horse-drawn vehicles, and farm equipment. That year, on the fourth of July, they both dressed up in period clothing and paraded their historic carriages through the streets of Dearborn. Clara is also said to have had a room in the tractor plant for exhibiting her collection of quilts, hooked rugs, china, pottery, silver, pewter, and glass. Henry's reputation as a collector of Americana had now grown to the point where he was being flooded with more antiques and homemade craft items than could be properly stored. Many were left in crates in a Ford Airport hangar.

Henry's vision of an educational institution was taking shape by 1925. He would have a "museum" to tell the story of man's technological progress through displays of inventions and artifacts and a "village" of early American life to show how such objects were made and used. Pupils would learn not only by reading books but also by using the tools and techniques of the past. "When we are through," he stated, "we shall have reproduced American life as lived in the past, and that, I think, is the best way of preserving a part of our history and tradition." The location for this educational institution was to be on 240 acres, with a 14-acre museum adjacent but not attached to the Engineering Laboratory; the village would contain nearly one hundred early American buildings next to the museum. The museum would be just a few steps from Henry's office in the Engineering Building. All of this was within a mile of Fair Lane.

While Henry and Clara were preserving the past in Dearborn, the Gaukler's Point property Henry and Clara had purchased in 1912, an equal distance east of Detroit, was being used in 1927 by Edsel and

Edsel Ford's estate on Lake St. Clair was built in 1926–27 on property once owned by Henry and Clara. Designed by Albert Kahn, the home faithfully reproduces the beautiful yet practical architecture of the Cotswold houses of Worcestershire, England. The property includes sixty-five acres with a shoreline of more than three thousand feet on the lake. (0.3399)

Eleanor as a site for their new family home on Lake St. Clair. Designed in beautiful Cotswold style, the home is faced with Briar Hill sandstone, with stone for the roof imported from England and installed by British craftsmen. Interior furnishings were selected with utmost care and artistic elegance, without limitations on cost. This would be Edsel and Eleanor's home for the rest of their lives.

On September 17, 1927, Clara received the following letter from the Woman's National Farm and Garden Association:

My dear Mrs. Ford,

I am commissioned by the Nominating Committee of the Woman's National Farm and Garden Association to extend to you an earnest invitation to accept the office of President and become its head for the following year. In this request the Committee is joined by many of the prominent members of the Assoc. whom I have consulted. The election will take place at the coming meeting in Boston Oct. 13th & 14th when I understand we will be having the pleasure of meeting you at the Wayside Inn.

As you know, the Association works on the problems of the rural women; seeks to bring them into contact with other women and, when necessary, to broaden interests in the words of the Charter to enable women to co-operate in furthering Agricultural & Horticultural interests; supplying scholarships to young women who need them for attending such schools & colleges. etc.

The detail work is largely done by the several Branches, altho there are scattered branches all over the country, the National Association holds them together; publishes the Magazine; holds about two meetings a year, Spring & Fall.

After a severe struggle, the Magazine is now on a good financial basis and is being well conducted and should serve more and more as a medium of exchange between members and branches.

There is available a good Executive Secretary if the President wishes to have her assistance who is a member of the Assoc. thoroughly interested, able to push the work, do the detail and conduct the headquarters business; she is now doing the work for the present President in an acceptable manner.

We have the prospect of strong Vice Presidents, Secretaries & Treasurer and will also elect a Council among whom the work may be distributed.

There is good work ahead for the Association and we urgently ask you to accept the office of President; we believe that by so doing you will greatly help the work and that you will find a loyal following.

Yours very truly
Emma Blakiston
Chairman Nominating Committee

On October 14, as the new president of the Woman's National Farm and Garden Association, Clara served four-thirty tea at Wayside Inn. Three weeks later, after Clara had paid the association secretary in Philadelphia her monthly salary check of $100, she was informed by letter that the salary was to be $50 per week. Clara would have none of that, and she assigned Jane Hicks, who had worked in Liebold's office, to be both her personal assistant and the association secretary.

Clara's first contribution to *Home Acres,* the association's magazine, read as follows: "I wish to extend my warmest greetings to members of the Woman's National Farm and Garden Association, and to thank them for the honor they did me in making me their President. It will be my pleasure in the coming year to do my utmost to please them, if possible make *Home Acres* bigger and better, enlarge the membership and other good things as they come along."

But Clara did not let her responsibilities with the Woman's National Farm and Garden Association tie her down. After celebrating the Edisons' forty-second wedding anniversary on February 25, 1928, in Fort Myers, Henry and Clara prepared for a trip to England. Sailing aboard the *Majestic* on March 31, registered as Mr. and Mrs. Robinson, they are said to have revolutionized the ship's dancing programs by leading passengers in old-fashioned dances. After arriving in Southampton on April 6, they motored to London. The next day, they saw London from the top of a bus. Henry was the guest of honor at a dinner given by the American Society in London on April 11; he made a thirty-one-word speech. The Fords met King George and Queen Mary for tea at the home of Lady Astor the next day. In the following days, Henry was received by the prince of Wales, met Lloyd George, and visited Morris Motors at Cowdrey. Henry and Clara spent the balance of their time traveling to literary landmarks and to Clara's ancestral town of Warwick, and it is said Henry visited the British Antique Dealers Association. They set sail for home on May 2, arriving in New York on May 9.

At home again, all was not tranquility. A disturbing affair erupted during the summer of 1928. Agnes Morton, a servant Clara had employed, was demanding more than $100,000 from Henry, using extortion by threats of public exposure. Henry was angry, and Clara was not immediately aware of the suit. The following letter was mailed to Clara by another servant, Saima Wanttaja, on September 8:

Henry and Clara, registered as Mr. and Mrs. Robinson, on the deck of the White Star Line's *S.S. Majestic,* on their way to England in March 1928. (P.0.19771)

Dear Mrs. Ford:

I am writing this in an endeavor to give you a clear understanding of the unfortunate affair in which Mr. Ford, your husband, and myself were the innocent victims of slander by two persons under your own roof who, if justice were not found wanting, could and should be punishable by law.

I feel that this was caused, beyond a doubt, by the jealousy in one of your servitors, because of the good will which always existed between myself and everyone with whom I came in contact while in your employ.

I know that Miss Agnes Morton has always succeeded in causing trouble among your employees, and now it is her scheme to cause trouble between yourself and Mr. Ford, to further her own ends.

I can honestly say that I have never had a breath of scandal touch my name in connection with any of my previous employers or anyone; and Mr. Ford has never manifested any signs of friendship towards me beyond a handshake, and that always in the presence of others.

While in your service, I have always done everything in my power to please you, therefore I feel that I am entitled to a reference from you.

This affair has almost brought me to the verge of a nervous breakdown.

Saima Wanttaja

Clara felt she should investigate. She tried to reach Agnes, who was already under surveillance in the case by the F.B.I. in Long Beach, California. Ray Dahlinger advised Clara not to communicate with Agnes, that Agnes had an aggressive lawyer who could be handled only by Ford lawyers. Just how the case was settled remains a mystery to the public.

Another situation troublesome to Clara concerned her sister Eva. George Brubaker, Eva's husband since 1907, who had been working for Ford Motor Company since 1915, suffered a nervous breakdown in 1927, left Ford Motor Company, and was recuperating in Utica, Michigan. Eva had left him in February 1923, after he had gone on a trip to Europe without her. Clara began helping Eva and her daughters, Grace and Bernice, with living expenses beginning in 1923 and extending for the rest of Clara's life. Between 1923 and 1928, George resided in rented apartments in Detroit while working for Ford Motor Company. Company records show George was in Europe again from December 1926 until March 1927. In January 1928, George Brubaker sued Eva in Macomb County Circuit Court. The Brubaker case dragged on for years. Clara had arranged for Ford Motor Company lawyers to insist on a divorce. Eva's daughter Grace testified that she did not believe her mother and father could be reunited amicably. The younger daughter, Bernice, testified in favor of her father. The court finally convened at Kate Raymond's home in Adrian to take bedside testimony from Eva. The case eventually ended in a divorce. But because of Clara's interference, Eva later blamed Clara for breaking up her marriage.

While Henry and Clara were in Florida during March 1928, Clara's brother Milton, age fifty-three, died in Munson Hospital at Traverse City, Michigan, after undergoing a hernia operation. He had been state representative from Grand Traverse County since 1924 and was president of the Grand Traverse Auto Company. The following January, in 1929, Bernice Robertson Bryant and the Bryants' two adopted children boarded the *S. S. Belgenland* for a three-month around-the-world cruise. Starting from New York City, the ship called at such ports as Havana, Balboa, San Francisco, Honolulu, Hong Kong, Singapore, Bombay, Cairo, Athens, and Naples before returning to the United States. The two children were tutored while at sea and went on some on-shore side trips. Clara received frequent cards and letters from Bernice and the youngsters. Bernice repeatedly stressed her sorrow at Milton's not being with them. They returned to Traverse City in April.

During 1928 and 1929, Henry acquired land in the township of Raritan, New Jersey, on which were located the buildings of the Menlo Park complex used by Edison between 1876 and 1886 for discoveries such as the incandescent lamp and the phonograph. After moving what he could of the buildings along with seven carloads of the red New Jersey soil to Dearborn, Henry recreated the Menlo Park buildings in Greenfield Village.

Both Greenfield Village and Henry Ford Museum were dedicated by Thomas Edison on September 27, 1928. The village dedication was held at the Fort Myers Laboratory, one of the first buildings moved to the Dearborn site, and the museum dedication was at the cornerstone, which had hardly been staked out. As with several of the buildings acquired by Henry and moved to the village, Edison's Fort Myers Laboratory was relinquished somewhat under duress. Neither Mina Edison nor the city of Fort Myers wanted the building taken from Fort Myers. Edison had previously succumbed to Henry's offer to build a new laboratory to take its place. Henry's gift of a Lincoln limousine to Mina in May 1927 may have helped his cause.

Henry and Clara with Thomas and Mina Edison (under the umbrella) standing beside Edison's Fort Myers Laboratory, about 1925. This building was
built by Thomas Edison's father in 1884–85, and Edison had used it for more
than forty winters. He was willing to give the building to Henry, and Henry
agreed to build Edison another laboratory to take its place. Shipped by railroad from Florida, it was the first building completed in Greenfield Village
and was dedicated on September 27, 1928. (188.5545)

The manager of Stein & Blaine, women's clothiers in New York,
wrote to Clara in July 1928, asking for quick delivery of a new Ford
Model A. Clara had maintained an account with Stein & Blaine averaging between $10,000 and $20,000, her average purchases having been
in the neighborhood of $5,000 on each visit to the store.

Henry and Clara, using the *Fair Lane,* headed for the South on
February 2, 1929. Her diary tells of the first few days:

February 2: Started for Florida went by way of Boston
"Wayside Inn." Bishop Page and Mrs. Page were on the same
train so went to Inn with us. Visited Boy's Trade School,

Mary's Lamb School, and Parmenter House, little old house over one hundred years old that we had restored, had dinner in old kitchen by the open fire, on bare table. They left at five o'clock for Boston to visit Bishop Page's mother who is an invalid.

February 5: Arrived in NY, Mr & Mrs Plantiff met us, I went direct to Stein & Blaine's to have fittings, then to Brentanies to get some books, to Tiffany's to order note paper, Yamanaka's for incense and flower bowls then to Mr. Ziegfelds office to look at Colonial suits he had ten elephants on his table and under. Then luncheon. Then to Carnige's Hall to see portrait of Henry.

February 6: Started south at 3:30, first long stop at Jacksonville 5 hours, poured rain. Henry went for walk, I stayed in car, after dinner we went for a walk under train cover. Arrived Fort Myers 9:45 Thursday.

February 7: Henry walked up to Edison laboratory. I went to house and started housekeeping. Mrs Edison called to offer her hospitality but preferred staying at home & getting settled. Evening cool, had nice grate fire.

February 8: Had electricians to change fixtures and curtain hangers to hang curtains, big job cutting all new poles.

February 9: Got pretty well cleaned up for Sunday.

February 10: Up late breakfast by the fire, then went on front porch and read aloud Old Man Adam and his Chillun. Mr. Edison came over at eleven, had dinner with us and then we went down by the river and sat until five o'clock just reminiscing.

February 11: Went over to Edison dock to meet Pres. Elect and Mrs. Hoover, their son Herbert, Mr. & Mrs. Ricard and Mr. Milbank owner of the yacht they all came on from Miami. Drove thru city of Fort Myers then back to the Edisons for dinner, wild turkey and a birthday cake with one candle. They all came over to our house after dinner. Mrs. Hoover loved our house in the orchard.

February 12: Mrs. Edison invited me to go to luncheon at Rotary Club, but was tired and declined. Went with her to meeting at Woman's Club, had good music. Mrs. Roundtree,

George Washington's Birthday very good, her little girl recited, It takes a Heap O'Living to make it home—splendid.

Henry was anxious to discuss with Edison the progress of the Edison Botanical Research Corporation's work on producing rubber from a domestic plant. Before returning home on March 6, Henry and Edison visited the Southern Sugar Company at Clewiston, Florida, to study cane processing. Clewiston was just a few miles beyond the 7,290-acre ranch Henry owned at Goodno, Florida.

Upon returning to Dearborn in March, the *Fair Lane* was sent to the Pullman shops at Hammond, Indiana, for servicing. During 1929, the *Fair Lane* had made four round trips to New York; two round trips to Ellsworth, Maine; a round trip to Jamestown, New York; a round trip to Marquette, Michigan; a round trip to Orange, New Jersey; a trip to Boston via New York; and a round trip to Pittsburgh.

The Fords' trip to Marquette that year may have had a noteworthy purpose. Several prominent Detroiters belonged to the Huron Mountain Shooting and Fishing Club, founded in 1889. It was located in the Upper Peninsula of Michigan about forty miles north of Marquette, near Big Bay, across the mountain from the Ford Motor Company lumber mills at L'anse and Pequaming. By 1929, fifty families had built cabins, all of primitive log construction with a well and pump, all equipped with electricity but without telephone service. In May 1929, Henry decided to join the club, paying annual dues of $250. Robert O. Derrick of Detroit was chosen to design the cabin, which would accommodate twelve. J. M. Goodwin of Marquette was hired as general contractor. A letter from Derrick to Clara indicated the cabin would be ready for occupancy by August 1930. Clara was purchasing furnishings from Tomella & Rupp of Marquette in May 1930. The cost of the cabin is recorded as $100,949. Henry and Clara remained members as long as they lived, and Clara seems to have enjoyed it as a summer home more than Henry did. It is reported that Henry did not hunt or fish and spent considerable time in Big Bay rather than at the cabin or at the clubhouse. Henry fell in love with the little town of Big Bay; in 1943, at age eighty, he would buy the entire town, including fifty-two houses, the large lumber mill, and the hotel.

In gathering antiques for Wayside Inn and Henry Ford Museum & Greenfield Village, Henry and Clara did business with dealers in both New England and Old England. In 1928, Herbert F. Morton found several priceless old engines for Henry in England, and purchases that year from Israel Sack in New York came to $70,100. In 1929, purchases from Charles Woolsley Lion, also of New York, came to at least $100,000. Many more items were bought in small lots by William Taylor, Ford's roving agent in New England with headquarters at

The Ford "cabin" at the Huron Mountain Club north of Marquette in Michigan's Upper Peninsula. This was Clara's favorite summer resort. Dozens of photographs show Clara feeding the deer which roamed the woods and came to the door for some tasty morsel given to them by either Clara or her personal maid, Rosa Buhler. Rosa is said to have greatly enjoyed taking an early morning swim in the frigid waters of Lake Superior each morning. Henry seems not to have especially relished living in such solitude in the woods, and neither Henry nor Clara was inclined to participate in social events held at the clubhouse. (0.2847)

Interior of the Huron Mountain "cabin." This well-furnished living room was lit by electricity as well as a fireplace. Following Henry's death in 1947, Clara continued to spend Augusts here, bringing friends and relatives to keep her company. (0.8543)

Wayside Inn. Ford's automobile dealers were also well aware of the Fords' interest in antiques and did their share of collecting on behalf of the Fords.

In May 1929, Henry and Clara visited Williamsburg, Virginia, which had been recently restored by the Rockefeller family. In July, they attended Lewis Miller's birthday celebration at Chautauqua, New York. Miller had been cofounder of the Chautauqua Institution and was Mina Edison's father. In mid-October 1929, the Fords visited the Edisons at West Orange.

The brick home of the Bryant family in which Henry and Clara were married was torn down in 1920; 9,500 bricks from it, together with some roof timbers, doors, and door hardware, were saved. When Greenfield Village was being built in 1929, architect Edward Cutler designed the chapel, which was named Martha-Mary Chapel after Clara's and Henry's mothers, and in it those remnants of Clara's home were used. The Bryant family Bible is said to have been placed on the Bible stand. The chapel was first used by the children of Greenfield

Martha-Mary Chapel at Greenfield Village. Named after Clara's mother, Martha, and Henry's mother, Mary, the chapel was designed by architect Edward Cutler and built in 1929, including bricks and door hardware from the Bryant homestead in Greenfield Township. The chapel bell was cast by the son of Paul Revere. Martha-Mary Chapel was used by the schoolchildren of Greenfield Village for daily morning exercises and for seventy years has served as a site for hundreds of weddings. (P.0.4031)

Village on January 26, 1931, and has served ever since as a popular site for weddings.

Near the chapel, Clara planted an herb garden with the help of Ellen Plantiff. In a letter to a friend, Clara states: "I have given the garden the name of one in Italy — 'The Garden of the Leavened Heart.' The herbs I have planted are: spearmint, peppermint, chives, thyme, summer savory, winter savory, borage, dill, sorrel, coriander, bee balm, horehound, lavender, sweet marjoram, pennyroyal, rue, chamomile, catnip, sweet basil." The design of the garden shows eight segments, four of them in heart shapes, all forming a circle enclosing the central cross. The point of the center held a brass sundial inscribed "Ye Shadow Teacheth." Bee hives close by completed the scene. Clara's enthusiasm for gardening was so great, she told this correspondent, that in the springtime she used a seed catalog for a pillow.

In Greenfield Village, elementary-school classes were started in 1929. The children of the village schools were treated as a privileged group, with transportation and all sundry expenses paid. About three hundred were eventually accommodated at levels through high school. But when Henry began to plan additional buildings for larger numbers, Clara put her foot down, saying, "I object to taking care of more school-children of the community while their mothers, relieved of the responsibility, have time to spend playing bridge and enjoying themselves."

In honor of Edison's invention of the incandescent lamp in 1879, a "Light's Golden Jubilee" celebration, organized by Henry and Edsel, was held on October 21, 1929. At this rainy daylong event, with President Hoover and hundreds of other notables in attendance, Edison reenacted the lighting of the first successful incandescent lamp in the reconstructed Menlo Park laboratory, and the museum and village were dedicated together as the Edison Institute of Technology. Mr. Edison was not at all well during the proceedings. Some say he nearly died at the banquet that evening and was revived with adrenaline by Hoover's physician. Mina Edison complained that the affair seemed all for the benefit of the General Electric Company. Clara was in attendance with Mina, but Eleanor and the Ford grandchildren were quarantined at home because of illness. The stock-market crash was to occur just four days later.

In the early spring of 1930, Clara was asked to give a speech for the National Garden Bureau of Chicago. Her talk was part of a radio program broadcast to attendees of the Chicago Garden and Flower Show. In her own handwriting, a rough draft of her speech reads as follows:

> Ladies and Gentlemen, you may be disappointed in my subject as it was advertised to be a talk on Country Beauty. I am going to talk to you about the Woman's National Farm & Garden

The banquet scene at Light's Golden Jubilee on October 21, 1929. This is a 17-by-6 foot painting by Irving R. Bacon, Henry's artist, who used individual photographs supplied by the more than four hundred guests to compose this diorama. Bacon worked for ten years between 1935 and 1945 on this project. Seventeen people were at the speaker's table, including Henry, Clara, and Edsel Ford; Mr. and Mrs. Thomas Edison; President and Mrs. Herbert Hoover; Madame Curie; Owen D. Young (Speaker); John D. Rockefeller; Gerard Swope; and George A. Eastman. Clara influenced Bacon's work by suggesting that Eleanor and the grandchildren be added to the painting although they were not at the banquet. The Jubilee painting is on exhibit in Henry Ford Museum. (P.A.2509)

Association, I'm sure many of you have never heard of it. This association was organized in 1914 by a group of women in Philadelphia to help the farm & country woman, at that time there were no good roads except main roads, & no radios. That was 16 years ago, many changes have been made in living conditions since then, many women are better off, but there are many far back in the newer country, and up north still.

During the war this association did notable work in food production & conservation for which it was awarded a medal by the National War Garden Commission. It helped organize the Land Army work, and in 1918 the Land Army placed 15,000 women on the land. You all know that when the war was on we all had to drop what ever work we were doing and take up war work, and during that time our organization suffered, many states had been organized and were doing good work, but after the war was over, it was very difficult to take up the work again,

Clara at the Hotel Pennsylvania in New York, with a model roadside market she had designed for exhibit by the Woman's National Farm and Garden Association. A pamphlet stated, "This model is made out of old boards and whitewashed, and so cheap no farmer can say he cannot afford it. With thousands of miles of good roads, the farmer can make more money from a neat, attractive building than he can from the ugly-looking shacks we see along our beautiful highways." (P.0.7145)

many states had disorganized, and it was difficult to get them started again. The New England states never disorganized entirely, but kept up the work as best they could, so that after the war was over they got started more easily.

Before I go any further I want to tell you that Mrs. Frances King was the first president and served for a number of years, 2 1/2 years ago I was elected National President, I felt at the time that I could not serve as I was so busy with other work, but I was persuaded, and as time goes on I get more & more interested in the work, the chief reason is that I have such excellent women all over the country to work with and our membership consists of more than three thousand.

Some of our purposes were, to stimulate an interest in, and a love for the country life, to cooperate with the Federal & State agencies, to assist women on the farm and women in the city to a realization of their interdependence and to better understand their mutual problems. To help women thru scholarships and expert advice to the best training in agriculture, horticulture, and to help women so trained, and by the way, we have a scholarship fund to be used by deserving women. The National fund to date is $12,000, and many states have started funds, Michigan has just started, and has about $700, during the first years we had sales of things women could make, and we all know that there are no better cooks in the world than farmer's wives, such farm jellies, butter, cake & pies and many things made with the needle, such as children's clothes, braided and hooked rugs and knitted things so these women were persuaded to get things ready and a sale was held. They all made a little pin money.

These sales grew so that the members of New England were brave enough to start a little shop, it has been running seven or eight years, and is very successful, it is at New Berry St. Boston. When you go to Boston, visit it, it is well worthwhile, it is called the Green Door Shop meaning the door of friendship between the country and city woman. There is another shop in Benson, Vermont, and we hope to have one in Michigan this year.

We also publish a magazine called *Home Acres*. The membership is $2.00 per year, and includes the magazine. Our last Annual meeting was held in New York, we had a three days' session, this next year we may hold the Annual meeting in Washington D.C. We have a council of thirty members and are obliged to meet twice a year in order to keep things going. Last spring we met in Sewickley, this spring we meet for council in Philadelphia at the home of our first vice-president Mrs. Howard Lewis.

In addition to our regular work this year, we are going to try working toward bettering Roadside Markets, both in looks and product, we have started one in Massachusetts, and hope to start one near Detroit, we hope to set a standard, calling for cleanliness, fair prices, and fresh goods, we expect members of our association to volunteer to visit these markets occasionally and see that the standard is kept up, two years ago I had made at my home, out of old boards a little Roadside market we whitewashed it inside and out, stained the roof dark green, and planted a few flowers around it. I have had many requests to exhibit it at flower shows in different cities, but that is too much responsibility for me. I exhibited it at the North American Flower Show in Detroit two years ago. I filled it with vegetables, fruit, nuts, eggs, butter, honey and some potted geraniums and it was very attractive. I wanted to show that one did not have to spend a lot of money to get an attractive roadside market. I also wanted to show that more people would stop to buy from an attractive stand than an ugly one, many times stocked from the city markets and commission houses. Our aim is to have them stocked fresh from the farms, we cannot expect to accomplish miracles at first, but hope to accomplish much good in the end. I thank you.

Chapter 9
Depression Days

enry and Clara planned another trip to Europe for September and October 1930. Leaving New York on the *S.S. Bremen* on September 6, Henry reported to the press regarding the economy: "It took a long time to get sick and it will take a long time to get well. What causes business is a man's thoughts and what he creates. You don't create anything when you sell stocks." In England, the Fords met with Prime Minister Ramsey MacDonald and with Philip Snowden, governor of the Bank of England. By September 11, they had arrived in France. While driving from Cherbourg to Paris, Henry learned of a 100-year-old threshing machine still operating in Normandy. He had to examine it, putting them hours behind schedule. In Paris, Henry was pursued all day by reporters with questions on everything from tariffs to Prohibition. He ignored them until Clara finally intervened, saying, "Aren't you going to tell them anything?" Henry then made the statement, "I'm hungry."

They visited Baden-Baden, Stuttgart, and Munich, where, on September 24, Henry spent hours taking apart an 1888 Benz automobile and refused politely to make a $5 million donation to the National Socialist Party. At Cologne, he laid the cornerstone of the new Ford factory, seizing a trowel to put the stone in place in a workmanlike manner. The Fords stopped at Rotterdam, where they met with the Dutch and Belgian Ford Motor Company directors, and then traveled by train back to England. While riding through the countryside, Henry noted the sorry state of agriculture in that part of England. The following year, he purchased Lord Kenyon's Boreham House and took control of some five thousand acres of land to demonstrate how farming could be done with up-to-date methods and machinery. The Boreham properties were managed by Sir Percival Perry; some of them are still under control of

September–October 1930
Fords enjoy a trip to Europe

March 7, 1932
"Hunger March" to Dearborn by Detroit's unemployed

1932–1933
"Garden Cards" are issued to Ford employees to encourage home gardening

February 14, 1933
"Bank holiday" closes all the banks in Michigan

January 15, 1936
Ford Foundation is established

February 3, 1936
Henry signs his will

Spring 1937
The Richmond Hill winter residence in Georgia is occupied

May 26, 1937
The "Battle of the Overpass" splits Fords into two camps

July 30, 1938
Henry's seventy-fifth birthday

April 3, 1939
Henry is reported to have symptoms of senility

Ford Motor Company. The Fords sailed home from England on the *S. S. Europa* on October 17; on board, when the band played a mazurka, Henry and Clara danced while the younger passengers stood by, asking what it was.

A letter to Clara dated October 4, 1930, must have warmed her heart:

Dear Mrs. Ford:

Mr. Coolidge and I are your self-bidden guests tonight, although you are far away. We stopped for tea on our way to Boston. It was Mr. Coolidge's first visit to the Wayside Inn. I had not been here for several years—not since Mr. Ford became its Host, or should I say Landlord?

Mr. Coolidge and I were married twenty-five years ago to-day. We found that we had to be in Boston on Monday and it occurred to us that it would be pleasant to drive this far upon our journey today and spend the night of our anniversary at the Inn. Had we known that custom closed the house on Sundays, we should not have asked to come but we were ignorant of that fact until after our arrival. However we received the most cordial and hospitable welcome and were made to feel at home, at once. Miss (or Mrs) Mirch opened your suite to us—and here we are.

What a delightful place to spend the night—any night—but especially the night of one's twenty-fifth wedding anniversary. It would not be complete without this expression of appreciation to you and Mr. Ford. We wished to have you know how happy we are. It is as though we had turned aside from the busy world and found a little corner of earth's heaven.

Sincerely,
Grace Coolidge

At home in Dearborn, Henry and Clara were not without financial buffers to counter the depression. Dated November 29, 1930, a list valued nine items of jewelry and furs at $440,822.80, not counting another two-strand pearl necklace purchased from John Kay for $275,000. Henry, in the meantime, was keeping $4 million of cash in a wall safe controlled by Liebold.

Others in the family were willing to benefit from the Ford exchequer. A letter from Frank Campsall, secretary to Henry Ford, dated January 28, 1931, reads as follows:

Mr. S. W. Raymond
S. W. Raymond Auto Sales
Adrian, Michigan

Dear Sir:

In accordance with your conversation with Mr. Ford recently we are enclosing a New York Draft No. 293938 payable to your order for the sum of $7,000.00

Very truly yours
Frank Campsall

The Raymonds set sail February 2 on the *S.S. Empress of France.* A wire to the ship from Clara read, "Love and best wishes for a comfortable, pleasant, and safe trip." On February 9, another letter from Campsall was directed to W. E. Hyslop of Ford Motor Company of Asnieres, France:

Dear Sir:

Mr. and Mrs. Samuel Raymond and daughter Violet are at the present time on a Mediterranean cruise. It is the writer's understanding that they will probably arrive at Paris in about two weeks and will call on you.

Miss Raymond is planning on locating in Paris for the purpose of attending an art school in costume designing. We will appreciate your rendering every possible assistance relative to the selection of a school and also in any other manner to make their stay pleasant.

As a matter of further information, Mrs. Raymond is a sister of Mrs. Henry Ford.

Very truly yours
Frank Campsall

Violet's parents sailed from Southhampton for home on April 18, leaving Violet in Paris. A letter from Violet in Paris is dated June 20, 1931:

Dear Mr. Campsall:
I am writing to ask you if you will please drop the Paris office a line again about my having a car occasionally? I feel certain that they do

business through the London office and feel that they have not the proper authority from headquarters.

Uncle Henry said I could have it when I wish but I always feel that Mr. Collins of the Paris office is not quite sure what to do. I don't use it often but a friend of mine is coming to spend the summer with me and I feel we will be wanting it more often. Will you just mention that I would like Mon. Pashe to drive us as he speaks English and the rest do not.

Then, too, will you ask Uncle Henry if it would be possible ever to have the car and chauffeur for a couple days at a time. He knows all the surrounding country so well and it would be very nice if when Virginia comes if we could go to Baden-Baden for example for a day or so. Not speaking the language it would be hard for us otherwise. If this does not fully meet with his approval be sure and tell me, because it is farthest from my intentions to do anything to displease him.

Oh yes, one more thing, please tell Uncle Henry I am still looking for the letter he promised me.

I do hope my requests are not too numerous!

My regards to Mr Ford, and thanking you, I remain

Sincerely
Violet Raymond

During that summer of 1931, Violet met a French-speaking man named Francois Audi who followed her to America. He was given temporary work in the foundry of Ford Motor Company, where he proved his worth. He learned to speak English and married Violet on August 22, 1932, with full approval of Henry and Clara and the Bryant family. Francois and Violet Audi had two children, Suzanne and Richard.

Exactly two years after the Light's Golden Jubilee in Dearborn, Thomas Edison died on October 21, 1931, in West Orange, New Jersey. Henry had visited Edison on July 24 and again just two weeks before his death, when they had talked at some length in the library at Glenmont. At the funeral, Henry preferred not to view the body, telling Charles, Edison's son, that he wanted to think of Edison as he remembered him in the past. In attendance at the funeral in West Orange were Henry and Clara, Edsel and Eleanor, and Harvey Firestone and his family. Edison was buried at sunset beneath a large oak tree on a hill overlooking his laboratory and factories.

The depression was less severe in Dearborn than in adjoining communities, thanks largely to the efforts of Henry and Clara Ford. Although the standard of living at Fair Lane seems not to have immediately changed following the market crash of October 1929, Henry and Clara were soon aware of the problems of others. Clara was still investing in more diamonds and furs in 1930, and the twenty or more annual trips on the *Fair Lane* did not diminish through 1931. On her January 1932 trip to New York, Clara had her Russian sable coat, purchased in 1927 for $63,600, remodeled at a cost of $9,500, and her combined jewelry and furs were insured in 1935 for approximately $1 million. There was a significant reduction in New York trips during 1932 and 1933, although Clara managed to get there about five times each year. Only six trips were taken on the *Fair Lane* during 1933, four of these to New York.

One of Clara's typical New York trips, in about 1928, is described in this letter back to Dearborn from the Ritz-Carlton Hotel:

Dear Henry-

We are here settled and living quite normal, having a very nice time. Mr. Moore met us at the train, took care of our luggage, and had Johnny to drive us so everything so far has gone well. Went to the theatre last night, and have just got up. The girls are still in bed, and it is nine o'clock. Met Dutee and Rose with some friends in the lobby of the Ritz Monday night. Dutee did not look well, and Rose said he has not been himself for a long time, told him he should come and make us a little visit at Dearborn. He sent us tickets for a play that he said we should see. I wonder if you have been for your R.R. trip yet, suppose you are dancing as much as ever. Weather is fine here but seems as if it would rain soon. Hope Agnes is looking after you as I told her. They are very nice to me at the Hotel, do not let anyone call me unless they ask for Mrs. C.J. Fisk.

Met Mrs. Edison at the dressmakers, did not have long to talk with her as she was going to have a fitting, was very sweet, said that Mr. Edison was well. Mr. Harrison at Stein Blaines said Mrs. Firestone had been in and ordered lots of clothes, and that Mr. Firestone came in and stayed two hours looking at clothes.

New York never looked as wonderful so many new stores, I wonder how they all make a living. I am feeling fine, no backache, think it is the change. Monday we all felt a little tired, so had our dinner in our sitting room, went for a long walk, and to bed early. I wish you liked N.Y. better, and would come with me.

Lots of love
Cally

Foreseeing depression trouble, Henry resigned as president of Dearborn State Bank in January 1931. Clara, in July of that year, was on the executive committee of the Girls' Protective League, which was helping families with children, girls in particular, who were poor but not eligible for public welfare. Some of the fathers were unemployed Ford workers. In October 1931, the supervisor of Nankin Township, a neighbor of Dearborn Township, appealed to Ford Farms to supply vegetables to a Red Cross soup kitchen for hungry families. Henry was farming hundreds of acres in Dearborn. In a matter of weeks, he had taken over the soup kitchen, furnishing both cooked vegetables and stew. At that location, he then set up a commissary where shoes, clothing, and grocery items were furnished, cooking and sewing classes organized, and a community cooperative established that lasted throughout the depression period. Other similar "welfare commissaries" were established in Garden City and St. Clair Shores, suburbs of Detroit.

From Ways Station, Georgia, Clara received this letter from Essie L. Burt on March 12, 1932:

My dear Mrs. Ford:

I hope this letter will find you and family enjoying the blessings of good health.

I am writing to inform that the Little Cherry Hill School will have an Exercise Wednesday Evening, March 30th 1932, at 7 o'clock P.M. You and family and friends are cordially welcome to attend should you be in the South at this time. We have been expecting you since the first of February.

The White School term is nine months, the Colored six months. Before the depression at times the patrons have paid the teacher from their pockets to extend the term a little longer, but at the present times they are not able, for work is very scarce. So I will have to close.

I regret this very much for the advanced pupils will not complete the books that they should.

I hope that you will come before the closing of school.

The Cherry Hill School was one of seven small, disorganized, ungraded schools for black children on Ford property. Within just a few years, Henry and Clara built two consolidated schools, one for blacks and one for whites. For the black school, a black principal and teachers were hired. Equivalent accommodations were provided in the two schools.

One of the roadside markets conducted by Ford Farms during the depression, this one in the fall of 1931. Melons, apples, peaches, pumpkins, and squash are being sold by the bushel at very low prices. (P.0.7146)

Henry had contributed $25,000 to the Republican National Committee to pay for time on NBC for speeches by Hoover. The year 1932 became worse. Henry did not like Roosevelt's restrictions on agriculture and refused to limit the acreage devoted to vegetables. In and near Dearborn, he planted 400 acres of carrots, 150 acres of onions, 80 acres of tomatoes, 60 acres of peas, and lesser acreage of other vegetable crops. Much of this produce was turned over to the Dearborn and Ypsilanti welfare departments. At least 1,000 acres were turned over to the city of Dearborn for the unemployed to grow vegetables for themselves. In addition, Henry sent tractor crews to any community in the Detroit area where garden plots needed plowing. For these individuals, their lots would be plowed and seed supplied. And the plowing was done well because there was the risk that Henry was likely to come and inspect the work. Some 63,468 Ford employees in the Detroit area were expected to have gardens. An estimated 1,500 acres were plowed for

Depression Days

227

Clara looks askance at what Dearborn Mayor John Carey and Henry may be conniving between them. The event is the dedication of Henry's and Clara's gift of Ford Field, a twenty-acre park in Dearborn, in April 1936. Carey was the choice of Harry Bennett and Henry to run the city during those years of labor strife. (Photo courtesy of Dearborn Historical Museum.)

employees, some as far as twenty miles from the Dearborn factory. During the depression years, Ford Farms' annual operational losses approached $1 million, exceeding that amount in 1937.

Although Dearborn supplied the largest number of gardens, in thirty-eight other cities throughout the United States, Ford Motor Company issued "Garden Cards" to 40,202 employees with the expectation that they would utilize a "Thrift Garden" in 1932. Of these employees, 7,617 wanted a company garden, 14,374 were planning a garden of their own, and 6,393 were assigned a company garden. Outside Michigan that year, Ford Motor Company gardens occupied 1,094 acres, and employee personal gardens occupied 3,882 acres.

Every last employee of the Ford plant in Iron Mountain, Michigan, accepted a Ford plowed garden. Here is what one employee had to say:

Aug. 11, 1938

Mr. Ford.
Dear Friend—
As I am an employee of the Ford Motor Co. I have a nice back yard garden which I would like you to see if you come to Iron Mountain.

I have tomato plants six also eight feet high and have had as high
as one hundred and sixty-five on one plant. Also cucumbers 8 feet
high. People from all over have come to see my garden. I have had
as high as 46 people on Sundays. Some take pictures. I have Dalihas
different sizes. I also have 2 Ford lots. I have gotten as high as six-
teen bushel of tomatoes from my small garden. I have a nice Hedge
and lawn I made myself. As I know you are interested in gardens I
would like you to visit mine while in Iron Mountain if you have
time. An employee.

Mr. Charles Hanson
Iron Mountain, Mich.

Only a few years earlier, the Ford Farms at Iron Mountain had
stored hundreds of bushels of carrots and potatoes in underground
trenches to be distributed to poor families during the winter months,
only to have some unknown person pour a caustic chemical into the
trenches and make the vegetables unfit for human consumption.

At this time, Clara, as president of the Woman's National Farm &
Garden Club, was promoting roadside marketing of flowers, baked
goods, and home-canned fruits and vegetables. Her object was to
encourage women who lived on farms to sell products on the roadside
to supplement their incomes. She had elegant architectural models
made of roadside stands and sponsored roadside markets in Dearborn.
Clara was also busy providing lists of people and institutions deserving
free vegetables and fruit from Ford Farms. A welfare list prepared by
Clara included fourteen homes and institutions to which Ford Farms
made weekly deliveries.

Many Ford Motor Company employees were working only three
days a week because sales of automobiles were slow. Henry put men on
an assembly line to recondition used Ford cars supplied by dealers. To
further bolster the economy, he announced in February, he would spend
$300 million to introduce a new V-8-powered automobile. But on
March 7, 1932, a group of three thousand unemployed Detroiters, led
by Communist activists, marched through the streets of Detroit toward
Dearborn. At the boundary, police told them they had no permit to
march in Dearborn and should disperse. The march continued, however, to the main gates of the Rouge Plant. The protesters threatened to
take possession of the plant. Water hoses and tear gas at the plant gates
were ineffective. At that point, Dearborn and Detroit police resorted to
gunfire, killing four of the march leaders. Known as the Hunger March,
this tragic disturbance upset Henry and Clara tremendously.

The kidnapping of the twenty-month-old Lindbergh baby at
around that time also put a scare into the Ford family. They were concerned about the vulnerability of the grandchildren. Harry Bennett was

instructed by Henry to institute additional safeguards. Among other things, a strong iron gate was placed at the tunnel entrance to Fair Lane.

In late November 1932, Henry was in the Ford Hospital recovering from an operation for strangulated hernia. The hospital bulletin read on the 29th, "Mr. Ford had a quiet, restful night. His temperature this morning is 98.6, pulse 70, respiration 18. It is expected that Mr. Ford may be able to leave the hospital within ten days."

The peak of financial crisis occurred in Michigan on February 14, 1933, when the governor declared an eight-day bank holiday, closing all the banks in the state. Banks had loaned money way beyond the now deflated value of the property mortgaged. The Fords had deposits of millions of dollars in the two major banks in Detroit, the Guardian Group and the Detroit Bankers organization; Edsel was an officer of the Guardian Group. Henry was asked to turn over his multimillion accounts to stabilize the banks and keep them solvent, but he refused, saying the federal government should correct the situation. On March 30, 1933, he did deposit $1 million in his own Dearborn State Bank to pave the way for its reopening.

Clara received a letter from her brother Harry in Boise, dated February 9, 1933:

Dear Sister Clara:

We earned $12,000.00 this year in our service dept. and new car sales costs to us exceeded that am't. by approx $500.00 and have barely made a living.

We have a strong Chevy. Dealer here that put a great deal of outside money into his business here which has cost us a neat sum in trade ins alone . . .

We need $50,000.00 to pay off bank before they foreclose . . . to put us back into a humble means of doing business . . .

If we cannot have the above we are to lose our all, and efforts for the last 21 years, and if the bank forclosed they take every thing including our homes, my home, what a disgrace, and all this because of our trusting the banks. We need new banking laws. We have untold misery; 1800 men out of work.

Our property is clear and you let me know by wire just as soon as you get this letter. There is a future to look forward to and we do not want to go back to what we went through 21 years ago.

Love to you all

Clara's younger brother Harry H. Bryant (1871–1938), who left the Bryant Greenfield farm to live first in Detroit and later at Anchor Bay on Lake St. Clair in Michigan, before going west and settling in Boise, Idaho. There he became a Ford dealer in 1913 and established the large Bryant Ranch near Yellow Pine, Idaho. (Photo courtesy Marvin Bryant, grandson)

Harry probably received help from Clara; the Boise dealership remained in business through the Depression.

In May 1933, the Adrian State Savings Bank, where Samuel Raymond had his dealership account, requested from Henry a deposit of $100,000 to protect the bank from failure. Henry apparently did not go to the rescue. In August 1933, the Fords together opened a new bank, Manufacturers National Bank, and General Motors established a new bank, the National Bank of Detroit. Nearly 4,000 banks in Michigan failed and did not reopen, many of those in the Detroit area. The city of Detroit for a time paid its workers in script, which was accepted at face value for taxes but was discounted by merchants for goods. Henry Ford paid his workers in cash. A survey of communities in southeastern Michigan showed unemployment ranging from 9.1 to 29.7 percent, with Detroit's percentage 15.7, Highland Park's 9.8, and Dearborn's 9.1. Henry was certainly trying to keep men at work either in the factories or on the farms; he was especially generous with the city of Dearborn. In June 1933, when his tax assessment on a piece of property was $15,000, he is said to have insisted it should be $54,000.

During the summer of 1933, Clara arranged a trip for Frances and Betty Bryant, daughters of Roy Bryant, on the *Vulcana* to Europe, where

The crowd of people on September 24, 1934, at the site of McGuffey's birthplace in Washington County, Pennsylvania. At this event, sponsored by Henry and Clara, a bronze marker on a granite monument was dedicated in honor of McGuffey.

Lord Perry entertained them in England. Roy was then using his Ford dealership to employ people to make small automotive parts. His Bryant Gear & Tool Division of Bryant Motors Sales employed Henry Ford Trade School graduates to supervise machine operators. Water pump gears, for example, were produced on two shifts at the rate of 10,000 per day. A good many dealerships employed this inexpensive K. R. Wilson equipment to make small parts and to rebuild Ford engines. Henry gave Roy a seven-passenger Lincoln limousine on February 1, 1934.

In May 1934, Henry inspected the Ford Exhibit at the Chicago World's Fair and is said to have told Arthur Brisbane, "I first met Mrs. Ford fifty years ago this month and if I had not met her I would never have amounted to anything."

It is said that Clara one day, on hearing schoolchildren shouting as they passed the Ford home, remarked to Henry, "Hear the children gaily shout." In response, Henry said, "Half past four and school is out."

Henry and Clara greeting members of the Federation of McGuffey Societies at its annual meeting in Greenfield Village on July 2, 1938. (P.188.23542)

Together these completed a quotation from the McGuffey Readers which they had both used in grade school. They began searching for those McGuffey books and soon amassed a sizable collection of the entire six volumes. Both Henry and Clara wanted to pass along the fundamental values offered by the McGuffey Readers, which Henry once said "taught industry and morality to America." They adopted the 1867 edition from primer through the sixth year as the standard reader in the Greenfield Village schools.

To stress the importance of William Holmes McGuffey as an educational leader, Henry and Clara purchased the 65-acre McGuffey Farm in Pennsylvania for $4,500 in January 1934. On the farm was the 1780 log-cabin birthplace of McGuffey with furnishings dating back to McGuffey's boyhood. Timbers from the birthplace and two log barns were moved to Greenfield Village, where the birthplace was reconstructed and a one-room log school built next to it.

Edsel Ford, in October 1934, received an extortion note demanding $5,000, the money to be left at a given time and at a given address in Detroit. A disguised detective delivered a one-dollar bill in a candy box and easily arrested a twenty-year-old man. The man, having used the U.S. Mail, had violated the recently enacted Lindbergh Extortion

Law, a federal statute, and was sentenced to ten years in Leavenworth penitentiary.

Gaston Plantiff, the head of the New York office of Ford Motor Company, and his wife, Ellen, were exceptionally good friends of Henry and Clara. Ellen was Danish and had come to America to be a singer. Gaston, who had been very valuable to Henry since 1915, retired in 1929 and, according to a 1937 affidavit signed by Ellen, "thereafter became subject to inebriation." Ellen also states in the affidavit that Henry Ford persuaded Gaston to set up a trust for herself and her daughter, Mary Ellen, which was signed March 31, 1932. Gaston died on October 19, 1934, at age fifty-nine, and both Henry and Clara attended the funeral, Clara accompanying Ellen and Henry accompanying Mary Ellen. Ellen's faithful and prolonged friendship with Clara no doubt stemmed in great part from the Fords' having promoted the trust for her and her daughter.

The Fords were headed to Ways Station, Georgia, on February 15, 1935. Since Thomas Edison's death in 1931, Henry and Clara no longer used the Mangoes as their winter home. In Ways, they resided in their private railroad car, the *Fair Lane*, parked on a railroad siding in the center of the little town. Henry was anxious to get his lumber mill operating and schools built; Clara was anxious to get her dream home constructed—one larger and more substantial than any of the existing homes of the former rice planters. She envisioned huge columns, wide verandas, magnificent staircases, and spacious rooms. Henry had bought the Hermitage for $10,000, had it demolished, and saved the salvaged bricks with which to build Clara's new mansion. Two of the slave huts from the Hermitage were shipped to Dearborn and erected at Greenfield Village. It was decided Clara's house would be situated on the site of the old Richmond Plantation overlooking the Ogeechee River. With those decisions made, the Fords returned to Dearborn on March 7, having lived in the *Fair Lane* for sixteen days.

As a function of the Edison Institute, in October 1935, Clara opened a School of Home Arts at the Nurses' Home of Henry Ford Hospital. The purpose of the school was to provide a place where a small group of high school graduates could live together and keep house. That first year, nine girls were given guidance in caring for a home: keeping it clean and orderly, cooking and serving wholesome meals, caring for their clothing, and learning how to care for infants and little children. Two groups of students a year were accommodated. Girls were chosen from rural districts by their teachers. The school operated until at least 1942, with several modifications of programs, a major one being to have the girls work at various assignments in the hospital to earn spending money. A similar program was in effect at Ways, Georgia, where high school girls lived together in the Ford Community House for two-week periods and, besides attending regular school, made their own clothing, cooked and served their own meals, and learned table etiquette and ballroom dancing.

Along with the Social Security Act of 1935, the federal government instituted the "wealth tax" of 70 percent on estates of more than $50 million. In consultation with family lawyers, Henry and Edsel adopted a scheme whereby their assets in Ford Motor Company stock would be divided between two classes of stock, voting and nonvoting. Those holding the voting stock would manage the company, and those holding nonvoting stock would have no say in company affairs. Six percent of their combined 3,452,900 shares were made voting and 94 percent nonvoting. A nonprofit (nontaxed) corporation called the Ford Foundation was formed on January 15, 1936, to accept the nonvoting shares as gifts from Ford family members either before or at the time of their deaths. In 1937, Henry and Edsel each gave 125,000 shares of nonvoting stock to the foundation, and the foundation in turn made donations to Henry Ford Hospital and the Edison Institute. At that time, the stock was valued at $5 per share. Edsel, in his will, left 1,153,809 shares of nonvoting stock to the foundation and his voting stock to Eleanor and the children. Henry, in 1944, gave another 1,400,000 shares of nonvoting stock to the foundation. While Ford officials and family members were on the foundation board, donations were made largely to domestic charities. Until Edsel died in 1943, more than $1 million was given each year to a list of twenty-seven domestic organizations. The largest benefactor by far was the Edison Institute.

According to a 1951 statement of Dr. Frank Sladen of Henry Ford Hospital, "Henry Ford's first serious accident was about January 1936. Mr. Ford was in the habit of having an osteopath, Dr. Lawson B. Coulter, massage him. The night before, Dr. Coulter had manipulated Mr. Ford's neck, putting pressure on the vessels in the neck. This was a very dangerous matter for a man of Mr. Ford's age. There resulted a cerebral vascular accident and consequent brain injury. The facial paralysis which followed was cleared up in about three weeks which was exceptional for his age and his condition."

On February 3, 1936, Henry signed a will which read, in essence, as follows:

I have heretofore provided generously for my wife, Clara J. Ford, and am satisfied that she is now in a position of complete financial independence.

I wish my wife to have, however, and I hereby bequeath to her, all of my personal effects in and about our home "Fair Lane," at Dearborn, Michigan, including all household furniture, automobiles, and everything used in connection with our home.

There has been heretofore organized, under the laws of the State of Michigan, a corporation known as the Ford Foundation, the purposes of such corporation being set forth in its Articles of Incorporation. To this Foundation I give and bequeath all my shares known as Class "A" [nonvoting] stock.

All of my real estate other than such as may be part of our home "Fair Lane," I give and devise to the Ford Foundation.

I wish to divide all of my voting stock in Ford Motor Company into five equal parts to be disposed of in the following manner: I bequeath one to my son Edsel B. Ford. The others I bequeath for the benefit of my four grandchildren, Henry Ford II, Benson Ford, Josephine Ford, and William Clay Ford.

I designate my son Edsel B. Ford to be executor of this my last will and testament.

On February 6, 1936, Clara signed a consent to Henry's will. Both documents were witnessed by Frank Campsall and H. R. Waddell, personal secretaries to Henry and Clara. A very similar will was signed by Clara on July 27, 1936, leaving personal belongings to Henry, nonvoting stock to the Ford Foundation, and voting stock and all the rest of her estate to Edsel. The grandchildren were not specifically named.

Records indicate that Henry and Clara left for Ways, Georgia, on February 6, 1936, by way of Jersey City, Washington, and Savannah. Clara's new home was being started. Henry was planning a large sawmill, homes for workers, schools, a community house, and another Martha-Mary Chapel—essentially rebuilding and expanding the entire town. While the house was under construction, headquarters were established at the nearby Cherry Hill plantation house. Clara participated in the design of her new home and selected the furniture, much of it to come from Fair Lane and the Henry Ford Museum in Dearborn, with additional furniture trucked up from the Mangoes. The house would be in Greek Revival style with elements of Federal and Georgian architecture.

On March 20, from Ways, Clara wrote to her Dearborn friend:

Dear Mrs. Ives:

I have thought of you so much since we have been down here. Spent a day with the Torry's and their guest book says that ten years ago we visited them with you and Mr. Ives, do you remember that Mr. Ives had his 70th birthday on the yacht; and now Mr. Ford is 73, how time flies. I met Mrs. Oemler, one of the sisters that owned St. Catherine's Island, she asked about you, has called upon me, and

*given me that good pudding recipe made with sweet potatoes.
Another neighbor had an oyster roast for us, and had about twenty
ladies from Savannah. Have had Dr. & Mrs. McClure visit us,
Mrs. Plantiff, and Miss Berry, her sister & husband and a number
of northerners have dropped in for the day. Expect Dr. & Mrs. Torry
tomorrow. Have just started our house and it is going to be lovely,
getting data on shrubs and trees, fruit trees are in bloom and the yellow jasmine climbs over everything. I am getting a great thrill out
of the garden end of it. I hope you have kept well this cold winter and
hope to see you when I get home, and tell you all about it.*

*Affectionately
Clara Jane Ford*

After forty-eight days in Ways, Henry and Clara were back in
Dearborn in time to prepare invitation lists for their old-fashioned
dancing activities. That year, about 160 couples were invited from
Dearborn and about 300 from Grosse Pointe. Not everyone liked old-
fashioned dancing, and many regrets were received.

The Fords were again headed to Georgia on January 19, 1937, via
New York and Washington. Clara's house was being completed, the
sawmill beginning to buzz, and almost 300 residential and commercial
buildings being started. The home was later valued at $362,736, the

sawmill at more than $100,000, and schools and chapel at $140,000. As at Fair Lane, Clara oversaw the house and grounds while Henry conducted his lumber and agricultural business. Martha Berry was among the visitors at Ways that year. Henry and Clara would stay until April 4, longer than usual, the normal stay said to have been "until the black flies began to bother."

Nineteen thirty-seven was an active year for labor unions all over the country. As a result of the Wagner Act, manufacturers were caving in one by one to union demands. On February 11, General Motors capitulated to the United Automobile Workers, and on April 8, Chrysler also surrendered. There were heated arguments between Henry and Edsel about how to handle the situation. Edsel wanted to negotiate with the U.A.W., while Henry insisted on fighting it out, using Harry Bennett as his commander-in-chief. Henry was convinced that unions were not necessary, that he was treating his employees fairly. Clara sided with Edsel, not wanting confrontation. She could see that Edsel's opinions were being cast aside for those of Bennett, and she exclaimed angrily, "Who is this man who has so much control over my husband and is ruining my son's life?" On May 26, leaders of the U.A.W. attempted to pass out union propaganda at the gates of the Rouge Plant. Henry instructed Bennett to prevent them. In a fracas known as the Battle of the Overpass, several were seriously hurt. The relationship between Edsel and Henry was never quite the same again. It was obvious Henry preferred Bennett as his adviser on plant personnel problems.

From Baden-Baden, Germany, that summer, a postcard with photographs of Henry II and Benson arrived at Fair Lane:

Dear Callie:

We have been here for three days and today we are going to Munich. From there to Copenhagen and Amsterdam and then back to London. The first time in London we had a marvelous time but Paris was rather depressing though we had a nice time. The trip over was very smooth and I am sorry I wasn't there when you called but I think I was in the movies. The commodore and Mr. Brenner asked us to give you their best wishes. Love to granddad and you.

Henry

Postcards weren't the only items arriving at Fair Lane. The butler was keeping a record. Of the hundreds of deliveries listed during 1937, these are a few noted following the Fords' return from Ways:

April 27: Maple sugar and can of syrup—John Burroughs, Roxbury, NY.

July 15: Crate of cherries—Mrs. M. D. Bryant, Traverse City, Mich.

July 21: Codeine, Empirin—Wachtels Drug Co., Savannah.

July 26: Incense sticks—Calcutta, India.

July 29: One crate peaches—Berry Schools, Rome, Georgia.

July 30: Green jardiniere with pink roses—Village students.

[The Fords left for Huron Mountains]

Sept. 20: One bushel peaches—Jack Miner, Kingsville, Ontario.

Sept. 20: One gallon honey—Frank Stout, Fort Myers, Fla.

Sept. 25: Avocados—Frank Stout, Fort Myers, Fla.

Oct. 2: Gloves—Henri Bendel, N.Y.C.

Oct. 14: Northern Spy Apples—Wayside Inn, Sudbury, Mass.

Nov. 1: Royal River Pears—Medford, Ore.

Nov. 8: Apples—Lord Perry, England.

Nov. 24: Oranges, grapefruit, and kumquats—Frank Stout, Fort Myers, Fla.

Dec. 1: Stark apples—Jack Miner, Kingsville, Ontario.

Dec. 14: Twelve boxes dates—Indio, California.

Dec. 15: Two boxes stationery—Tiffany, N.Y.C.

Dec. 21: Christmas gifts—Mrs. Prunk, West Orange, N.J.

Dec. 21: Christmas gifts—M. B. Bryant, Boise, Idaho.

Dec. 23: Four jars pickles—Mrs. M. D. Bryant, Traverse City, Mich.

Dec. 23: Christmas pears—Wm. M. Hughson, Medford, Oregon.

Nearly all of these shipments were addressed to Clara. Frank Stout was manager of the Mangoes at Fort Myers. The property was rented, but Clara asked him to supply her with fresh fruits from Florida. Flowers arrived throughout the year, and a multitude of gifts came for birthdays and at Christmas time. For every year recorded there are citrus fruits from Fort Myers; pears from Oregon; apples or peaches from Ontario; cherries or fish from Traverse City; fruit or cotton from Rome, Georgia; and wine, flowers, or vegetables from Ways, Georgia. A constant stream of candy, books, and feminine notions arrived from Clara's friend Ellen Plantiff and from Grace Prunk, her sister Eva's daughter.

Henry and Clara were off to Ways again on January 23, 1938, and stayed until March 24. Clara's mansion was finished, and she began to invite Savannah socialites for gatherings. There was always much excitement when the Fords and their party arrived. Fifty additional people were hired to handle the extra work of cleaning, cooking, serving,

A front view of the Richmond Hill residence. Henry and Clara sometimes brought their Dearborn musicians to Richmond Hill, and old-fashioned dances would be held on this front lawn. (P.0.5628)

arranging flowers, and keeping the grounds neat and trimmed. Benjamin Lovett and the Ford musicians organized dancing events, with some dances held on the lawn. Every nook and cranny of every building on the premises had to be ready for a glance from Henry, who was fast of foot and sharp of eye, known to show up at unexpected times and places, ready to talk to whoever was about. Clara was more inclined to limit herself to the mansion. One of Clara's many charitable deeds concerned an elderly black lady known as Old Aunt Jane. Janie Lewis, who had once been a slave, lived in a hovel and had no income. Clara provided a small, modernly furnished home and arranged for food, clothing, and medical care for the rest of Janie's life.

When Herman Cooper, the black principal of the Black High School in Ways, Georgia, was recently asked how blacks were treated by whites at Richmond Hill during the time the Fords managed the town, his answer was that blacks were treated better when the Fords were there, but they were there only a small fraction of the year. Cooper also tells of a time when Clara was being driven through the farm lands and she saw blacks working in a field with a white foreman watching them. She told her driver to stop and issued instructions for the foreman to work along with the others.

This was a year of anniversaries. For her seventy-first birthday on April 11, Clara received a miniature silver service from Eleanor and Edsel. This day was also Henry and Clara's fiftieth wedding anniversary, attracting a large number of flowers and gifts. Henry and Clara visited Wayside Inn in late April, and Clara spent July 24 through 26 in New York. Henry's seventy-fifth birthday fell on July 30, and all of Detroit

A view from the veranda of Richmond Hill, facing the Ogeechee River and land owned by the Fords on the opposite side. (P.0.6568)

celebrated, with City Hall decked out in banners, a mammoth children's party at the State Fair Coliseum, and a banquet at Detroit's Masonic Temple.

One of Henry's gifts on his seventy-fifth birthday was the Grand Cross of the German Eagle, which was presented to him by the German vice consul in Detroit. This caused quite a stir as reported by the press. People wondered why an American of Ford's stature would accept such an acknowledgment from Hitler, who was at that very moment ruthlessly pillaging Europe and trying to annihilate the Jewish people. The only response Henry provided was that he accepted the medal from "the German people," for whom he had no resentment. (On October 19, 1938, Charles Lindbergh would accept an even higher award, the Service Cross of the Order of the German Eagle, presented by Field Marshal Hermann Goering.)

On December 12, 1938, Henry and Clara granted a warranty deed to Harry and Esther Bennett conveying riverfront property on the west shore of Grosse Ile. Although valued at $53,134, payment for the prop-

Clara and Henry leaving the banquet honoring Henry on his seventy-fifth birthday, July 30, 1938. Henry would wear patent leather but not white shoes. (188.23829)

erty was one dollar. The Fords had purchased this property on West River Road in 1924 for $47,481,70. The house might have been purchased for use as a summer home by the Fords or as an antique to be dismantled and moved to Greenfield Village. However, there is no evidence that either use was made of the property.

The Fords reached Ways, Georgia, on January 31, 1939. Their *Fair Lane* railroad car was left as usual on a siding in Ways during their stay until March 16. In town, the sawmill was producing more than 200 prefabricated homes for the development of two subdivisions at prices of about $3,500. The rents for these homes were ten to fifteen dollars per month to Ford employees or free to poor families. The people of Ways were very appreciative of the new schools for both black and white children and of the new clinic which had rid the community of malaria and hookworm.

Clara organized a buffet supper for eighty-six guests at Richmond Hill on February 21, 1939. Savannah Kitchens of 202 East 31st Street provided the following refreshments:

50 shrimp salad sandwiches
50 almond and celery sandwiches
50 Old English cheese sandwiches
100 toasted peanut butter and bacon sandwiches
100 rolled toasted Virginia ham paste sandwiches
100 cheese biscuits
160 cakes—sponge cakes, Creole kisses, almond crescents
Salted pecans, small cucumber pickles
Coffee, cream, sugar, hot chocolate, whipped cream

86 guests @ .80:	$68.80
Two maids and gasoline:	$15.00
Total:	$83.80

Clara entertained many well-to-do Savannah guests as well as friends and relatives from Detroit and Dearborn.

On April 3, 1939, Dr. Sladen attended Henry at the request of Clara. As Dr. Sladen recalled in 1951, "The major trouble was general weakness and related complaints. This is also a symptom of developing senility. Also it should be noted that Mr. Ford had hard arteries and used them hard. Senility, of course, is a very gradual development although there may be a sudden change."

On April 28, Henry and Clara, with Edsel and Eleanor, traveled to New York to attend the opening of the World's Fair. In fact, there were no fewer than seven round trips to New York during 1939. One of these was in connection with "Dearborn Days" at the fair in mid-May, when

While the Fords were in Georgia during February 1939, young John Dahlinger was tooling around Dearborn in his custom-made sports racer. (188.24575)

the 27-millionth Ford car arrived. A stop at Fort Edward, New York, on August 23 was to witness a tractor demonstration, and the six days the *Fair Lane* was parked at Worcester, Massachusetts, from August 25 to 31, no doubt meant the Fords were visiting Wayside Inn.

In June, a large group of women visiting London from forty countries belonging to the Associated Country Women of the World and including representatives of the Woman's National Farm and Garden Association of America, received the following invitation:

Mr. & Mrs. Henry Ford
and the
Woman's National Farm and Garden Association
invite you to visit the Henry Ford Institute of Agricultural
Engineering, Boreham, near Chelmsford, and the Fordson Farms
adjacent thereto on Sunday, June 4th, 1939.

That same month, the Woman's National Farm and Garden Association held its national meeting at the Hotel Statler in Detroit. Clara entertained members at a luncheon in the Clinton Inn at Greenfield Village on June 8.

Anna Bryant speaks up for her husband, Clara's brother William, in a long letter to Clara dated November 2, 1939:

Clara's brother, William Bryant, at about the time Henry had labeled him a "Play Boy" and William's wife, Anna, wrote her letter of complaint to Clara. (William remained active in the Masonic Lodge, and when he died two years later, the burial was conducted with full ceremony by his lodge.) (64.167.1.96)

Dear Clara:

Clara, I am deeply hurt that Henry considers Will a "Play Boy." He has always worked and worked hard, with the exception of a few years after he gave up the trucking, and he sure needed a rest and we had saved enough to have him take it a little easier. You surely will agree that everyone has to have some recreation, and if Will got his at his lodge club rooms, he might have gone to a worse place, don't you think so? He never could afford to belong to a Country Club, and his lodge work has brought him many hours of enjoyment and he is loved and respected by many. I am more than proud of what he has done and I should think you would be too. He is a brother anyone can be proud of. I don't agree with you that he neglected his business for lodge and bowling. He wasn't educated for business. You know Clara how very little schooling the older boys got. After the depression and bank closing took about all of our income, Will got the work he is doing now, and if you think riding around on street cars and buses 8 hrs a day 5 days a week packed in with all kinds of people isn't hard work, I do, and he has been doing that for almost five years. I don't blame him for getting tired of it, and with all of

Depression Days

245

your resources I think he is justified in thinking you might give him something to earn our living with that wouldn't be so tiring.

I often wonder Clara if you realize what it means to be related to one of the wealthiest men in the world and live on 35 a week. So much is taken for granted and expected of you. We even had to stop going to Church. They expected so much more than we could give and pestered us to ask you for this and that. And just as soon as a store finds out who we are, up goes the price on things. I am even criticized because I do my own washing. Oh I could tell you lots more it does, but you can see what we are up against all the time. Clara I was so upset about this, it just made me sick. What with Florence having her arm broke and Will having his teeth out and me having to have Past Noble Grands Club here yesterday, I was just in the work of getting ready when I got your letter. Next week Wed we will have been married 46 years and they have all been happy years in our home and I wouldn't change places with anyone in the world. (Nuf sed)

I am sorry you don't like Will but then I love him so much it will do for all the family I guess. He always has and always will be very dear to me and you know we all have some faults so we must over-look them and make the best of the good that is in everyone. Now dear, I hope you won't let this make any hard feelings between us as I love all the family and am more than grateful for all that you have done for us. Will close with best wishes and love to you both.

Anna

Chapter 10
Life at Fair Lane

Henry and Clara Ford's greatest enjoyment is said to have been their home life, gardens, and flowers. By the early 1930s, Henry and Clara had developed somewhat routine household habits at Fair Lane. Some of these rituals are quite well described by Clara's household help—her maid, Rosa Buhler, and her butler, John D. Thomson. Fair Lane's electrical engineer, Charles Voorhess; the chauffeur, Robert Rankin; and the gardener, Alphonse de Caluwe, also have much to tell in their reminiscences. Clara's nephew Edward L. Bryant has provided lengthy firsthand accounts of Aunt Clara and Uncle Henry at Fair Lane.

At home, Henry and Clara discussed their problems with each other, sharing good advice. In decision making, Henry's nature was "Go ahead and do it right," while Clara's was "Be sure you're right before you go ahead." Clara had full responsibility for the staff at the residence. Her staff normally consisted of houseman, gardener, chauffeur, butler, second butler, cook, and maid. The staff always referred to their employers as Mr. Ford or Mrs. Ford. Edsel called his parents Father and Callie, and the children and grandchildren always called her Callie. Very few people called Henry by his first name. Old farm acquaintances might, but company executives did not.

Clara has been described by relatives as "frugal but not stingy" and "tenacious and not lazy." Wages paid by Clara were not especially generous. In the twenty years between 1929 and 1949, Rosa Buhler's pay increased from $100 per month to $125 per month, while John D. Thomson's increased from $145 to $160; they must have been excellent employees to have satisfied Clara for that length of time. Alphonse de Caluwe, head gardener from 1923 until 1950, and also a conscientious

September 17, 1927
Clara elected President of the Woman's National Farm and Garden Association

July 8, 1929
Clara entertains members of the American Rose Society

October 25, 1929
Stock market crash; beginning of the Great Depression

October 21, 1931
Henry and Clara attend funeral of Thomas Edison

May 26, 1937
Battle of the Overpass at the River Rouge plant

April 11, 1938
Henry and Clara celebrate their fiftieth wedding anniversary

March 1, 1942
Henry and Clara attend funeral of Martha Berry

worker, seems to have carried on a continuing dialogue with Clara concerning the need to pay his helpers more. He insisted they were not getting as much as workers from Ford Farms. Ford Farms furnished twenty or thirty men during summer months for outside work in the greenhouses and on the grounds of Fair Lane, including Clara's elegant rose gardens. These men, who were paid by Ford Farms boss Raymond Dahlinger, were subject to instructions from Alphonse, which often were followed by countermands by Clara, which, of course, were final. Some of these employees say they tried to hide from Clara when they caught sight of her; they considered her overly particular. By the same token, when Clara was showing her gardens to her friends, she did not want a gardener in sight.

Henry was usually first up in the morning, going out for a bicycle ride or a walk. He kept a bicycle at the front door and one in the powerhouse garage. He would often be out of the house by six o'clock — sometimes before dawn — driving to the laboratory or the factory, where he would perhaps have breakfast. He would check on what his engineers were doing, or sometimes travel to his farms or village industries to assess progress there. Some of the engineers working directly for Henry would put in long hours, never knowing whether Henry would be checking on them the first thing in the morning or the last thing at night. Quite regularly, however, he would meet with his top executives at exactly one o'clock for lunch. He would have with him a small notebook and stubby pencil; he might tie a knot in his watch chain to help him remember things. When he returned to Fair Lane later in the day, he would whistle a bird call to let Clara know he was there. As Henry aged, his hours and meals became more like Clara's: breakfast at eight-thirty, lunch promptly at noon, and a light supper at about six-thirty.

From boyhood, Henry was inclined to demonstrate his vigor by jumping over fences and running races. In his fifties, at Fair Lane, he delighted in showing his grandchildren how to chop wood and climb a tree. As Henry aged, he would challenge younger men to foot races. Not wanting to embarrass Henry, some would deliberately lose to him. Henry tried to prove his youthfulness by insisting he did not need glasses; he was hardly ever photographed wearing them in public. He would take a penny from his pocket and show it to people, saying he could read the date on it. Some say he carried the same penny, showing it over and over. He told a visitor, "For forty years, every time I think of it, I rub around my eyes. If you would do that, you would never need glasses."

Both Henry and Clara needed full-time chauffeurs. Clara liked to relax in the car, sitting in the back seat and "knowing when the car stops I'm there." She liked to talk about movies, chauffeur Rankin has recalled, adding, "When we sometimes came close to Edison Avenue, we would drive by for a look, and she would say, 'Ah, the old homestead.'

Henry and Clara taking it easy on the front lawn at Fair Lane in June 1923.
Young Henry II, squatting between them, is full of energy, while Grandpa
holds the younger Benson on his lap. Behind them is Clara's magnificent
peony bed, said to have contained twelve hundred plants of forty varieties.
(P.0.4552)

She had a wonderful sense of humor. Henry never had to tell her a funny story for a second time. On the other hand, Henry had an awful habit of sitting up in the front seat with me. And that front seat had to be leather, not mohair, which he detested. He was restless and wanted to be on the go all of the time. He didn't like to be alone, and he didn't like to be with many people. If he was interested in anyone, he would stick right with them. He liked to talk to the little fellow. He was stubborn, stubborn as a mule.

"Henry was a talkative person according to his mood. If he wanted to draw someone out, he could be very inquisitive, and he was a good listener to most people. He answered questions in short telegraphic style and avoided any lengthy public speaking. His favorite topic of conversation was likely to be mechanics or farming, but he also had a keen interest in people, especially young people. He used to say he enjoyed being with children because they would keep quiet, and they would not ask him for favors."

Meals, which had to be on time at Fair Lane, were prepared by the cook with close supervision and sometimes rather severe criticism by Clara. Henry liked very plain cooking, nothing fancy, while Clara's tastes were the opposite. She clung to her mother's English style of cooking, which her cooks found difficult to follow. Clara hired a new cook almost every year. For breakfast, Henry was very fond of buckwheat pancakes with kernels of corn fried in butter and lots of maple syrup or honey, until he switched to oatmeal in later years. He preferred to eat his meals at a small table in the dining room rather than at the big long one.

According to maid Rosa Buhler, the Fords always had meat for lunch, which was their big meal for the day. They liked their meats done so well they fell apart. Clara liked her food highly seasoned and included a cream sauce with almost everything she served, yet she was very concerned about her figure, Buhler says. Clara's weight during 1935, for example, as recorded in Clara's own handwriting, varied from 105 to 109 pounds. Both Henry and Clara were fond of oysters, cooked and raw. When they were alone for supper, they would have milk toast or something light.

Henry was much more abstinent than Clara, who liked beer and wine. Dahlinger remembers being asked to bring her favorite Rolling Rock beer from Pennsylvania, and she insisted on having Scuppernong wine available at their winter home in Georgia. Clara would accept a cocktail at an outside event and would offer drinks to guests at Fair Lane. Henry sometimes used alcoholic mixtures as medications and insisted on water, without ice, with his meals. Clara once suggested that her guests have a glass of sherry, whereupon Henry immediately left the table as if in disgust. To the guests' surprise, however, he was soon back, riding into the dining room on his bicycle and carrying a bottle of champagne under his arm. His aversion to liquor may have been a response to his father's habits; in his reminiscences, Earl Ford states that William Ford had a drinking problem.

Henry's complete soybean diet was not at all popular with Clara, but she did like soybean bread. To get her to try one of his soybean crackers, Henry served some to her with a glass of sherry, knowing she would not refuse. Clara was inclined to complain that her husband "doesn't enjoy his meals," and further that "Henry could eat sawdust and enjoy it as much as apple pie." Clara once remarked, "You could give Henry a slice of the tenderest roast beef with the fluffiest mashed potatoes and a piece of apple pie that would melt in your mouth, and he wouldn't know what he was eating." No one at Fair Lane relished the weed sandwiches recommended by Dr. George Washington Carver of Tuskegee Institute. Clara was opposed to buying fruits and vegetables out of season and much preferred to have them from her own garden or orchard.

For invited guests, Clara provided very differently. A memo from the Women's Exchange and Decorative Art Society of Detroit on June 19, 1939, offers this estimate for a luncheon for sixty guests to be served at Fair Lane at one o'clock on Thursday, June 22:

Fresh fruit plate on table.
Creamed chicken in tiny pates.
Rice croquettes.
Glazed apricot.
Individual aspic salad.
Hot rolls. Hot coffee or iced coffee.
Salted nuts.
Raspberry ice with French pistache.
Individual iced cakes.
Rental of ten tables with Italian cloth.
Silence cloths and napkins.
Sixty chairs and green covers.
All dishes, silver, linen, goblets, etc.
The services of ten waitresses and our kitchen force.
Delivery and pickup to Dearborn and transportation for our force.
Total $294.00.

Some prominent guests who were entertained at Fair Lane over the years included John Burroughs, the Duke of Windsor, Sir Percival Perry and family, Thomas and Mina Edison, President and Mrs. Herbert Hoover, Charles A. Lindbergh, George Washington Carver, the Gaston Plantiffs, Freeman F. Gosden, Charles J. Correll, Mickey Rooney, and

Clara and Henry at Fair Lane on their fiftieth wedding anniversary, April 11, 1938. On the wall behind them are framed enlargements of photographs taken at about the time of their wedding. Clara was seventy-two years old when this photograph was taken, and Henry would be celebrating his seventy-fifth birthday in July. (P.0.589)

others. Clara invited members of the various garden clubs to Fair Lane each year when her rose gardens were most attractive. On such occasions, Henry would sometimes welcome the guests as they arrived at the door. During World War II, Clara invited some sailors from the nearby Naval Training School and gave them not only dinner but cigarettes, much to Henry's astonishment. The estate freely welcomed close relatives of both Henry and Clara. Clara's relatives came often, but Henry's brothers, John and William, are not known to have visited Fair Lane. Henry's sister, Margaret, who had known Clara well in their youth, stopped in to visit her several times following Henry's death. When Henry met with his brothers, his sister, and cousins who lived close by, it was at their homes. Ford family reunions were held in and near Dearborn but not at Fair Lane.

Henry had little to say about the decorations and furnishings at Fair Lane; that was Clara's responsibility. In household matters, Henry's motto was "Peace at any price." Henry was aghast when, during the depression years, Clara commissioned Charles of London to redecorate Fair Lane, including the off-white painting of expensive wood-grained walls. Edward Bryant states, "Of course, like other women, she had to have a change, and so on occasions she painted the woodwork — I didn't like it as well, but she knew what she was doing and what she liked, but in my opinion it spoiled things. On occasions she had the paint brush through the entire house, with the exception of the staircase and the dining room. Uncle Henry put his foot down there. She had to have new furniture, and so she had to have what she thought was the best. She went from modern to antique. Those putty walls were awful, I thought."

Henry normally gave in to Clara's tastes. However, in the case of his mother Mary's homestead in Greenfield Village, he did insist he knew what was right. When Clara attempted to change things there, Henry was really upset — upset to the point where Clara chose to stay out of the building.

Apparently, neither Clara nor Henry wished to decorate the walls of Fair Lane with paintings by the Old Masters, as did many of the wealthy in Detroit and elsewhere. One enterprising English art dealer presented Henry with a handsome photograph album depicting paintings he would like to sell. The only response he received was, "That was a fine book you gave me; I'm going to keep it in my library." Other than perhaps *The Stirrup Cup* by Cuyp and a couple of landscapes by Corot, Fair Lane walls were quite devoid of the Old Masters. Clara did not want her home to seem too formal; she preferred the lived-in look to some degree. She once remarked, "No, indeed, I never object when my husband puts his feet on a fine chair or table and scratches it. Nothing in this house is too good to use. Our home is not just a showplace but a place to live in and enjoy."

Over the years, many rooms at Fair Lane were used very little if at all except for storage. The billiard room was converted to a study for Clara. Edward Bryant reports, "Aunt Clara appropriated the room as a hide-out and office and personal business room. She put in cabinets and bookshelves and a desk in place of the billiard table, and she did a great deal of her writing and personal correspondence there. She kept things up, and the doors were closed and locked. In the later years, you weren't even supposed to see in this place, and it became very untidy and cluttered."

The bowling alley was used very little because there was no automatic pin-setting machine. And the swimming pool was used only when the grandchildren came, never by Henry, it is said. The grandchildren were there quite a bit, however, usually for two or three days at a time. Every imaginable attraction was provided to keep them there: ponies and carts, little automobiles, miniature steam engine and threshing equipment, a play house, a tree house, a maple sugar shack, and Santa's workshop. As the grandchildren grew up, the Greenfield Village children were always invited to Christmas parties at Fair Lane.

Clara was very particular about the library and her books. They had to be taken out and dusted about once a month, and every Monday the second butler was assigned that task by Thomson. The books included the hundreds of classics Clara had purchased while she was at 66 Edison in Detroit. There were about 700 volumes in all, including a dozen or so of the Alger books, also *Our Friend John Burroughs, Wake Robin, My Boyhood, Summer Sunshine, The Three Little Pigs,* and *The Five Little Peppers.* Larger offerings included *European History, Oberammergau Passion Play, The Pageant of America,* and the proceedings of the President's Committee on Home Building and Home Ownership. Clara had been a member of that committee. Other books on the shelves were *Robert's Rules of Order, Valve Gears for Steam Engines,* and *Cyclopedia of Electrical Engineering.* Henry didn't care to read fiction, other than comics, but he read Emerson over and over.

There was a phonograph in the library, and Henry and Clara would dance to some of their favorite waltzes. They didn't care to listen to classical music, preferring folk songs such as those sung by Burl Ives or songs by Henry's favorite, Stephen Foster. They also liked some of Edison's favorites such as "I'll Take You Home Again, Kathleen." At times, Henry would be alone in the library and would dance a bit by himself to such tunes as "The Horse with the Green Eyes" or "Who Threw the Overalls in Mrs. Murphy's Chowder." On weekdays during the 1930s, Henry's musicians often practiced for the old-fashioned dances in the laboratory area over the powerhouse. Henry would drop in on them, try out new steps, and perhaps join them with his own violin or mouth harp.

Between 1925 and 1943, the Fords' major social events were their own early American dances conducted fortnightly by Benjamin Lovett

Clara with Josephine and William Clay Ford, children of Edsel and Eleanor, at Fair Lane in 1932. "Jodie" is about nine years old and "Bill" about seven. They are wearing Bavarian costumes. (0.7603)

in Dearborn. Held first rather informally in the Engineering Building, they later became more formal when they were moved to beautiful Lovett Hall. These dances normally began about nine o'clock and lasted until midnight. Attendance was by invitation, the Dearborn list compiled by Henry and Clara and the Grosse Pointe and Detroit list by the Edsel Fords and by Sarah Burnham, the leading social arbiter in Detroit at that time. Invitations were almost entirely to married couples. Most of the evening was spent in straight dancing. Although there was

You are cordially invited to attend

a class in

Old Fashioned Dancing

sponsored by

Mr. and Mrs. Henry Ford

Friday, January the Nineteenth, 1934

at nine o'clock

The Administration Building at Dearborn

An invitation to an
evening of dancing,
1934. (D.807)

Lovett Hall, between Henry Ford Museum and Greenfield Village in
Dearborn, is the finest of the several ballrooms provided by Henry and Clara
for old-fashioned dancing. It was opened on October 26, 1937. (B.113018)

Henry and Clara, toward right and not facing the camera, dance with their guests at Lovett Hall in 1937. The orchestra is at far right on the stage. Henry and Clara appear to have a bit more dancing space than the other couples. (188.21862)

no program for the exact order of the dances, many participants lined up a few dances in advance. Typically, there would be a break for refreshments of cocoa or coffee and some sandwiches at about eleven o'clock, with two or three dance numbers to follow. People would leave about midnight. The old-fashioned dances were discontinued by the Fords after Edsel's death.

Henry and Clara would sometimes leave the house together unnoticed by the staff and disappear for hours at a time, causing the staff to become quite alarmed when their absence was noticed. Especially on Sundays, they would walk long distances along the extensive pathways of the estate. Clara would sometimes carry a walking stick. Both Fords were interested in birds and animals. And there were many—maybe too many. Ducks had multiplied until they were so noisy Clara had some of the drakes killed off. The flock of white peacocks, fed three bushels of corn daily, were for some reason attracted to the lawn mowers, and Clara was afraid they would be killed by the rotating blades. At night, the peacocks screeched terribly by the front door.

Clara spent a lot of time in the flower gardens. This was her chief hobby, with perhaps cooking coming second. Her nephew Edward Bryant declares, "Aunt Clara could hold her own when it came to discussing roses, geraniums, or bulbs." Clara insisted on fresh flowers for decoration at all times and spent considerable time improving floral arrangements—a skill at which she felt very capable.

By the 1930s, Clara's gardens were fully developed. The "Blue Garden" next to the house was filled with a variety of blue flowers, beautiful when viewed from the dining room. The "Early Rose Garden" had a wrought-iron gate, lily pond, and teahouse. The "Peony Garden" was near the entrance drive and the miniature farmhouse built for the grandchildren. Upstream from the residence was the boathouse, where Clara kept the *Callie B,* the electric boat she sometimes used to visit her upstream neighbors. There was "Burroughs Grotto," a terraced area with a small statue of Burroughs and a heated birdbath at its base. On the way to "Hidden Lake," Jensen's man-made pond provided for Henry to skate on in the winter, one passed Clara's "Rose Garden."

Clara must have spent considerable time keeping up with her various botanical memberships. By the 1930s, she was a member of at least a dozen, starting in 1915 with the Garden Club of Dearborn, of which she was both president and life member. She became a member of the American Iris Society in 1921 and an honorary member of the Grosse Pointe and Eastern Michigan Horticultural Society in 1925. By the following year, she was on the board of directors of the American Nature Association. Her favorite and most demanding group was the Woman's National Farm and Garden Association, of which she was elected president in 1927. Beginning in 1928, Clara became a life member of the

Clara cutting irises at Fair Lane on May 27, 1939. George Ebling, the Fords'
personal photographer, took this picture. He was especially conscientious and
meticulous. Henry often stated that Ebling was the world's best photographer.
(188.71369)

Although this is an excellent photograph of Clara arranging flowers, Ebling has commented that Clara's requests were quite a problem for him. "Clara expected very flattering photographs, but she was not particularly photogenic herself, and the flowers with which she often posed were not always in the best of bloom."

Massachusetts Horticultural Society. In 1929, as life member, she became a trustee of the American Rose Society. In 1931, she belonged to the American Horticultural Society. The New York State Fruit Testing Co-operative Association struck Clara's fancy in 1938; from this group, as a member, she purchased plums, apples, cherries, nectarines, apricots, and grapes. By 1939, Clara was a member of the American Delphinium Society and the Greater Detroit Gladiolus Society.

Among Clara's notes is the following:

Go make thy garden as fair as thou canst,
Thou workest never alone;
Perhaps he whose plot is next to thine
May see it and mend his own.

Clara almost always took an afternoon nap on the sun porch, and sometimes Henry did as well. In later years, Clara usually went to her room upstairs for an afternoon rest. Edward Bryant explains their use of the sunroom: "The Fords spent a great deal of time there. In the sunroom, they had the mail, the envelopes from the clipping bureaus, the

Clara and Henry at the entrance gate to the English Garden at Fair Lane in September 1939. The gate was acquired in England during one of their trips abroad. (P.0.1001)

notes and recommendations from the office, pictures, and the daily newspapers. Don't think Henry Ford wasn't informed, and he was pleased to see what he had said to, or the recommendations that he had made to, the newspaper reporters in their stories. Here in this room was the lounge where his slippers were, his pillows were, his Locksley Hall, Longfellow's poems, his McGuffey Readers, his Luther Burbank plates and drawings, seed catalogs, and John Burroughs articles. He always had a little pad or book and a stub pencil. He wore glasses, and he enjoyed sweaters. He had fine wool blankets to draw over his feet if he wished to. He could sleep at the drop of a hat. He could relax or tense up and start an argument at will. He could be rough. He swore and was

Clara takes a friend for a ride in her electric boat, the *Callie B,* on the Rouge River upstream from Fair Lane. (P.0.03205)

blasphemous on occasions, which I didn't and don't like, but I never heard him swear in the presence of women, but he told some very dirty stories. He could make you sick with his soy bean creations. On this porch would be concentrated foods including special candies and nuts, which he would nibble at, but he always passed things around. He had fine manners, and he was courteous and considerate, and he was very kind to my Aunt Clara. It was here that he was at his best, as far as I was concerned."

According to Thomson the butler, Mr. and Mrs. Ford's evenings at home seldom varied. For entertainment, neither of them liked tragedies at all, preferring radio programs that were simple, lovable, and humorous. Clara always listened to *Beulah;* she never missed it. She was fond of Jack Benny and the *Quiz Kids* programs and followed *Dr. Christian* until her death. Both Clara and Henry were fond of comedies like *Amos 'n' Andy* and regularly listened to Ford Motor Company programs such as the *Ford Sunday Evening Hour.* If Clara was listening to one of her favorite radio programs and not one of his, Henry would leave her and go to his research laboratory in the powerhouse. If Henry found Clara with some of her friends, he would usually manage a hasty retreat to his laboratory.

Clara liked to read and would often read aloud to Henry either from a newspaper or from books such as *Bambi* or *The Yearling*. Thomson recalls Clara spending a month or more reading *Gone with the Wind* to Henry. She often read to him on the *Fair Lane* during trips to and from New York and Richmond Hill. She loved to read biographies, especially of royalty. Although there seems to be not one photograph of Clara wearing eyeglasses, in March 1915, she had gone to Dr. Robert W. Gillman in Detroit, from whom the bill to her listed three dollars "for Professional Services" and two dollars for "Lenses." Henry also had eyeglasses, but he was not seen in public wearing them. Henry read the *Reader's Digest* quite regularly on his own and insisted on following "Little Orphan Annie" in the newspaper; once he contacted the cartoonist to learn how Annie would cope with an especially trying situation. "Jiggs" was another favorite of Henry's.

Clara liked to go to movies locally and to plays in New York. After reading *Gone with the Wind*, she and Henry both saw the movie, and Clara went to see it again four or five times, according to her chauffeur Rankin. Henry did not like to go to New York, where he would invariably be recognized and bothered by reporters. Clara loved to go and often went with her own friends in the *Fair Lane*. She had favorite actors and actresses, including Lionel Barrymore and Billie Burke. Both Henry and Clara appreciated the help of Gaston Plantiff, manager of Henry's New York office, who knew the town thoroughly and escorted the Fords to many enjoyable spots. Clara would shop with friends, often having items delivered to the *Fair Lane* parked at Mott Haven Storage Yards near Grand Central Station. They often slept in the railroad car, but when Clara would stay at the Biltmore or the Ritz, she likely registered as "Mrs. Henry."

Clara liked to knit. Henry complained that his feet suffered because of his overly darned socks. Rankin tells of having to go into dime stores to get a new pair of socks for Henry, whereupon Henry would change his socks in the car, saving the darned ones so as not to upset Clara. During World War II, Clara started an afghan of red and brown wool but never finished it. She got some wool from the Red Cross to knit socks for the soldiers, but she could never do the heels and quit. Rosa Buhler says she did the heels for her.

It is said that Clara was more likely to want to go out to parties than Henry. Although the Fords received hundreds of invitations, they usually offered "regrets" and were home more evenings than they were out. Both Clara and Henry enjoyed going to weddings, however, and seldom missed one to which they had been invited. They were especially busy during June. Thomson reports, "In winter, Henry would dress in formal clothes and a top hat for a wedding. He'd come prancing down the stairs, Ted Lewis style, especially if Mrs. Ford wasn't there." One of Henry's last public appearances was at a wedding with Clara.

The Fords did not like games such as checkers, chess, dominoes, or cards, or outdoor games such as croquet. Birdwatching was more to their liking. They were not at all interested in watching outdoor sports, although Edsel occasionally would entice his father to attend a World Series baseball game or the Indianapolis races. Henry was left-handed and obtained a set of left-handed golf clubs. It is said that he tried them once, but the ball hit his niece, Violet Audi, who was standing too close, and that was the last of his playing golf.

Henry and Clara subscribed to all three Detroit newspapers but spent little time reading them. Clara handled her own correspondence most of the time. Henry read very little of his mail; the amount was so tremendous he required several secretaries to screen and answer almost all of it. Some fifty form letters helped with that task. He was interested, however, in what the press was saying about him and he employed a clipping service.

Henry never wanted a valet. He picked his own clothes each day, except sometimes his tie, which he liked to have Clara pick for him. She purchased his pajamas, underwear, shirts, socks, and ties—always four-in-hand. He preferred gray suits for everyday wear and dark formals, and he didn't mind dressing up. Clara bought some of the suits, but most were custom-made. Henry is said to have acquired about five suits a year and may have possessed at any one time a total of one hundred suits. About seventy-five out-of-season suits were kept in cold storage at Henry Ford Museum, with twenty-five on hand at Fair Lane. Clara once gave away forty-five of Henry's suits to Mariner's Church and to Good Will Industries.

Henry's shoes were handmade of very soft leather, sometimes by the Greenfield Village cobbler and sometimes by Mattew Brothers in Boston. He took off his shoes and put on house slippers as soon as he arrived home. He kept his shoes a long time and stored them in wooden boxes at Fair Lane, where he had about sixty pairs.

Henry shaved himself with a safety razor until very late in life, when his barber would come to Fair Lane; Henry had a barber chair placed in the swimming pool area. Clara was quite upset when she found Henry was paying the barber six dollars for a shave.

Henry was far more giving of his money than Clara. He was especially generous to children. When his niece Grace Brubaker was about four years old, Henry gave her one hundred silver dollars to play with. At Fair Lane, Rosa Buhler relates that each day an envelope containing $200 in cash was prepared by the office cashier, and she would put it into Henry's coat pocket for spending money. It was seldom spent, but each day a new envelope and cash were supplied. At the end of the week, the envelopes and remaining cash were returned to the office to start another week of the same process.

A somewhat informal portrait of Clara taken on one of her trips to New York around 1930. She is wearing a jaunty sailor straw hat and a single strand of pearls with pearl earrings. This copy of the photo was sent to Nellie (Pierce) Bryant of Boise, Idaho, wife of Clara's brother Harry. Nellie's grandson, Marvin Pierce Bryant, donated the photo to the Dearborn Historical Museum.

Wilbur Donaldson, a young protégé and driver for Henry, recalled: "He was, let's say, a poor driver. Mr. Ford didn't concern himself with such things as stop signs and stop lights. He went right past them, and he'd drive over curbs to pass cars. Before I was old enough to drive, Henry said, 'Get in, Wilbur, I'll drive you home.' It was a frightening trip. I hung on. It was exciting but certainly not safe. Later I got bawled out. I was told no one ever let Mr. Ford drive. Ever! He always rode in a plain, black four-door sedan, but they had leather seats, not mohair. He didn't like his coat to pull when he slid out. He liked young people because they were not after his money and didn't try to talk when he did-n't want to. He and I would ride in the car together for hours and hours and hours and not speak a word. Mrs. Ford liked to ride in a chauffeur-driven limousine, but Mr. Ford got tired of Cadillacs in his garage. He bought the Lincoln Motor Car Company so she could ride in one of his cars. Mr. Ford always wore gray suits, with a vest, even at his farms when he worked in the field or when he tinkered in the machine shop. He wore a felt hat in wintertime and changed to a straw hat on Memorial Day. On Labor Day, he went back to a felt hat. Mr. Ford was not a humorous man. I never heard him laugh. But he was a kind man. He was concerned about others, and he helped a lot of people."

Clara was petite, with dark hair and hazel eyes, which were "not snappy but rather soft." Her only makeup was lipstick and a natural fingernail polish, according to Rosa Buhler. She was always meticulously dressed and was very careful of her clothes. Clara had favorite dresses, one or two in particular which she was photographed wearing each year for ten consecutive years. She favored maroon dresses because that was Henry's favorite color. In Detroit, she purchased many of her dresses from Walton-Pierce; in New York, she bought from Stein and Blaine or other shops recommended perhaps by Ellen Plantiff. Rosa Buhler says she spent a good deal of time lengthening and shortening Clara's dresses. She normally would keep a dress four or five years. Although Clara had the money to buy anything she wanted, she was still thrifty and took pleasure in thinking she was getting her money's worth. She is said to have gone to more than one store to save on a twenty-five-cent hair net. As for jewelry, she was especially fond of her pearls. She seldom wore some of her more elaborate jewels.

Clara's height, said to be only four feet, eleven inches, without high heels, had always been a problem to her. Although older than her sisters Kate and Eva, Clara was three and four inches shorter. She was inclined in her younger days to wear conspicuously high hats and, later, fairly substantial heels on her shoes.

Bedtime for the Fords was ten o'clock; in later years, it became nine o'clock. They slept on their backs with tiny down pillows. According to Rosa Buhler, "they were both very good at snoring. We could hear them downstairs." In later years, each of them had to take a sleeping pill. For minor illnesses, neither wanted a doctor; they usually tried to remedy their own little colds and ailments. For a cold, Clara would use an old English remedy made from black currant jam dissolved in water and swallowed hot. Although Henry seldom had a bad cold, he did have a slight cough all the time which was thought to be a habit. For either colds or upset stomach, Henry would put himself on a milk or water diet.

At Fair Lane, Clara kept hundreds of little slips of paper. Some of these contained advice for keeping house:

"Sal" for moths, spray every few weeks.
"Slents" for your ears to stop noise.
"Renuzits" for dry cleaning.

Clara in a dress and hat she liked so well that she was photographed in them for ten consecutive years. This is the first photo, from 1933.

"Ever Keep" canning compound, follow directions.
"One–a–Day" B complex.
"Dirt Doom" cleans everything.
"Miles Nervine" for wakefulness.
"Fitches Shampoo" for dandruff.
"Westphale Hair Tonic" yellow liquid — good.
"Plasticote" can be used on linoleum, applied with brush.
Oil of Golden Rod made by Shakers of Shirley, Mass.
Creme de Cocoa, get at Detroit Club or Penobscot Liquor Shop.
Mercks Calcium Pantothene — one grain — for retaining present coloring of the hair.
To bleach handkerchiefs — one tablespoon cream of tartar, one quart of water, soak overnight.
Shellac cretonne ten times, two or three days between times.
To sprinkle runways for rats — one pound lime, one pound copperas, one pail water.

Some of the slips of paper were reminders of things to do: chores for Rosa, some for Campsall, some for herself:

Find deed for Mr. Liebold.
Picture of ourselves for Mr. Cameron — one of mother for old church.
Mrs. Barbour wants picture of Henry in wheat field and photo of me in cap and gown.
Cut out pictures from old magazines and paste on parchment lamp shades for lamps.
Make chest for Fort Myers.
Send for measurements of arch for curtains.
Bernice would like to take boat trip any time after this week, would like to board boat at Mackinaw.
Send Eufalie plant, eggs, cheese, chicken to Maggie.
See if we have a feeding table for birds for Miss Sibley.
Send Mrs. Plantiff log swing.
Please take care of clothes in Mr. Edsel's closet — look for moths, brush well.
Cut down tree across river.
I wonder if you could find out anything about him, if he has been fitted with artificial limbs.
Send League Women Voters $400 for State, $100 County.
$500 toward fund for Mrs. Brotherly League.
Try to give some kind of party for old ladies, ask Miss Hulbert to help.
Send Miss Sajo some of my clothes, also some furnishings for young couple and family who have nothing — St. Agnes girl.

Take plants to Marine Hospital or flowers.
Mr. Ford to present Mr. Edison with 50th anniversary watch.
Have on hand for Santa's Cabin—two dolls, umbrellas and rain
capes, five jigsaw puzzles.

Spring of 1936—
Four Dreers trowels
Six Magic weeders
One pr thornproof gloves 10 1/2
One pr 11 1/2
One pr double cut pruning shears

Clara also recorded some favorite sayings:

When you sit on a tack it is a sign of an early spring.

Why can the Duke never be an Admiral? Because he is the third
mate to an American Destroyer.

How they do it in Hollywood: Ketchum, Hitchum, Ditchum.

Custom is what keeps people from doing what they want to, because
they're afraid other people also doing what they don't want to do
will object to their doing what they do want to do.

A kiss of the sun for pardon,
a song of the birds for mirth,
One is nearer God's heart in a garden,
Than anywhere else on earth.

I wish I was a stone
a settin on a hill
a doin nothin all day long
but jist a settin still,
I wouldin eat, I wouldin sleep
I wouldn't even wash,
I'd jist set still a thousand years,
and rest myself, by gosh.

Chapter II
World War II

Back in the 1930s in England, a group of war veterans at Oxford University called themselves the Beer and Beef Club. Known in this country as the Oxford Group, they had adopted the four standards of "honesty, purity, unselfishness, and love" in order to counteract the influence of the Nazis and Communists. The movement spread to the United States, where, on May 14, 1939, in the name of "Moral Re-Armament," a meeting was held at Madison Square Garden, with a radio broadcast by Betsey (Mrs. James) Roosevelt. On June 4, General Pershing issued a statement: "This Moral Re-Armament should enlist the support of all thinking people. There is a spiritual emotion which underlies all true patriotism, and good citizenship itself is dependent upon the high sense of moral obligation of the people. Today, confronted by conditions so threatening to world peace, we must re-dedicate ourselves to the faith of our forefathers if we are to be worthy of our heritage."

On Henry's birthday in 1939, he received a greeting from Frank N. D. Buchman, leader of the American group:

To Mr. Henry Ford on his seventy-sixth birthday:

Seventy-six years old today
Henry Ford will lead the way;
In the spirit of seventy-six again
He'll build God's world through God's new men
All join with you in loud Hurray!
This is spirit of MRA

July 13, 1940
Wedding of Henry Ford II and Anne McDonnell

June 20, 1941
Signing of labor contract with the United Automobile Workers

April 26, 1943
Edsel dies

June 1, 1943
Henry named president of Ford Motor Company

April 10, 1944
Henry II named executive vice president of Ford Motor Company

July 1944
Ford Homestead moved to Greenfield Village from its original site on Ford Road in Dearborn

March 1945
Doctors pronounce Henry to be in very poor health

On November 28, 1939, Clara received a letter from the Moral Re-Armament group asking that she have William Cameron, spokesman on the *Ford Sunday Evening Hour*, talk on the need for a spiritual revival in America. By this time, MRA was estimated to have reached one million people throughout the world. The Fords were undoubtedly members, as were the Harvey Firestones.

Leaving Dearborn on Valentine's Day, 1940, Henry and Clara went to Ways by rail. Clara's four-day diary reads:

> Wednesday 14th — Left for Georgia, Grace with us.
> Thursday 15 — Arrived in NY half day late, bad storm, much
>   snow. Went to theatre — "Life with Father."
> Friday 16 — Shopped with Mrs. Plantiff. Left Jersey City
>   9 P.M. Horace, Grace, Tommy & Carrie with us.
> Saturday 17 — Arrived Ways Station P.M. Everyone surprised
> and a little cross, as they were not expecting us before
> Sunday.

Both the Seaboard and the Atlantic Coast Line railways passed through Ways, which was one reason Henry wanted that location for his sawmill. Lumber from Ways found its way not only to Dearborn by rail but also up to Sudbury, Massachusetts, where a Martha-Mary Chapel was built with Ways Station lumber. Church pews, schoolroom desks, and caskets were other products of Henry's sawmill. In March, George Washington Carver visited Ways to dedicate the Carver School, built for black students and supervised by a black principal and teachers. Starting with 150 pupils, it was soon educating 300.

When the Fords returned to Dearborn on April 1, the specter of war was ever more close. Hitler had invaded Denmark and threatened Norway. Henry's previous stance of avoiding conflict in Europe changed abruptly. He now stated that a friendship with England was necessary, with a slogan: "Hold the fort, for we are coming." But Henry was inconsistent. After first offering to build 1,000 fighter planes a day to aid the Allies, he turned down a plea to build Rolls-Royce aircraft engines for Britain. Edsel was very embarrassed over the situation. He did not understand his father at all. The consensus was that Henry was "cracking up."

Clara, in the meantime, had received for her birthday the usual cakes, candies, roses, and, from Martha Berry, a sunbonnet. She was looking ahead to the wedding of her grandson, Henry Ford II. Trips to New York in April, May, and June prepared her for the "wedding of the century," scheduled for July 13, 1940, at Southampton, Long Island. Henry and Clara with their friends left Dearborn on July 11 on the *Fair Lane*. The bride-to-be was Anne McDonnell, a member of a large and

Henry and Clara
dancing at the wedding
of Henry Ford II on
July 13, 1940, at
Southampton, Long
Island. (P.0.4638)

Posed on the stage of the Henry Ford Museum Theater are Clara and Henry (front row center) with the June 6, 1940, graduating class of the Edison Institute. World War II would soon diminish male enrollments in the upper grades of the school. (188.27674)

prosperous Irish family who lived during the winter in a twenty-nine-room apartment on Fifth Avenue in New York and had as their summer home a fifty-room mansion on the ocean at Southampton. Anne had thirteen brothers and sisters and eighty-three first cousins, lots of new in-laws for young Henry to meet. Her father ran the well-known brokerage firm of McDonnell and Company.

Edsel and Eleanor arrived from Seal Harbor for the wedding on their yacht, *Onika*, three days before the ceremony in order to attend a series of prewedding parties. There were more than eleven hundred wedding guests, many more than the small church could accommodate. Sixteen armed guards were on hand to protect the two rooms full of wedding gifts. One of the gifts was from Henry and Clara: a custom-built Ford car with paid chauffeur included. Henry Ford, Sr., was at first annoyed that his grandson was marrying a Catholic, but after dancing with Anne following the wedding, he seems to have made no further comments regarding her religion. Henry and Clara would welcome great-grandchildren Charlotte, Anne, and Edsel II.

After Henry received a cake and a bouquet of yellow roses for his birthday from Edison Institute students, Henry and Clara on August 6 left from the Rouge Plant on the ship *Henry Ford II* going to Duluth for ore. They stopped off at Marquette to stay at their Huron Mountain lodge for the rest of the month. Clara made trips to New York during September and October, and both Fords visited Boston and New York during October.

During 1941, Henry built a house in an elegant section of Dearborn for his sister, Margaret Ruddiman, using brick and woodwork from an earlier Ruddiman home at a cost of $38,435.90. She had been living in Detroit since 1928.

Henry and Clara left for Ways on January 26, 1941. Clara's only diary entry was: "Left Detroit — Sunday January 26, '41. Arrived Savannah Tuesday 28th, 5 P.M. Had dinner at Richmond Hill — Horace, Grace, and Tommy." The Fords were now employing 320 blacks and 351 whites on the Ford Farms. Although wages were less than in Dearborn, Dr. C. F. Holton, the community physician, remarked, "Henry Ford, by means of his health clinic, his schools, and employment, has changed the population from a sickly, suspicious, illiterate, and undernourished group into one of the healthiest communities in Georgia." Henry and Clara returned from Ways on March 13, after stopping at Tuskegee, Alabama, to visit Dr. Carver and at Rome, Georgia, to visit Martha Berry. On May 1, 1941, after much negotiation with the two railroads and the U.S. Postal Department, the people of Ways Station were able to change the name of their village to Richmond Hill, the name of the Ford residence, in honor of Henry and Clara.

Back home, the Fords found labor trouble in Dearborn. The U.A.W. had filed election petitions with the National Labor Relations Board to hold votes at the Lincoln, Highland Park, and Rouge plants, and the Supreme Court had judged the petitions valid. Henry vowed he would close the plants rather than let the union conduct a vote. But the tide was turning against Ford inside the Rouge Plant. On April 1, 1941, workers stopped working, union officials declared an official strike, and the workers left the plant. Henry instructed Edsel to leave the labor situation to Bennett. On April 3, the union made an offer of settlement. Although Bennett ignored the offer, Edsel insisted on negotiations.

In all this, Clara undoubtedly played a major role. When Henry had decided to close his plants rather than submit to the U.A.W., Clara was terribly upset. She could visualize riots and bloodshed. It is said she threatened to divorce Henry if he didn't side with Edsel and negotiate. Henry himself never did negotiate. After the spontaneous strike on April 1, the plant had shut down and negotiations began. The strike vote required by federal law resulted in a large majority voting for the union. Ford officials and union leaders settled the dispute in Washington on June 20, 1941, when a contract of unusually generous

terms was signed. Henry was crushed by the overwhelming number of workers who voted for the union. The labor conflict had been a strain on the health of both Edsel and Henry.

On July 27, Henry and Clara started their annual lakes cruise, summarized by Campsall as follows: "Dearborn to Pequaming, stopped off two hours, then through the Portage to Superior to load ore, back down the lake, through the Soo, over to the Straits, turned around and proceeded down Lake Huron and docked at the Great Lakes Engineering Works where the passengers were discharged August 2. The cargo was delivered at Cleveland."

At Christmastime, Clara joined the China Relief Legion headed by Pearl S. Buck, national director of United China Relief.

The bride, Edith McNaughton, and the groom, Benson Ford. (N.O. 19044)

(Left) Clara and Henry attending the wedding of their grandson Benson
Ford to Edith McNaughton in Grosse Pointe on a warm and breezy July 9,
1941. About two hundred relatives and friends filled Christ Church Chapel
for the ceremony, while crowds of onlookers filled the streets outside.

Henry's younger brother, William, on the left, with Henry at a tractor convention at Dearborn Inn in 1940 promoting the Ford Tractor with "Wheel-Less Implements." William was then sixty-nine and Henry seventy-seven years of age. (188.27022)

The United States was now, in 1942, directly involved in the war. Because of Henry's erratic mental state, it fell upon Edsel and Charles Sorensen to carry on the business. Sorensen had made an earlier agreement with Henry that he would retire in 1941 at the age of sixty, but with the health of both Henry and Edsel being poor, and considering the deluge of war work, Sorensen felt it best to continue with the company. Dozens of war contracts to be implemented by Ford Motor Company had to be handled by Edsel and Charles Sorensen, who had been an outstanding production manager for many years. Contracts totaling nearly a billion dollars were being negotiated with the government. The largest of the war contracts were negotiated during this period.

At the first of the year, civilian passenger-car production was stopped in Ford plants, and Greenfield Village was closed to the public. On February 28, 1942, Henry and Clara left for Georgia, heading first to Berry College, where Martha Berry had died. This time, their private secretary, Frank Campsall, accompanied them. The war was already affecting operations at Richmond Hill. Several hundred acres were taken by the army for Camp Stewart, and provisions were made for an aircraft guidance system. The plantation's cabin cruiser was taken by the Coast Guard, and no more cars, trucks, or tractors could be obtained. Government regulations restricting materials, manpower, wages, rents, and new taxes made life more difficult. The Fords came home after three weeks, stopping on the way at Tuskegee Institute to visit with Dr.

Standing from left to
right: Henry, Clara,
and Roy Bryant.
Seated are Harry
Wismer, Mary
Elizabeth (Betty)
Wismer holding little
Henry Wismer, and
Katharine Bryant.
Betty was one of the
five children of Roy
and Katharine Bryant.
This photograph was
taken at the Bryant
home about 1942.
(P.0.14353)

Carver. This was Henry's last trip on his private railroad car.

Leaving Dearborn on April 26, "Mrs. Ford and party" traveled to New York and Atlantic City, returning April 30. This was Clara's last trip on the *Fair Lane,* for the government had ordered a ban on the use of private railway cars for the duration of the war. Chauffeur Rankin stated, "When during the war, the government had taken away their private railroad car, Mrs. Ford missed it very much." Liebold was instructed to sell the car and did so for $30,000. Clara removed her belongings, including dishes and linens. Henry and Clara continued to travel by rail, but during the next five years they traveled together on each trip and used rail transportation at most three times a year. One of those trips each year was to Richmond Hill.

For her birthday in 1942, Clara received a silver set from Eleanor and flowers from Roy and Katharine Bryant. Following the late-April trip to New York, an Irish punchbowl arrived at Fair Lane from the Steuben Glass Company and was placed on the dining-room table. On Henry's birthday, he received a cake from the Richmond Hill Bakery

A 1942 photograph
of Henry Ford II in
naval uniform with
his wife Anne
McDonnell Ford
and their daughter
Charlotte.
(N.O. 13109)

and peaches from Berry Schools. Henry and Clara left immediately for
the Huron Mountains, taking the *Henry Ford II* to Marquette. They
returned to Dearborn on August 28.

Their trip to Georgia in late February 1943 was by way of New
York, using New York Central, Pennsylvania, and Atlantic Coast Line
railroads. As in the previous year, Frank Campsall was with them. On
their return trip, they again paid Berry Schools a visit and arrived back
in Dearborn on March 26.

During the winter, Edsel, who had been bearing the brunt of Ford
Motor Company responsibilities, had been quite ill. Henry did not seem
to take Edsel's illness very seriously, but Clara was more concerned. On
April 26, 1943, Edsel died at his home on Lake Shore Drive in Grosse
Pointe Shores, at age forty-nine. He had first been diagnosed with gas-
tric ulcers but finally was found to have stomach cancer aggravated by
undulant fever, possibly caused by drinking unpasteurized milk delivered from Ford Farms. Rites were held at Christ Church in Grosse
Pointe and confined to approximately six hundred family members and
close friends. At two-thirty that afternoon, the Ford plants, including
the giant Rouge, were silenced for two minutes. Interment was in

Clara and Henry seated on a sofa at Edsel's home at Gaukler's Point in early 1943, just before the death of Edsel. Standing, from left to right, are Henry II, Eleanor Ford, Eleanor's niece Katrina Kanzler, Anne McDonnell Ford, Josephine Ford, and Edsel. The baby held by Clara is Charlotte Ford, daughter of Henry and Anne Ford and Edsel's first grandchild. Henry holds the baby's doll. (P.833.77863-13)

Woodlawn Cemetery on Woodward Avenue in Detroit. Because Edsel's death was so unexpected, his body was placed in the mausoleum of Eleanor's uncle, J. L. Hudson, until his own could be constructed.

Shortly after Edsel's death, Eleanor put the Lake Shore Drive home up for sale but then changed her mind about selling it. When Eleanor died in 1967, she left an endowment which maintains the

Clara and Henry
at Fair Lane in the
fall of 1943.
(P.188.71580)

beautiful home as a museum. At the time of Edsel's death, Henry II
was in training at the Naval School in Chicago. On June 1, the Ford
Motor Company board of directors met, adding as new members
Eleanor Ford and others including Harry Bennett. Although some
thought the new board would put Bennett in charge of the company,
the collective voting power of Clara and Eleanor made Henry Ford I
again president of Ford Motor Company. Henry II was released from
the Navy and was made a Ford vicepresident in December 1943.

Henry Ford I now found it necessary to revise his will of February 6, 1936, in which Edsel had been appointed executor. A codicil dated June 1, 1943, named Clara J. Ford as executor. Likewise, Clara found it necessary, by means of a similar codicil dated July 23, 1943, to replace Edsel's name with Henry's on her will of July 1936.

On June 5, 1943, Henry is said to have admitted, "Maybe I pushed the boy too hard." From the old Edison Avenue home, Henry was able to obtain some of the bricks from the garage workshop built for Edsel in 1908. Then, in Greenfield Village, Henry used these bricks in building a replica of Edsel's workshop as a permanent memorial to his son.

Clara had her brother Roy's family for close company, but Henry was not very friendly with his relatives. Liebold stated, "Mr. Ford's mind began deteriorating about 1942 or 1943. There were signs before Edsel's death. His son's death and the labor vote about that time greatly affected him." Henry's mental and physical frailty led the federal government to consider taking over Ford Motor Company in order to protect its defense contracts. If it had not been for Sorensen's position on the board of directors, this probably would have happened.

For Henry's eightieth birthday, he received greetings from President Roosevelt. Henry and Clara left by boat for their annual Huron Mountain vacation on July 28, 1943, returning September 3. The first week of November and the first few days of December were spent in New York City. Campsall traveled with them on both New York trips. It is said Campsall was spending so much time with the Fords that his wife felt like a widow.

Shortly after Christmas 1943, Clara wrote to a longtime friend as follows:

Dear Mrs. Dunlop:

Thank you very much for the good little pies you sent us just before Christmas. They are as delicious as ever. Our Christmas was easier to get through than we expected, without our boy. His wife was to be with us but came down with the "flu" the day before. The youngest grandchild came. We had breakfast across the river, and saw the little children with their tree, had supper with the Bryants to help Carol celebrate her birthday. Home at ten, plenty tired. Thanking you again,

Sincerely,
Clara Ford

In 1944, Henry and Clara left for Richmond Hill on February 9, returning on March 22. On March 2, Charles Sorensen had retired from Ford Motor Company, leaving control to the vacationing Henry and to Harry Bennett. Clara was not particularly perturbed at Sorensen's leaving, because for years he had been somewhat harsh with Edsel. With support again from Clara and Eleanor, on April 10, 1944, Henry Ford II was named executive vice president of Ford Motor Company. Henry I's influence was diminishing.

A strange document came to the attention of Henry Ford II during 1944. It was a codicil to the will of Henry Ford I drawn up by Ford Motor Company lawyer I. A. Capizzi, calling for a board of trustees to operate the company for ten years following old Henry's death. Named on the board of trustees were Capizzi, Frank Campsall, Edsel Ruddiman, and Roy Bryant, with Bennett as secretary. It was Bennett who possessed the original copy. When questioned about it, Bennett is said to have taken it from his pocket and burned it, saying it was of no value anyway.

Until 1944, the Fords had traveled to Richmond Hill by train. This year, they drove, leaving the first week of February. They used three automobiles, the first driving far in advance to handle arrangements, the second a Lincoln carrying Henry and Clara, and the third carrying baggage.

From Richmond Hill that year, Rankin drove Clara down to Clearwater, Florida, to see her brother Fred and her sister-in-law Jo. Clara had helped finance their Clarkston, Michigan, farm before they retired to Florida, and she helped pay their hospital bills. In December 1946, Fred died, and Clara paid for funeral expenses including a marker in Dunedin Cemetery. Jo died in Florida in 1949. On the way back to Richmond Hill that March of 1944, Clara and Rankin had lunch at Daytona about two-thirty in the afternoon, and Clara asked Rankin how much farther they had to drive to reach Richmond Hill. When he said it was too far to drive that day, Clara insisted that they try it. They arrived at Richmond Hill at six-thirty after averaging sixty-five miles an hour.

A four-day trip to New York was taken in mid-May. In the meantime, Campsall had obtained from Capizzi a list of eighteen properties with their "book values" owned by the Fords for which some disposition should be made. These ranged from a $500 school lot to the $692,988 Dearborn Country Club. Also among them were the Botsford Tavern, which was sold to Seaboard Properties Company for $229,050, and Ford Island near Traverse City for $30,000. The total value came to more than $1.7 million. Henry and Clara decided most of the properties were to be sold, but several were to be gifts. As an example, by means of a warranty deed dated July 1, 1944, Henry and Clara conveyed 140 acres of Dearborn Township land to Raymond and Evangeline Dahlinger for the sum of $1.00.

The first building Henry Ford had restored was his birthplace in 1920. It was also the last building he moved to Greenfield Village. In

Seemingly pals, Henry Ford II and Harry Bennett are seen here together in Bennett's office in the Ford Administration Building on April 4, 1944. This was the day Henry Ford II was made executive vice president of Ford Motor Company. The power struggle between the two men would go on until September 1945, when Bennett left the company. (P.833.79986.4)

July 1944, the house and windmill were moved and reinstalled in the village. The house was finally removed from its original location at Ford and Greenfield roads because of the fear of vandalism and the cost of guards needed to protect the property.

Also in 1944, Henry donated 1,400,000 shares of Ford Motor Company stock worth $7 million to the Ford Foundation.

Henry and Clara's vacation to the Huron Mountains occupied all of August. In October, a disastrous hurricane struck Fort Myers, taking down electric wires, blowing down trees, destroying the fruit, and leaving the Fords' tenant without water, gas, or phone. The tenant added: "The *Reliance*, Mr. Edison's electric launch you planned to take to Dearborn, was washed away and is down the beach about a mile a total wreck." The Ford home had not been especially damaged, and no immediate action was taken regarding the property. A pre-Christmas trip to New York and Boston seems to have completed the Fords' travels for the year.

Nineteen forty-five would be a difficult year. In January, financial secretary L. J. Thompson examined the Fort Myers property, giving alternatives of renting or selling. It was decided to sell the Mangoes that year. According to Rankin, he drove the Fords by automobile to Richmond Hill that February. But Henry was not at all well, and a doctor attended him.

Dr. John G. Mateer had found Henry "so physically weak he could not walk upstairs." He was given tonics and vitamins and in the next few months picked up in general vitality. He had lost initiative in starting conversations, however, and was limited to yes-and-no answers to questions. This was in striking contrast to his normal character. Dr. Mateer characterized Henry as a "pleasant vegetable."

Clara had sheltered Henry to quite an extent since the signs of senility in 1939. Now she was somewhat embarrassed and protected him even more. Mateer has stated, "During 1945, Mrs. Ford recognized her husband's mental impairment and protected him from any business talks. Henry Ford probably would not have been able to conduct business conversations intelligently. During May 1945, Mr. Ford did recognize his immediate family but probably not many others beyond the family." It was Mateer's feeling that "Mr. Ford was doing no reasoning." Instead of Clara's keeping track of him to see that he didn't get into trouble, he now had a tendency to follow her about.

On February 21, 1945, Campsall was informed that four pieces of property occupied by members of the Roy Bryant family had been appraised and that Roy and two of his daughters agreed to buy the properties at the appraised value. Henry and Clara must have decided differently, however, because between April 24 and June 29, they signed warranty deeds for the same pieces of property, charging one dollar in each case. Roy's family had been very close to Henry and Clara for years. Fred Black, a trusted employee, said that Clara wanted especially to take care of them because she was afraid that if she died, Henry might not do so.

On August 2, 1945, Henry and Clara boarded the ore boat *Henry Ford II* for a Great Lakes cruise. They traveled through Lake Huron to Lake Michigan, down past Milwaukee, then turned around and came back up to Green Bay, through the Straits of Mackinaw and the Soo Locks into Lake Superior, through the Portage between Hancock and Houghton, and on to Superior, Wisconsin, to load ore. From there, they proceeded up to Fort Williams, Port Arthur, and Isle Royale, then back through the Soo Locks and Lake Huron to the coke dock at the Rouge Plant, where they debarked on August 11. The cargo was then taken across Lake Erie to Huron, Ohio. There is no record of Henry and Clara having gone to the Huron Mountains that year.

Henry Ford II was gaining considerable authority within Ford Motor Company despite the hold of Harry Bennett and his cronies. Although Clara had tried to induce her husband to relinquish the presidency to Henry II, the older Henry was reluctant. It was Eleanor Ford who turned the tide when she proclaimed she would sell all her voting stock if her son were not given the presidency. Old Henry then agreed he would step aside. Campsall prepared the letter of resignation, and on September 21, 1945, a board meeting was called. At the meeting were Henry Ford I, Henry Ford II, Harry Bennett, Meade Bricker, B. J. Craig, Eleanor Ford, and Frank Campsall. Bennett hastily left the room as soon as the vote was taken, but he found time to remark to young Henry with much anger, "You're taking over a billion-dollar organization here that you haven't contributed a thing to!"

Chapter 12
Henry's Declining Years

The stay in Richmond Hill in the winter of 1946 was somewhat hectic. An abbreviated "anonymous" diary of events (found in a collection of office papers) reads as follows:

Monday, January 21st. Mr. and Mrs. Ford and Mr. Frank Campsall left Detroit by private car at 11:45 P.M. via Cincinnati and Atlanta, arriving at Richmond Hill on Wednesday, January 23rd. Chef Foster and Porter Woodley.

Monday, January 28th. Aunt Jane died (aged colored woman lived near Darien).

Tuesday, February 5th. Two children of Mr. and Mrs. Henry Ford II with nurse Muriel Donahan and Tom Laughran arrived at Richmond Hill. Lady Nancy Astor — Yeaman's Hall, Charleston, S.C. Robert Rankin called at home of Mrs. W. S. Nelson in Savannah for Lady Astor and brought her to Richmond Hill for luncheon. Mr. and Mrs. Ford rode in with Lady Astor to Savannah.

Friday, February 22nd. Two children and nurse leave for New York City, also Tom Laughran.

Monday, March 4th. Mr. Roy Bryant, Mr. and Mrs. Harry Wismer wired from Atlanta would call at Richmond late that day. No record or a witness of their arrival. (Farr — watchman at Cherry Hill gate.) Mr. Campsall was taken to the Central of Georgia Railway Hospital in Savannah about 3:00 P.M.— Room #228 — where he remained until

Thursday, March 7th. Frank Campsall returned to Cherry Hill with Rankin about 3:00 P.M.

Sunday, March 10th. Mr. Campsall was again taken by ambulance to Hospital in Savannah.

March 16, 1946
Frank Campsall, Henry's personal secretary, dies in Savannah

March 26, 1947
Clara receives an honorary Doctor of Humanities degree from Berry College

April 7, 1947
Henry dies at Fair Lane

November 23, 1948
A meeting is called regarding ownership of the Ford Cemetery where Henry is buried

December 17, 1948
The Clara J. Ford Fund is organized

Frank Campsall, personal secretary to Henry and Clara, in Dearborn with Henry not long before Campsall's death on March 16, 1946, in a Savannah, Georgia, hospital. (P.0.13275)

Monday, March 11. Operation — serious condition.

Wednesday, March 13. H. R. Waddell (Clara's secretary) arrived at Richmond Hill in the company plane. That same evening drove to Savannah with Dr. McClure and Robert Rankin. Visited Frank Campsall at the hospital. Dr. McClure stayed at the DeSoto Hotel for several days.

Friday, March 15th. Received instructions from Mr. and Mrs. Ford to make arrangements for leaving Richmond Hill for Detroit on March 20th.

Saturday, March 16th. Frank Campsall passed away at 6:10 A.M. Mrs. Plantiff arrived. Met by Mr. and Mrs. Ford and Rankin in Savannah. Met Dr. McClure — called at Sipple Funeral Parlors.

Monday, March 18th. Mrs. Plantiff drove to Bradenton, Florida, by Carmi.

Wednesday, March 20th. Leave Richmond Hill at 8:00 P.M. in

private car for Detroit via Atlanta and Cincinnati — Mr. and Mrs. Ford, H. R. Waddell, Paul Foster, Roger Woodley. *Friday, March 22nd.* Arrived Dearborn, 9:00 A.M.

Even in his somewhat dazed condition, it must have been a severe blow to Henry to lose his faithful secretary Frank Campsall, who had worked for him for thirty years and, since Liebold's retirement in 1933, had been Henry and Clara's personal secretary.

Clara was considerably occupied during 1946 in seeing that Henry, in poor health, was sheltered from the public and from responsibilities with which he could not cope. Henry possessed very little of his old initiative and merely trailed Clara from place to place.

Because of Henry's weak condition, in June 1946, an elevator designed by the Ford Motor Company and manufactured by the Inclinator Company of America was installed at Fair Lane. It was a custom model identified as an "Elevette" and was installed just inside the entrance of Fair Lane. It was a personal elevator that would carry the Fords up one level to the main stairwell landing. It had a cable lift powered by a one-horsepower electric motor. The platform with an accordion gate enclosure at each end accommodated a maximum of four pas-

Clara (left) and Ellen Plantiff visiting the cemetery at White Hall Plantation near Richmond Hill, Georgia. This is believed to be on March 16, 1946, the day that Frank Campsall died in a Savannah hospital. Ellen left for Florida on the 18th, and Clara returned to Dearborn two days later. Henry was not at all well at that time. (P.0.12708)

sengers on the eight-foot vertical trip. Passengers entered one end of the car and left by the opposite end without having to turn around in the car. A person in a wheelchair could have been accommodated easily. The elevator's "lift speed" of twelve feet per minute indicates the eight-foot trip would have required a lengthy forty seconds. It was not a speedy elevator. Shortly after Henry's death in 1947, the elevator was removed.

H. Rex Waddell, Clara's secretary, handled the Fords' personal mail and somehow managed to excuse Henry from attending nearly all public events. Henry did, however, attend the Automobile Golden Jubilee on June 15, where he sat with his old friends Charles B. King and Ransom E. Olds, and a party at Ford Field where 50,000 Dearborn people sang "Happy Birthday." He did not speak at these events and was escorted by Clara and Waddell. Clara also took him to a Grosse Pointe wedding, but Henry showed little interest.

In late summer, Henry and Clara took their usual vacation by boat to Marquette and the Huron Mountain Club, leaving July 31 and returning September 4. In September, Clara was ordering lilacs from Brand Peony Farms in Faribault, Minnesota. A railroad schedule shows Henry and Clara traveling to Framingham, Massachusetts, on October 14 and on to New York on October 17, returning to Dearborn October 21. Another trip to New York occupied the first week of December. Late that December at Fair Lane, Henry, as usual, dressed up as Santa Claus and passed out presents to Greenfield Village schoolchildren.

Clara had made personal contributions of $7,952.57 to twenty-five charitable organizations during 1946. The larger donations were to the Y.W.C.A. of New York, Christ Episcopal Church of Dearborn, and Hindman Settlement School.

Nineteen forty-seven started out as usual for Henry and Clara with a rail trip to Richmond Hill by way of Cincinnati and Atlanta, leaving Dearborn on January 27. With them were secretary H. R. Waddell, chef Paul Foster, and porter Roger Woodley. They arrived at Richmond Hill on January 29 and stayed until March 24. For a few days in February, Lord and Lady Perry visited, and in mid-March Roy Bryant and some friends from Dearborn stayed for a few days before continuing on to Florida. During this period, Henry's vitality fluctuated from day to day, but he did take a ride with Roy and Rankin through the countryside to the villages of Hinesville and Midway, while Clara entertained six ladies from Savannah.

On March 24, the Fords left for home by way of Rome, Georgia, and Berry College. On March 26, at the college Clara was awarded the honorary degree of Doctor of Humanities. The only other time the college had awarded such a degree was to its late founder, Martha Berry. In conferring the degree, the president of the college said: "You, Mrs. Clara Bryant Ford, have long been active in many diverse and useful projects.

In this photograph, Henry, with hat in hand, and Clara in her cap and gown are standing with college dignitaries on the Berry College campus. This was Henry Ford's very last public appearance. On this occasion, Clara had received an honorary degree of Doctor of Humanities from Berry College, and Henry had been invited to help plant a magnolia tree in Martha Berry's Memorial Garden. The tree is shown planted at right in the picture. (N.O.1016)

Henry and Clara on Henry's original Quadricycle on May 23, 1946, when Clara was entertaining the Woman's National Farm and Garden Association and visiting Greenfield Village. (P.0.18715)

Henry and Clara watching the dirigible mooring mast at Ford Airport in Dearborn being toppled on October 26, 1946. The days of the dirigible were over. This was one of Henry's last public appearances. (P. O. 18695)

Outside Santa's Workshop at Fair Lane, Henry, in the background dressed as Santa, distributes gifts to Greenfield Village children. This photograph was taken on December 23, 1946, his last Christmas with the children. (P.188.74407)

You have been a gardener of growing things both human and horticultural. You have been very close to God's heart." In accepting the degree, Clara stated: "It is always a pleasure to come to Berry. I am happy to accept this honor, and am more honored in knowing that Miss Berry wanted me to have this degree from Berry College." Following Clara's award, Henry planted the first tree in the Memorial Forest, which had been planned by Miss Berry before her death. The tree, a magnolia, was planted near the archway entrance to the school. With students to assist him, Henry made certain it was planted straight.

It was a rainy April in Dearborn. By April 7, the Rouge River had overflowed its banks, inundating the Fair Lane powerhouse so that the residence was without heat, electricity, or telephone. Henry was offered breakfast at Rankin's house nearby; he had a hearty meal of oatmeal, prunes, bacon, toast, and coffee. Later, he asked Rankin to drive him around Dearborn to various locations, where he assessed the damages done by the flood. Each situation offered a degree of excitement and a mental challenge. He seemed to be enjoying himself. Henry also asked to see the cemetery where his grandfather, Patrick Ahern, was buried and the Ford Cemetery where his parents were buried, mentioning that he was to be buried at the latter one.

In early evening, the engineer was able to turn on the power momentarily, and Henry was about to fool Clara into thinking he had fixed it himself, but the power went off again. Later that evening, Clara read to Henry by a fireplace with only candle and oil lamps for illumination. They retired upstairs at about nine. At eleven-fifteen, Henry complained to Clara of a headache and a dry throat, whereupon she called Rosa Buhler and asked her to call Dr. Mateer. Henry died at eleven-forty, twenty minutes before the doctor arrived. Henry Ford II was told of his grandfather's death and hurried to Fair Lane. The press was notified immediately and the world knew of Henry's death the next morning. The death certificate indicates "cerebral hemorrhage (massive)."

Reverend Hedley G. Stacey, pastor of Christ Episcopal Church in Dearborn, which Henry and Clara had attended since 1915, delivered a short service at Fair Lane the day after Henry's death. He stated in his reminiscences:

> Mrs. Ford held up very well under it; there's no doubt about it. No one but herself knows how much she missed him. She missed him tremendously. In fact, she spoke to Mrs. Stacey and I about how much she missed Henry, and then she would tell little things, you know, that he used to do and so on. She was sort of remembering. She missed him very, very much. Mrs. Ford left me the prayer book Mr. Ford gave her the day they were married. She called me up one day, after his death, and asked me if I would take charge of it. She wrote a letter, giving the book to me, certifying that it was given to me by her, and she called it her most precious possession. She said, "I don't want this to be kicked around or to be lost. If you don't mind, I'd like you to have it, and I know you will look after it."

(Further statements by Reverend Stacey concerning the Fords are in Appendix 2 of this book.)

Funeral arrangements were handled by the William R. Hamilton Company of Detroit, with services scheduled at Detroit's St. Paul's Cathedral for April 10, 1947. There were ninety-seven invitations issued, including forty-seven relatives, twenty-seven friends, fourteen top executives of Ford Motor Company, five doctors from Henry Ford Hospital, and four people from the Edison Institute. Thousands more came, filling the streets outside the cathedral. Dean Kirk B. O'Ferrall delivered the following appreciation:

Few great men are appreciated by the generation in which they live. Their ideas are generally far in advance of their contemporaries and arouse incredulity in many minds. The creative geniuses of the race are often maligned and persecuted. I imagine in the early days of Henry Ford's great career this may have been true, but as today in humble, simple fashion he is laid to rest with his fathers, the world is able to see and recognize as a great boon to humanity the ideas he set himself to realize many years ago. Those better versed than I are estimating his industrial greatness and the new age in industry which his ideas inaugurated.

I wish to speak of the qualities of his later years which impressed themselves upon me. First, his dislike of ostentation and pomp; the continuance to the end of his simple personal tastes and habits in an age given to luxury and extravagance in this country. These good habits may well impress themselves upon our youth of the land. Then, I must mention also the humility and depreciation of personal praise which always characterized him.

Secondly, I doubt whether any man of great wealth ever gave more away without the knowledge of the world and his fellows generally. He once told me if his own conscience was clear in such matters, that was all he wished.

Thirdly, his lifelong devotion to his home, the fine example of home life he set, his devotion to his early surroundings, the city and community he did so much to make great and powerful. He did not desire to change his home to dwell among the financial princes of the world; the words home and children in every sense meant much to him.

And lastly, his belief in Everlasting Life. His firm faith that his life was but a preparation for another and greater one, which he often discussed with me; so that I have no doubt that now after the more than four score years which by clean and healthy living, he was permitted to live, and now that the "silver cord has been loosed" and "the golden bowl broken," he has gone to his long home which shall know no end, in the infinite Eternity of God.

Henry was buried where he expected to be — in the little cemetery on Joy Road near Greenfield Road in Detroit. Clara, however, was concerned about the openness of the location and the need to guard the

St. Paul's Cathedral on Woodward Avenue in Detroit, where crowds
gathered for Henry's funeral on April 10, 1947. (833.84160-43)

grave. A guardhouse and twenty-four-hour protection were immediately established. She had given thought to placing Henry's grave next to the Episcopal Church at Military and Cherry Hill streets in Dearborn. And consideration was given to moving the entire Ford Cemetery onto Greenfield Village property.

It was generally assumed that because Henry and Clara owned the property around the cemetery, they also owned the cemetery, but that was not the case. The cemetery was the property of descendants of Samuel, George, and John Ford, who settled in the area in the 1830s and 1840s. It had been part of Samuel's original farm. Clara's solution to her cemetery problem was to establish an Episcopal church next to the cemetery. A meeting of approximately ninety representatives of the three branches of the Ford family was called for November 23, 1948. New directors were added to the board of trustees of the cemetery, and attendees were invited to quitclaim their rights. Most of them did; most of them had no further need of the cemetery.

Henry Ford II offered to take care of the Henry Ford Museum if Clara would handle Greenfield Village. Clara gave responsibility for the village to Raymond Dahlinger, who was to follow her suggestions. Among her suggestions were the removal of the windmill at the Ford Homestead and the equipment from the Village Chemical Laboratory. According to H. S. Ablewhite, a former Lutheran minister appointed by Henry II to manage the museum, Clara was at the same time interfering with his operation of the museum. He stated, "Definitely, I don't think Mrs. Ford really understood the philosophy behind the village and museum. I don't think she sensed the greatness of the opportunity here of the institution as an educational institution. Her interest was purely in the preservation of her husband's hobby. She remained a little farm girl all her life. She was completely unspoiled by all her money; that's my personal opinion."

Very fond of her summer home, Clara, with the Roy Bryants, sailed on the *Henry Ford II* to Marquette and spent the month of August 1947 at the Huron Mountain Club.

Clara's contributions to charities during 1947 totaled $8,669.23, with the largest being to the Sister Elizabeth Kenny Foundation. A total summary of "charitable gifts" by the Fords from 1917 through a portion of 1947 adds up to nearly $37 million. Of this amount, $10.4 million had been given to the Edison Institute, $10.5 million to Henry Ford Hospital, $9.45 million to the Ford Foundation, and $775,000 to the Y.M.C.A. A total of $1.95 million had been given to individuals, and $336,000 had been paid for patients in Henry Ford Hospital. Until 1944, charitable deductions were limited to 15 percent of the taxpayer's net income. Less than half ($15 million) of the contributions by the Fords were allowable as deductions from their income taxes. Henry's estate in 1947 was valued at $500 million.

In October 1947, Clara personally delivered the following note to Henry's sister, Margaret Ruddiman, and Margaret's daughter, Catherine, both living at 44 River Lane in Dearborn.

Dear Margaret and Catherine:

Since Henry's death I have been continuing, in a rather loose way, the financial help he has been giving you for many years. Meanwhile, I have been thinking of some way to put his financial arrangement with you on a better and more regular basis.

I have decided to buy you an annuity which will pay you $150 a month as long as either of you is alive. I know it was Henry's intention to make some provision for you the rest of your life, and this will simply follow out his intentions. Mr. Waddell has some papers which you should sign so that this can be done. You are both in such good health that I have a suspicion the insurance company will lose money on this deal.

Based on ages of eighty and forty, the cost to Clara of the annuity purchased from Connecticut General Life Insurance Company was $50,143.35. Margaret died in 1960, Catherine in 1992.

In November, Clara was granted a widow's allowance of $300,000 per annum. At Christmastime, the Roy Bryants stopped at Fair Lane, and Rankin drove Clara over to the Bryants' to watch the Bryant children open their presents, with Roy acting as Santa Claus.

Clara offered her jewelry, estimated to be worth $1,035,602 in 1947, and much of it given to her by Henry, to her Ford grandchildren.

Henry's sister Margaret came to visit Clara at Fair Lane quite often after Henry died, but the families of Henry's brothers, John and Will, offered little solace. Will's son Burnham stated: "The Fords were not a closely knit family. There was a very strong strain of independence in all of us. Outside of the usual funerals, outside of the usual happenstance meeting and things like that, I've talked to Mr. Edsel Ford twice in my life. Actually, there was no love lost between our family and Mrs. Henry Ford. We didn't know her. Uncle John managed very well for himself."

On January 5, 1948, Clara wrote a note to her nephew Edward Bryant, then a lawyer in Detroit, as follows:

Dear Edward:

You wrote me a kindly note last April, and said you would call me, and come to see me some time. I haven't been too well the past months, took a cold in May, which developed into pneumonia, and took my strength, then this fall, took another cold which put me back again, nothing special, just have no strength, but am getting better. Dr. says it all came from the shock of losing Uncle Henry. I will tell you about it when I see you.

With best wishes
from Aunt Clara

The seventh Medal of Liberty was conferred on Clara by Haakon VI, king of Norway, for her meritorious work on behalf of the Norwegian people during the war. The medal was dated at Oslo on January 9, 1948.

In mid-January, Roy Bryant and family booked a tour by land, water, and air from New York to Panama, Ecuador, Peru, Chile, Argentina, Paraguay, Brazil, and Trinidad. Clara wired good wishes to Katharine on the *S. S. Santa Luisa* on January 21 as it passed through the Panama Canal.

Clara planned to visit Richmond Hill, this time without Henry.

A total of thirty-five men were employed by Ford Farms to take care of Clara's Dearborn property. On each of three shifts, security men guarded the residence (inside and outside), the front gate, the back gate, and the river bank across the dam. Road patrolmen constantly checked various buildings including the Bungalow. A group of five engineers kept the powerhouse in operation. Grounds crews included a house boy, a game warden, a garden leader, four gardeners, a truck driver, and two laborers. Clara's costs per month added up to $9,731. Labor rates averaged about $1.40 an hour for a forty-eight-hour week.

Inside staff, paid by Clara, were offered the following new rates beginning in February 1948:

> Robert Rankin, lives inside, Chauffeur, hired 11-9-37 at $200; new 2-1-48 salary $220.
> John M. Thomson, lives inside, Butler, hired 6-10-36 at $145; new 2-1-48 salary $180.
> John M. Whelan, lives inside, Second Butler, hired 12-8-41 at $110; new 2-1-48 salary $140.
> Mabel C. Thompson, lives inside, Cook, hired 10-16-47 at $150; new 2-1-48 salary $200.
> Rosa Buhler, lives inside, Maid, hired 9-20-33 at $100; new 2-1-48 salary $140.
> John Williams, lives outside, Houseman, salary $270.

Henry Ford Farms records for "Mrs. H. Ford (Residence)" for June 1948:

30 quarters of skim milk
78 quarts of whole milk

67 pints cream
20 pounds butter
4 quarts buttermilk
30 pounds cheese
20 dozen eggs

Leaving Detroit on Sunday, June 6, Clara and friends took a one-week trip by private railroad car to Williamsburg, Virginia, and back, stopping for a day each way in New York City, where they occupied a suite of rooms at the Carleton House. On August 2, Clara boarded the *Henry Ford II* for her annual trip to the Huron Mountain Club; she returned on the same ship to Dearborn the first week of September.

Clara transferred ownership of Dearborn's Valley Farm, a useful appendage of Women's Hospital of Detroit for thirty years, by means of a quitclaim deed dated December 17, 1948. All during that thirty years, Clara had been maintaining the property.

Also on December 17, articles of incorporation were drawn up for the Clara J. Ford Fund, with the first meeting of the board of trustees convening on December 29. The board of trustees consisted of Clara, H. R. Waddell, L. J. Thompson, and H. I. Armstrong, Jr. Waddell, Clara's secretary, acted as chairman of the fund, and Armstrong was secretary. Articles of incorporation stated the purpose of the corporation as: "To receive gifts, donations and bequests exclusively for religious, charitable, scientific, literary or educational purposes, or to give or disburse the funds and properties so received from time to time exclusively to corporations, trusts, community chests, funds or foundations organized and operated solely for any one or more of the above purposes, and no part of net earnings of which inures to the benefit of any private shareholder or individual, and no substantial part of the activities of which is carrying on propaganda or otherwise attempting to influence legislation; and for the purpose of aiding the orderly and efficient disbursement of said funds for such purposes, to invest and reinvest such funds and accumulations thereon or additions thereto in any property or assets in the Trustees' sole discretion." The office of the fund was at the Ford Engineering Laboratories on Oakwood Boulevard in Dearborn. Clara donated $200,000 to the fund at the start. Her contributions to thirty-three organizations in 1948 totaled $20,386. The largest was $11,000 to Christ Episcopal Church of Dearborn.

Chapter 13
Clara's Declining Years

Clara had a heart attack in January 1950. The front page of the *Dearborn Press* of February 17 reported that she was suffering from a moderately severe heart condition and had been in Henry Ford Hospital for two weeks. Ellen Plantiff stayed for a week at the Hotel Statler in Detroit in order to visit Clara at the hospital. In late February, in the hospital for a periodic examination, Clara fell while walking across her room and suffered shock which kept her in the hospital six weeks. One of her nurses stated: "There were very few evening visitors at the hospital. Those who came would usually come in the afternoon before supper. In the hospital, I would bring the visitors in then leave and check back at short intervals to see how Mrs. Ford was. We did not allow them to stay long." Rosa Buhler stated that she took flowers to Clara every day she was in the hospital.

Clara was not really satisfied with the little Ford Cemetery located in Detroit without the protection of a church as the burial place for Henry. A new Episcopal church was being planned for Dearborn, a building Clara had supported but Henry had been reluctant to support. Clara would have liked to have had Henry reburied near the new church to be built at Cherry Hill and Military streets. Henry and Clara had previously given three and a half acres as a site for the church. According to Rev. Stacey in his 1951 reminiscences:

> Mrs. Ford called me up when she was in the hospital. I had been down to see her a couple of times, and she asked me to come down and see her. I was to have tea with her that afternoon, but a relative in Adrian died. [Clara's sister Kate Raymond died in Henry Ford Hospital on September 17, 1949.] That ended that, because in a very short time she passed

January 1950
Clara suffers a mild heart attack

May, 16, 1950
Ford Motor Company handles all arrangements for the Garden Club of America visit to Dearborn as guests of Clara

August 11, 1950
Clara signs her last will

September 29, 1950
Clara dies at Henry Ford Hospital

March 15, 1951
The Fair Lane Estate is deeded to the Ford Motor Company

October 17–20, 1951
Fair Lane furnishings are auctioned in New York

June 2, 1952
Ground is broken for the construction of St. Martha's Episcopal Church beside the Ford Cemetery

Clara is honored at a birthday luncheon at Berry College, probably in 1948. She is joined here by college officials and served by college students. Clara is occupying the ornate high-backed chair previously occupied by Martha Berry at such events. (Martha Berry died on February 27, 1942, at age seventy-five.) (0.9710)

on. She had been thinking about further contributions to the church. In fact, I was asked from the office whether I would consent to the establishment of the monument right next to the church on Cherry Hill. At that time, Mrs. Ford was very much taken up with that idea to have it right there on the property next to the church. Difficulties arose in regard to the [Ford] cemetery itself. There was quite a bit of involvement of other people in the cemetery. They found it was practically impossible to ask to move Mr. Ford, and any such relatives that they thought of, anywhere else. They came down to the fact that it had to be maintained where it was, and Mrs. Ford talked to me several times as to the best way of preserving the sanctity of the place there. She decided that a nice church and a parish house built in connection with the cemetery would be one of the nicest ways of preserving the whole business, and that, as far as I know, was the origin of establishing what would be St. Martha's.

Clara is shown here at the City Club in Detroit where an heirloom exhibit and afternoon tea were held on October 24, 1949. The heirloom she is holding is the *Buckeye Cookbook* given to her by her mother as a wedding present in 1888. She is looking at a citron recipe which was one of her favorites. (B.113513)

In April, Clara underwent a minor operation but was released from the hospital and returned to Fair Lane. In an April 22 letter to Clara from Dr. F. Janney Smith of the Cardio-Respiratory Division of Henry Ford Hospital, she was told:

This is to let you know our opinion regarding the matter of visitors.

In your present condition, an excessive number of visitors may be very injurious to your health. Therefore, you should not have more than three or four a day, and it is necessary to forbid you to mingle in crowds.

On May 12, Katharine Bryant, in a letter from Moana Hotel in Hawaii, wrote as follows:

Clara at the twenty-fifth anniversary banquet of the Henry Ford Hospital
School of Nursing and Hygiene on January 28, 1950. From the left are
Elizabeth S. Moran, director of the school; Benson Ford (standing), chairman
of the board of trustees; Mrs. Alfred Schmitt; Dr. Roy D. McClure, chief of
surgery; Clara; Frank Sladen, chief of medicine; and Eleanor Ford.
(Photograph courtesy of Henry Ford Hospital)

Dear Clara:

*I feel ever so conscious over not having written you but it has been
very hard to find spare minutes when we were not too tired to write.
We were so happy to hear about your successful operation and what
a help it has been. I do hope you will gain steadily—better weather
should help.*

*We were awfully proud to know that you were selected "Mother of
the Year" which seems a great honor, well deserved. Roy seemed to
be exceedingly proud to have the honor of accepting it for you. We
both love Hawaii very much . . .*

Meanwhile, Jack Mullaly, manager of the Ford Motor Company
Special Events Department, was planning for Clara a luncheon for the
Annual Meeting of the Woman's Farm and Garden Association to be

Fair Lane as seen from across the Rouge River in the early spring of 1950. The master bedroom is on the third floor of the rotund portion of the house centered in the photograph. The entrance to the underground boathouse, where Clara kept the *Callie B*, is clearly visible at lower left. (Photo courtesy of Dearborn Historical Museum)

held at Lovett Hall in Greenfield Village on May 16, 1950. Ford Motor Company was picking up the tab. Floral decorations consisting of 5,000 roses and several large bouquets of apple blossoms were purchased from Harry Miller of Dearborn at a cost of $1,776,75. Clara was informed that the roses had come from the Joseph H. Hill Company of Richmond, Indiana, and were known as "Better Times." Details of the development of that particular rose were also forwarded to Clara. Because she was not well enough to handle the event herself, Eleanor Ford and Benson's wife, Edith, volunteered to serve as hostesses.

Attending the event were 535 delegates. Following the luncheon, they were taken to Fair Lane on fourteen buses to view the gardens of Clara Ford, their past president for many years and now their honorary president. Clara had been out of the hospital and at home for several weeks. She was moved in a wheelchair by a nurse to a window in her third-floor bedroom, where she waved to her guests. Dozens and dozens of thank-you letters came to Clara from members following the event.

On June 22, 1950, Clara addressed the following letter to the Clara J. Ford Fund:

Gentlemen:

The Diocese of Michigan of the Protestant Episcopal Church is acquiring a site on the south side of Joy Road between Southfield and Greenfield roads in the City of Detroit, Michigan, for the establishment of a new parish to be known as St. Martha's Episcopal Church. To aid this project, I am establishing from my own resources a trust under which not less than $700,000 will be raised and made available for the construction of the church, associated buildings and improvements and its maintenance thereafter.

Heretofore I have made contributions to the Clara J. Ford Fund to be disbursed by the trustees of that fund for religious, charitable, etc. purposes. At the present time the funds on hand total almost $300,000. As one of the trustees of the Fund, I recommend to my co-trustees the distribution of all or a substantial part of its existing funds to the Diocese to be added to my personal contribution of $700,000. The total sum of approximately $1,000,000 should be sufficient to establish said St. Martha's Episcopal Church in a suitable and proper manner and probably provide a fund for maintenance.

Very truly yours
Clara J. Ford

On July 11, 1950, Reverend Richard S. Emrich, Bishop of the Diocese of Michigan, wrote to Clara:

Dear Mrs. Ford:

Mr. Waddell came to my office this afternoon, bringing with him your letter with its enclosures, namely:

1. Original deed from Ford Motor Company to the Executive Council of the Diocese conveying approximately eight acres of land. This is a gift by Ford Motor Company.

2. Two copies of the Trust for Building St. Martha's Episcopal Church dated June 23, 1950, wherein you have placed certain property in trust for the purpose of raising $700,000 to be used in building the church and future maintenance.

Two copies of the Perpetual Trust for Maintenance of Cemetery and St. Martha's Episcopal Church, dated June 13, 1950, wherein you have placed 1,000 "A" shares of Ford Motor Company stock in trust, the income over cemetery maintenance requirements to be distributed to the Diocese for building and maintaining this church.

In addition to the enclosures, I was, of course, moved and delighted to read that you believe the Clara J. Ford Fund will appropriate $300,000 for building and maintenance, so as to make the available funds total approximately $1,000,000.

You may be assured that as a member of the Committee of Trustees I will do everything in my power to carry out your wishes in this matter.

The Diocese of Michigan accepts with deep gratitude your noble gift.

Sincerely yours,
Richard S. Emrich

An undated statement by Clara includes the following additional information:

It is my desire to create a permanent, dignified and attractive memorial to my late husband. For this purpose I have arranged that the required funds and land be made available.

It is my understanding that the Executive Council of the Protestant Episcopal Church have agreed to the following plan; that I arrange for the financing, design, and construction of a suitable group of church buildings on the above mentioned property, the buildings to include a church, a parish hall for religious education, a rectory, a sexton's house, together with accommodations for parking automobiles; the church grounds and cemetery to be landscaped and enclosed with a suitable fence. The entire group of buildings shall be of a modified Gothic style or order of architecture, unadorned and of plain design. It is my wish that the group of buildings be constructed of stone of the general appearance and durability of the material used in my residence at Fair Lane.

I request that if any changes or additions become necessary at any future time that they conform in style, construction, materials and architecture with the original buildings.

Although frail and ill, Clara maintained a lively interest in the plans being drawn for the church. St. Bartholomew's Mission was responsible for the parish in this new area of Detroit, and Clara's suggestion of the church being named St. Martha's after her mother, Martha Bryant, was somewhat of an imposition. The parish chapel was dedicated as St. Bartholomew's Chapel, however.

Dated August 11, 1950, is a will signed by Clara, witnessed by Waddell, Clifford B. Longley, and L. J. Thompson. In brief, provisions of the document were as follows:

To the Edison Institute — an amount of $4,000,000 for educational purposes.

To Mrs. Walter Buhl Ford (Josephine) — 3,000 shares of nonvoting stock of Ford Motor Company.

To William Clay Ford — 3,000 shares of nonvoting stock of Ford Motor Company. (These to equalize gifts made some years ago by Edsel to Henry Ford II and Benson Ford.)

To her great-grandchildren, of whom there were nine—the remainder of her nonvoting shares of Ford Motor Company stock. (Clara had earlier given her few shares of voting stock to other members of the Ford family and was not participating in management of the company.)

To all four grandchildren she willed her personal effects: household furnishings, jewelry, equipment, and any other tangible personal property as her grandchildren might select within one year after her death.

To Nettie M. Scott — $5,000.
To Martha B. Pardee — $5,000.
To John H. Williams — $5,000.
To Rosa Buhler — $2,000.
To John D. Thomson — $2,000.
To Alphonse de Caluwe — $1,000.
To Robert Rankin — $1,000.

Of those receiving cash, Nettie Scott was daughter of Clara's uncle Nelson Bryant, and Martha Bernice Pardee was daughter of her sister Eva; the others were Fair Lane employees.

Principal assets of the estate, consisting of 63,260 shares of nonvoting Ford stock and the 1,200-acre Fair Lane estate, were together estimated to have a value of $8,500,000.

Ellen Plantiff came from New York several times to see Clara; during August, she stayed at Fair Lane for about ten days. Annie Green, one of Clara's afternoon nurses in Fair Lane and at Henry Ford Hospital, stated, "The routine at Fair Lane called for the evening meal about six o'clock, after which Mrs. Ford retired early. It was rare for her

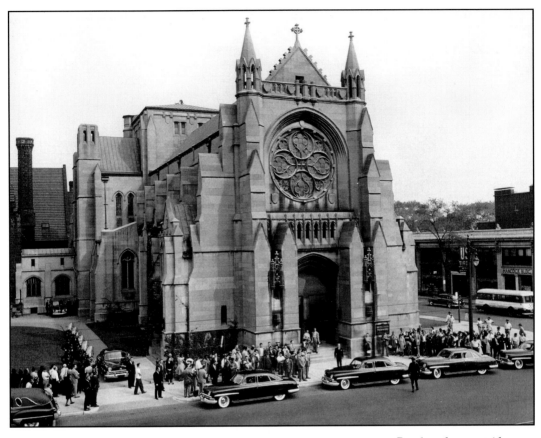

People and cars outside St. Paul's Cathedral on Woodward Avenue in Detroit during Clara's funeral on October 2, 1950. (833.93782-11)

to have any visitors after supper. She remained upstairs most of the time, although we brought her downstairs in a wheelchair three or four times a week, and once in a while had a picnic or took her through her rose garden. I remember some of the visitors as Mr. and Mrs. Roy Bryant, Robert Bryant, Mrs. Wismer, Mrs. Prunk, Mrs. ImOberstag, Mrs. Scott, Mrs. Plantiff, and Mr. and Mrs. Audi."

Nettie Bryant said that on September 22, she was invited to Fair Lane by Clara to join a small group to watch a movie. Nettie was driven to Fair Lane by Rankin. After some of Clara's guests had left and Nettie was waiting for Rankin to take her home, Clara called in a manicurist and had her fingernails done.

At noon on Thursday, September 28, Clara was rushed by ambulance to Henry Ford Hospital when her physician, Dr. F. Janney Smith, decided she needed emergency treatment. She died early Friday morning of heart failure. Clara was eighty-four years of age. Katharine Bryant took care of funeral arrangements, scheduling them for the following Monday. The mayors of Detroit and Dearborn proclaimed Monday an official day of mourning, with flags flying at half mast and with govern-

Family members enter the Ford Cemetery on Joy Road in Detroit for Clara's burial. Heading the group are Roy and Katharine Bryant. Following them are Anne McDonnell Ford, Charlotte Ford, Henry Ford II, Eleanor Clay Ford, Benson Ford, Edith McNaughton Ford, Walter Buhl Ford II, Josephine Ford, William Clay Ford, and Martha Firestone Ford. Eva Bryant Brubaker, Clara's only surviving sister, refused to leave her home in California. (P.833.93782-15)

ment offices closing between the hours of one and three o'clock. All plants of the Ford industrial empire suspended operations for three minutes during the services in respect for Mrs. Ford.

Services were held in St. Paul's Episcopal Cathedral, with Rev. Richard S. Emrich, Bishop of Michigan, delivering the following address:

We are gathered to say an earthly farewell and to give into God's hands, with our prayers, the life of Mrs. Henry Ford. The Lord gave her life to us: the Lord has taken her away. Blessed be the name of the Lord.

Since what the Lord takes away he first gave to us, our attitude today should be one of sorrow at parting mixed with a deep thanksgiving. As this earth knows human life, hers was full, happy, gracious, and blest. She had all that this life can give—length of days, the love of family, friendships, the joy of accomplishment, and beauty of surroundings. We say farewell then, and give into God's hands, with gratitude, a gracious friend who made all of our lives better by her life.

But we gather to say our farewell in a holy spot, consecrated to God. It is a holy spot, filled with prayers, memories, and hopes, where men gather to worship God and to think about the ultimate meaning of their existence. We said at the beginning of this service, "We brought nothing to this world, and it is certain we can carry nothing out." Therefore, because we try to see things from God's point of view, we look at the things of the heart, at character. "The captains and the kings depart; still stands thine ancient sacrifice, an humble and contrite heart." So within this holy place, we are grateful to God for a life's task honorably discharged; for simplicity in the midst of fame; for humility when it would have been easy to become proud; for character that did not change in the midst of success or sorrow; for steadfastness in a changing world; for loneliness endured without defeat; for generosity. Since today we see things in this holy spot from God's point of view, we know that all that matters in the end is this quality of life.

But this is also a place of hope, of faith, of triumph. "In my father's house are many mansions." "I am persuaded that neither death, nor life, shall be able to separate us from the love of God, which is in Christ Jesus our Lord." We believe in life everlasting, and in victory won.

And so, for the Church and for all of us, I say these ancient words:

Depart, O Christian soul, out of this world.
In the name of God the Father Almighty who created thee.
In the name of Jesus Christ who redeemed thee
In the name of the Holy Ghost who sanctifieth thee
May thy rest be this day in peace, and thy dwelling place in the Paradise of God.

Clara was laid to rest beside Henry's grave in the little Ford Cemetery. The church buildings she had been planning beside the cemetery had not yet been started. Approximately 160 floral tributes were presented at the funeral, in addition to hundreds of cards, letters, and telegrams.

Clara's will was admitted to probate on October 12, 1950. Her estate was now in the hands of lawyers and her three appointed executors: grandsons Henry II, Benson, and William. Clara's resources on the day of her death were estimated to be as follows:

Cash	$3,069,516
Bonds	42,475
Stocks	12,652,000
Real estate	2,583,004
Personal property	458,888
Total	$18,805,883

For the same date, liabilities were also estimated:

Taxes—Federal Gift	$3,872,367
Federal Income	662,279
Michigan Intangibles	43,760
Michigan Sales and Use	571
Municipal	10,470
Other	74,604
Total	$4,664,051

Clara's 1950 expenses through September had totaled $1,868,629:

Charities	$103,536
Income tax	1,516,057
Salaries	160,070
Personal	15,304
Intangibles tax	25,962
Labor	47,700

Under the direction of Henry Ford II, the work of administering Clara's estate was carried out by the firm of attorneys Bodman, Longley, Bogle, Armstrong & Dahling of Detroit. Tax consultants were Meredith & Meredith of Detroit. Appraisals of individual household furnishings were carried out, item by item, by Fidelity Appraisal Company.

A Fair Lane cost-reduction program outlined in an early November memorandum was fully implemented by December 1, 1950. This resulted in the number of watchmen being reduced from twenty to five, powerhouse personnel from six to one, gardeners from ten to none, and elimination of the houseman and game warden. The powerhouse had been converted to oil to be operated by one employee. The greenhouse and gardens were inactivated and all personnel transferred, including Alfonse de Caluwe, who had stayed awhile to handle sales of the plants. Sales of

At Clara's gravesite, officials of the Edison Institute attend a memorial service, probably on April 11, 1966, the anniversary of her birth. From the left are Dwight Buffenbarger, Adrian DeVogel, Mark Stroebel, Lyle Hughes, Robert Wheeler, Gustav Munchow, Robert Dawson, Frank Caddy, Ester Shelley, Donald Shelley, an Episcopal representative, and the pastor of St. Martha's Church. (B.61683.2)

greenhouse stock had amounted to $1,464.65. Peony plants from the gardens, numbering 1,077, were sold at fifty cents each, while Clara's rose bushes brought a bid of only fifteen cents each. As for Fair Lane's wildlife, the seven adult peafowl and four chicks were given to the Detroit Zoo. Thirty-six hives of bees were sold for $105, and as soon as the thirty-five deer had been shot and the carcasses sold for $1,272.35, the game warden was dismissed. More than one Ford Motor Company executive appears to have had venison for Thanksgiving dinner.

A few weeks after Clara's death, her sister Eva in California wrote as follows to her niece, Edward and Laura Bryant's daughter in Detroit:

St. Martha's Episcopal Church and the Ford Cemetery on Joy Road near Greenfield Road where Henry and Clara are buried. The tall 1876 obelisk to the left marks the grave of Henry's mother, Mary. The long flat stones near the obelisk mark the graves of Henry and Clara. The photograph was taken in May 1954, only a few months after the dedication of the church. Henry's sister Margaret and brother William are buried in this cemetery, but not his brother John. Clara is the only Bryant in the cemetery. (Photo courtesy of Dearborn Historical Museum)

Dear Doris:

It was so nice to hear from you but am very sorry indeed to hear of your mother's illness. Grace said she looked very well at the funeral.

Yes, Doris, I am very proud of my girls, they are so good to me.

Well Aunt Clara died as she lived, hating her own family, and no reason for it as I can see. I did not feel obligated to take that long trip to attend her funeral.

How are you getting along, you always had to work so hard I always felt sorry for you but now that your family is grown up you may have it easier I hope.

I had a short note from Edward, he seems to be happy.

Yes, I would have liked to see your mother, every trip I took back east I wanted to visit her but no one seemed able to take me out to her house, so I never did get to see her, we would have had lots to talk about, I used to like to visit her in the early days when you were little. How we do drift apart not intentionally either.

I am so happy out here in Calif. I have my own house and a lovely Mountain Cabin that I go to each week and where I usually have a crowd for a charcoal broiled steak dinner. We can eat outdoors the year around and it is such fun.

Write and tell me about yourself and your family. Perhaps we can get acquainted again.

My love to yourself, your dear mother and all who inquire for me.

Aunt Eva

At Fair Lane, domestic employees to whom separate residences had been provided were asked to leave their premises by mid-October. Raymond Dahlinger knew he was dismissed when he was locked out of his office at the Engineering Laboratory. He did, however, get a pension of at least $12,000. John Williams was kept at Fair Lane for six weeks. John Thomson and Rosa Buhler, however, were allowed to remain for eleven months. Fair Lane was restricted to government appraisers for three months. The Ford grandchildren did not inspect Fair Lane until January 1951. When they did, they were shocked at the accumulation of "stuff." Rosa Buhler stated that "Clara couldn't part with anything. Any vacant space was in no time cluttered up."

On March 16, 1951, a deed issued by Henry Ford II, Benson Ford, and William Clay Ford granted for "one dollar and other valuable considerations" their right, title, and interest of the estate of Clara J. Ford, deceased, to Ford Motor Company. Description of the property contained approximately 1,346 acres, including the site of Fair Lane but excluding the property previously deeded to the Roy Bryant family. On April 4, 1951, Roy served notice that he would file a claim against the estate based on the contention that Clara had promised she would leave her possessions to his family. Clara had omitted from her will her only living siblings, her sister Eva and her brother Roy. To Roy, she had apparently insinuated on several occasions that he would eventually have possession of Fair Lane. The suit against the estate, asking for $10 million or more, proceeded until March 1955, when it was settled out of court for a relatively small amount in cash.

As part of the housecleaning process at Fair Lane, more than a thousand mementoes and personal belongings accumulated over the years by Henry and Clara and stored at Fair Lane, which had not been claimed by the Ford grandchildren, were donated to the Henry Ford Museum in 1951. A few of these have been put on display, but most are still in the endless process of being catalogued.

When the Ford grandchildren had their pick of Fair Lane furnishings, they seemed to take very little. The bulk of the holdings were shipped off to be auctioned to the public by Parke-Bernet Galleries in New York. Among the items were *Twelve Minuets* autographed by W. A. Mozart and *Andante con Variazione* autographed by L. von Beethoven. During the afternoons of October 17–20, 1951, sales of 867 items were scheduled, described in the catalog as "Furniture, rugs, and decorations removed from three residences of the late Mrs. Henry Ford. Sold by the order of the executors of her estate." The three residences involved were Richmond Hill, the Huron Mountain residence, and Fair Lane. Proceeds amounted to $172,117. Some of the items were purchased by J. N. Anhut, who was associated with Botsford Tavern, for $11,500. These were various items of personal property, mainly furniture and objects identified with Ford markings. Anhut has been very helpful in arranging for the return of many of these items to Fair Lane.

Another advertisement by the same auction house, dated November 19, 1952, announced the sale of jewelry: "Two magnificent necklaces—unique emerald and diamond necklace, divisible into a parure, and a superb ruby and diamond necklace and other fine pieces. Property of the late Mrs. Henry Ford of Dearborn, Michigan. Sold by the order of the executors Henry Ford II, Benson Ford and William C. Ford." Proceeds from this sale of jewelry, said to have been gifts to Clara from Henry, amounted to $157,595.

In June 1952, at a special afternoon ceremony, ground had been broken for Clara's St. Martha's Church next to the Ford Cemetery, and on October 5, the cornerstone was laid. The first rector was Walter Fry, who served from 1952 to 1969. One year later, on October 18, 1953, the first Sunday service was held. The church was dedicated January 19, 1954, although not all of the organ pipes had yet been installed. The organ was built by Casavant Freres Limited of Saint Hyacinthe in Quebec, Canada. Following Clara's plans, the buildings are modified English-parish style, consisting of church proper with attached parish house, the rectory, and the sexton's residence and garage. There is ample parking as Clara requested. The church seats 400 persons: 258 in the nave, 50 in the chapel, 28 in the baptistry, another 43 in the gallery, and choir seating in the chancel for 27. Clara would have been very pleased.

Henry Ford's youngest brother, Will, died in Whitehall Convalescent Home in Novi, Michigan, on May 5, 1959, at age eighty-seven. Since his retirement from the tractor implement business in Dearborn in 1937, he had owned and managed a 500-acre farm on Pleasant Valley

Road near Brighton, Michigan. Funeral services were in Dearborn. Surviving him were his wife, Frances, and three children, Burnham, Myra, and Edith.

In 1963, Roy Bryant was engaged in a court battle with his son-in-law, sportscaster Harry Wismer. Roy was an original stockholder of the Detroit Lions football team, and Wismer claimed Bryant had reneged on an option to sell him his shares for $20,000—the original cost. Bryant claimed Wismer was not eligible to be a stockholder under National Football League rules. Bryant kept his Lions stock, but Wismer was awarded $100,000 in a settlement. On July 4, 1966, Katharine Wright Bryant died in Dearborn. Her husband, Roy, lived until May 1, 1976, dying at the age of ninety. They are both buried in Woodmere Cemetery in Detroit, where Melvin and Martha and several other Bryants are buried.

Epilogue

When Ford Motor Company took over Fair Lane in March 1951, arrangements were made for consulting archivists from the National Archives in Washington and professional librarians to come to Dearborn and organize the Ford papers. Loads of these materials were first taken to the Ford Engineering Laboratories, where preliminary sorting began on the Fair Lane papers. Following the sale of Fair Lane furniture, as the house became empty, the archives staff took over the mansion for its work. The Fair Lane papers and the Henry Ford office papers were then all moved to Fair Lane for processing. The basement was used to classify the half-million photographs. The swimming pool was drained and filled with sand, a floor installed, and the space converted to a stack area for books and papers. Various private rooms in the mansion were converted to staff offices. Some say the interior of Fair Lane was considerably altered by the archives occupancy.

To further augment the historical records of Henry Ford and the Ford Motor Company, Henry Ford II commissioned Owen Bombard of the Oral History Section of the Ford Archives in 1951 to conduct oral interviews with nearly 300 friends, relatives, acquaintances, and employees of Henry Ford. These reminiscences supply facts, opinions, and anecdotes on nearly every aspect of Henry's life, on company operations, and occasionally on Clara's and Edsel's lives.

Between 1951 and 1953, Sidney Olson, then vice president in charge of forward planning for J. Walter Thomson Company, took advantage of the monstrous photographic collection to prepare a pictorial biography entitled *Young Henry Ford: A Picture Story of the First Forty Years*. The book contained dozens of photographs never before published, many of them taken by Henry himself. Published by Wayne State University Press, this book is still in print.

March 1951
Archivists are called to Fair Lane to organize the papers saved by Henry and Clara

November 1954
The first book based on the Fair Lane papers and Henry Ford office papers is published

January 17, 1956
Ford Motor Company stock is offered to the public

February 17, 1958
Ford Motor Company donates the Fair Lane residence to the University of Michigan

March 1963
The Committee for the Development of Fair Lane is organized

September 15, 1964
Ford Motor Company donates its archival collections to Henry Ford Museum

May 25, 1967
Fair Lane is designated a National Historic Landmark

June 8, 1975
A life-size statue of Henry is dedicated at Dearborn's Henry Ford Centennial Library

By November 1954, the organization of documents had resulted in the first volume of Allan Nevins's monumental trilogy which summarizes the history of Henry Ford and the Ford Motor Company as gleaned from Fair Lane records together with Ford Motor Company office records. Henry Ford II had commissioned Nevins, of Columbia University, to write these books, and he was satisfied enough with the first volume, *Ford: The Times, the Man, the Company,* to give each of his management personnel a personal copy. Using these same archival resources, succeeding volumes by Nevins and his associates, Frank Ernest Hill, William Greenleaf, and George B. Heliker, were published between 1957 and 1964. Also, the scholarly book *American Business Abroad: Ford on Six Continents,* authored by Mira Wilkins and Frank Ernest Hill and published in 1964, is based on materials found in the Ford Archives.

On February 17, 1958, the Fair Lane residence with 210 acres was given to the University of Michigan to be used as a new Dearborn campus. A cash gift of $6.5 million also was given to the university by the Ford Motor Company Fund for construction of academic buildings. At that time, the Fair Lane archival material was moved from the Fair Lane residence to the north wing of the Ford Rotunda on South Schaefer Road in Dearborn, and the Ford Motor Company files were moved to storage in Highland Park. The archives then became a function of the Ford Motor Company public relations office. After surviving, almost miraculously, the disastrous 1962 fire when the Rotunda burned, the Fair Lane papers were also put into temporary storage.

To provide a useful location for the archives, both the Fair Lane papers and the Ford Motor Company papers were donated by the company in 1964 to the Edison Institute (Henry Ford Museum & Greenfield Village), where they are now housed and available for use by the public. For tax purposes, the entire collection was assigned a value of $4,485,000. Henry Ford Museum & Greenfield Village is not property of Ford Motor Company, a fact that often confuses people. Ford personnel get no special treatment. By now, hundreds of articles and dozens of books, including this one, have been written on research accomplished in the Henry Ford Museum & Greenfield Village Research Center, the present home of the Ford Archives.

Starting a long and continuous restoration project, the University of Michigan–Dearborn has attempted since 1958 to make use of the Fair Lane residence as a conference center catering to meetings of industrial, business, labor, civic, and cultural groups. Eventually, the swimming pool was converted to a restaurant for the use of conferees, university faculty, and the public, the goal being to preserve Fair Lane without draining state-derived educational funds.

In March 1963, the Women's Committee for the Development of Fair Lane was organized. The group included many prominent

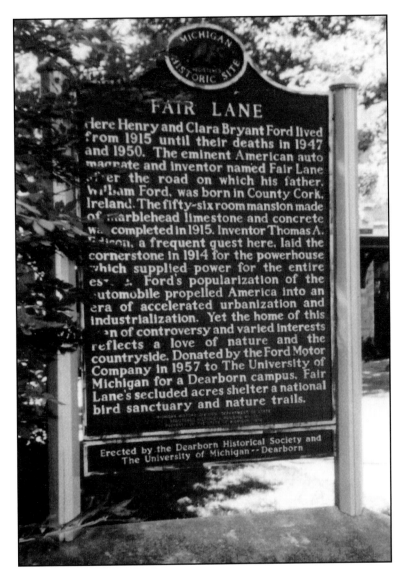

Clara and Henry's home, Fair Lane, was declared a National Historic Site in 1967. (Photograph courtesy of G. Palm, Dearborn)

Dearborn women. A summary of their first year's work as reported by a member of the executive board is as follows:

This was a volunteer group representing women from all areas of Michigan who would be considered as Friends of Fair Lane. The objective of the group was to acquaint all people with the plans for the Conference Center and solicit aid in developing good will, create ideas of cooperation and encourage donations to finance the much needed repairs for the building. When approached by the Centennial Committee (in 1963) asking for

The Marshall M. Fredericks memorial to Henry Ford, including a life-size statue of Henry. The memorial is located on Michigan Avenue in Dearborn facing the Henry Ford Centennial Library. The four bronze reliefs flanking the statue tell the story of Henry's life. Counterclockwise from top left are depicted his childhood, his youth and marriage, his early vehicles, and the various buildings important to the Ford empire. (Photo courtesy Dearborn Historical Museum)

assistance in hostessing tours of the home during the 100th Year Celebration, we were delighted to cooperate with them and the University of Michigan. This was our perfect opportunity to pay personal tribute to Mr. Ford.

During June, July, and August, Women's Committee hostesses were happy to conduct tours and to be of service in any way. Thousands of guests were escorted through the residence and gardens on guided tours with informational talks on interesting facts from the past and plans for the future. In addition to Sundays, Tuesdays, and Thursdays, the hostesses functioned for "Open House" and occasions where thousands of people were present. Among these delightful, impressive events were:

The Henry Ford Centennial Celebration Concert by the Rackham Symphony Choir, a choral Concert.

Symphony Concert—Interlochen Orchestra, Modern Dance and Ballet Groups reminiscent of the Ford Sunday Evening Hour.

Tours followed the luncheon for honored guests at Lovett Hall, Greenfield Village and the marker dedication.

The Pilgrimage Tour of Ford-built cars from Greenfield Village, including the Model T Ford Club International, the Lincoln Owners Club and others of the Antique Car Owners Clubs.

Many bus tours, special groups of local, national, and international guests.

It was a privilege to participate in the Centennial Committee Program, and we all appreciate the courtesies and cooperation afforded us.

On May 25, 1967, Fair Lane was designated a National Historic Landmark, and a marker was placed in front of the residence.

After three years of fund-raising and guiding visitors on tours of the residence, the Women's Committee for Fair Lane disbanded as the university insisted on management of the projects initiated by the women. In 1985, however, the women were asked again to help raise money for Fair Lane. Annual social events were sponsored by the committee for the next three years, before again being taken over largely by university personnel.

The Henry Ford Statue Committee gathered funds between 1968 and 1972 to commission Danish sculptor Marshall M. Fredericks to produce a life-size statue of Henry Ford. To quite an extent, the funds, which amounted to nearly $50,000, were contributed by the schoolchildren of Dearborn. The statue was placed next to the new Henry Ford Centennial Library, which had been donated to Dearborn by Ford Motor Company.

Hundreds of unnamed volunteers over the years have contributed an untold amount toward the restoration and attractiveness of Fair Lane since the death of Clara Ford. As Fair Lane was gradually renovated and made presentable to the public, the university assigned a "coordinator" to train volunteers to guide visitors through the residence, beginning with first-floor rooms and later the second-floor rooms as they were made presentable. There were an average of sixty to sixty-five guides working at Fair Lane during those years. By far the most conspicuous group of volunteers have been those docents who conduct visitors every day of the week through Fair Lane. After being thoroughly coached, their knowledge of the premises and about Henry and Clara is astonishing. (There are still one or two volunteer docents who knew Henry and Clara personally.)

Other groups of volunteers have been active in restoring the premises. A group of University of Michigan engineering students, during a four-year project beginning in 1977, restored the powerhouse equipment to operable condition. Powerhouse operation and interpretation are handled by another group of volunteers. There are groups of volunteers who for years have worked hard to take care of the gardens and greenhouses. This work is continuing. Classes for hundreds of elementary schoolchildren are provided by other volunteers, as are decorations for Christmas and other holidays.

In 1990, some of these Fair Lane volunteers organized the Henry Ford Heritage Association, an international society with a membership of about seven hundred people with the purpose "to foster interest in the life and accomplishments of Henry Ford, and the preservation and interpretation of landmarks associated with his life." In addition to publishing *The Legend,* a periodical, and arranging interesting field trips, each year at Fair Lane they hold a party to celebrate the birthday of Henry Ford.

Under the university's stewardship, a considerable amount of money has been invested in restoration of Fair Lane. For several years, an annual dinner dance sponsored by the university and chaired by volunteers has raised several hundred thousand dollars for restoration of the residence and acquisition of some of Clara's furnishings which had been sold at auction in 1951.

In 1993, the University of Michigan inaugurated a billion-dollar fund-raising campaign, of which $24 million was for the University of Michigan–Dearborn and $4 million was for the Henry Ford Estate. Of the $4 million, an amount of $1.5 million is earmarked for "preservation," $1.5 million for "restoration," and $1 million for "education" projects associated with the Henry Ford era. Edsel Ford II led the five-year campaign for the estate. A recent donation by the Ford Motor Company Fund has paid for restoration of the roof of the residence. Descendants of Henry and Clara, as well as descendants of Roy Bryant, have been major donors.

By 1997, campaign financial goals were met, and Henry's power-house garage had already been restored with some of his historic vehicles on display. The number of visitors to the estate is now approaching 150,000 annually. There are more than 160 volunteers helping with the work at Fair Lane—ten times the number of paid staff members. Volunteers are listed as filling twelve types of positions, with almost half of them trained and available for more than one type of duty. On visiting Fair Lane these days, one will most likely be met and guided through the premises by one of these enthusiastic volunteers, and upon occasion the visitor may be very surprised to meet "Henry" and "Clara" in person, impersonated now by volunteers.

Appendix 1
Bryant and Ford Family Histories

CLARA'S FAMILY

Clara's grandfather John Bryant was born in Canada in 1809, thought to have been the son of Polly Bryant, born in Vermont in 1790. Clara's grandmother Jane Bogert was born in Cherry Valley,   New York, in 1813. John Bryant is reported to have purchased large tracts of land in Wayne County, Michigan, as early as 1835. This land was about ten miles northwest of Detroit in Greenfield and Redford townships. There is some evidence John Bryant may have been an innkeeper. John and Jane Bryant's children were Melvin (or Melville) Samuel, Caroline (Aunt Car Line), Henry Dexter (Uncle Deck), Nelson Amos (Uncle Ness), Arvilla, and John R.

After Jane Bryant died in 1865, John did not remarry. He began to sell off his property. In 1872, there were four forty-acre parcels deeded to his four sons. Melvin paid $1,000 for his. Melvin's property was located in Greenfield Township about one-half mile north of Grand River Avenue on Monnier Road (now Schaefer Road). Next to Melvin's, to the south, was Henry's parcel. The two parcels of John and Nelson were in Redford Township. John's daughters apparently received no land.

Melvin Samuel Bryant, Clara's father, was born in Michigan in 1836. He married Martha Bench on July 16, 1860. Martha was the daughter of William Bench and Mary Ann Godfrey of Warwickshire, England. She was born in England on March 11, 1839, and came to the United States with her father when she was eight years old. The ten children of Melvin and Martha Bryant were Frederick, Edward, Clara, William, Harry, Kate, Milton, Marvin, Eva, and Edgar LeRoy. There is evidence that a child named Cary was born on July 1, 1870, but there is no further record.

This light-colored stone house in Warwick, England, is said to be where Martha Bench Bryant was born on March 11, 1839. Her parents were William Bench and Mary Ann Godfrey. The photograph was taken by Edsel Ford on a trip to England in 1912. (P.0.2522)

The first five children of Melvin and Martha, including Clara, were born in a two-story frame building on the southeast corner of Grand River Avenue and Greenfield Road. Living quarters were on the upper floor, with a general store below. It has been known as the Blanchfield store. On the forty acres purchased from his father in 1872, Melvin Bryant built a small frame house, where children Kate, Milton, and Marvin were born. In 1880, a new and much larger brick house was built on the same land. Eva and Edgar LeRoy were born there. Bricks and hardware from this home were used in 1929 to build Martha-Mary Chapel in Greenfield Village.

An excellent and much more detailed account of Bryant family history, "The Bryant Homestead and the Martha-Mary Chapel," is found in the series of articles by Edward L. Bryant in *Michigan Heritage* magazine, volume VII, 1965.

JOHN BRYANT
1809–1893
JANE BOGERT
1813–1865

Melvin S.	Caroline	Henry Dexter	Nelson A.	Arvilla	John R.
1836–1917	*1839–?*	*1840–1888*	*1844–1922*	*1846–1916*	*1849–1926*
m.	m.	m.	m.	m.	m.
Martha Bench	Edward	Charlotte	Mary Ann Bench	Angus	Ellen
1839–1911	Monnier	Ward	Sarah O'Brien	Turner	

Children born at Greenfield and Grand River

Frederick H.	Edward L.	Clara J.	William R.	Harry H.	Kate Dell
1861–1946	*1863–1913*	*1866–1950*	*1868–1941*	*1871–1938*	*1873–1949*
m.	m.	m.	m.	m.	m.
Johanna	Laura Bell	Henry Ford	Anna	Nellie	Samuel
Seidel	Kennedy	*1863–1947*	Wolfertz	Pierce	Raymond
none	Lloyd – Arthur	Edsel	Florence	Melvin	Russell
	Martha – Wallace			Harry	Milton
	Doris – Marguerite				Harold
	Edward – Warren				Violet
	Melvin				

Children born on Monnier Road

Milton D.	Marvin R.	Eva G.	Edgar LeRoy
1876–1928	*1879–1922*	*1881–1953*	*1885–1976*
m.	m.	m.	m.
Bernice	Mabel	George	Katharine
Robertson	Millett	Brubaker	Wright
Jean	none	Grace	Frances
Richard		Bernice	Mary Elizabeth
(both adopted)			Carol
			Robert
			Katharine

The church in Warwick, England, attended by Clara's mother, Martha
Bench, when she was a girl. The photograph was taken in 1912.
(Photo courtesy Marvin Bryant, grandson of Harry H. Bryant)

On Fair Lane stationery and in her own handwriting, Clara applied the following caption to this picture: "This is William Bench, grandfather of Mrs. Henry Ford. He came from England in about 1839 with his wife and four daughters. The oldest, Martha, was the mother of Mrs. Ford. He would be the great-great-great-grandfather of the children of Henry Ford II." A large painting of William Bench (1811–1897) now hangs on a wall at Fair Lane. (B.40869)

This photograph of Clara's mother, Martha Bench Bryant, was probably taken between 1900 and 1905. She came to America from England in 1847 with her parents. On July 16, 1860, she married Melvin Bryant, a hardworking Greenfield Township, Michigan, farmer. On their farm facing Monnier (Schaefer) Road just north of Grand River Avenue, Martha and Melvin raised ten healthy children — seven boys and three girls, including Clara. Martha died on that same farm on October 13, 1911; Melvin outlived her by six years. Both Martha and Melvin are buried in Woodmere Cemetery in Detroit. (P.0.485)

HENRY'S FAMILY

Henry's grandfather John Ford was born in 1799. With his mother, Rebecca, in 1819, he renewed a family lease on a poor twenty-three-acre plot of land near Clonakilty, Ireland. John married Thomasina Smith in 1823. Twenty-four years later, in 1847, they were induced to emigrate with their family to America during the great potato famine. Before reaching America, Thomasina died at sea. John, with the children, continued to Michigan, where relatives of both Fords and Smiths lived. Of their seven children, Rebecca, William, Jane, Henry, Mary, Nancy, and Samuel, William was the oldest boy.

John Ford purchased eighty acres of forestland in Redford Township near Detroit from Henry Maybury in 1848. The Mayburys are said to have come from Ireland on the same ship as the Ford family and were closely allied with the Fords for many years. For his land, John paid $200 down, subject to a mortgage of $150.

Henry's father, William, born in 1826, had been trained as a carpenter in Ireland and spent some time in Michigan working on the Michigan Central Railroad stations between Detroit and Chicago, in the meantime helping his father pay off the $150 mortgage in December 1850. One of William's neighborhood employers was Patrick Ahern, who was building a house on ninety-one acres in nearby Dearborn Township. William helped Patrick build this house. In 1842, Patrick and his wife, Margaret, had adopted a three-year-old child who had been orphaned. Her name was Mary Litogot, and she was the daughter of William Litogot of Wyandotte, Michigan. She had three brothers, Sapharia, Barney, and John. Living with the Aherns, Mary attended the Scotch Settlement School. She was thirteen years younger than William, but he took a liking to her, and they were married in the home of Thomas Maybury on April 21, 1861, at about the time the Ahern home was completed. William moved in with the Aherns, and they lived amicably for many years. This house, in which Henry Ford was born on July 30, 1863, and which Henry always said belonged to his mother, is now in Greenfield Village.

The book *The Fords of Dearborn* by Ford R. Bryan (Wayne State University Press) provides a detailed description of Ford family history.

WILLIAM FORD
1775–1818
REBECCA JENNINGS
1776–1851

Samuel Ford	John Ford	George Ford	Henry Ford	Robert Ford
1792–1842	*1799–1864*	*1811–1863*	*(?–1832)*	*1803–1877*
m.	**m.**	m.	?	m.
Nancy Smith	**Thomasina Smith**	Alice Good		Jane Hornibrook
1795–1873	*?–1847*	*1810–1893*		

Rebecca	William	Jane	Henry	Mary	Nancy	Samuel
1825–1895	*1826–1905*	*1829–1851*	*1830–1901*	*1832–1882*	*1834–1920*	*1837–1884*
m.	**m.**	m.	m.	m.	m.	m.
William	**Mary**	Henry	Katherine	Henry	Thomas	Nancy
Flaherty	**Litogot**	Smith	O'Leary	Ford	Flaherty	Kennedy
?–1861	*1839–1876*	*1828–1884*	*1829–1912*	*1827–1914*	*1829–1905*	*1844–1890*

Infant son	Henry	John	Margaret	Jane	William	Robert	Infant son
1861	*1863–1947*	*1865–1927*	*1867–1960*	*1869–1906*	*1871–1959*	*1873–1877*	*1876*
d.	**m.**	m.	m.	(unmarried)	m.	m.	d.
	Clara	Mary	James		Frances		
	Bryant	Ward	Ruddiman		Reed		
	1866–1950	*?–1932*	*1865–1909*		*1874–1965*		

	Edsel	Robert	Catherine		Lewis		
		Clarence			Burnham		
		Ethel			Mary Ellen		
					Myra		
					Edith		

Remains of the dry-stone cottage near Clonakilty, Ireland, where William Ford, father of Henry, was born in 1826 and from which the John Ford family moved when they came to America in 1847. The photograph was taken in 1912. (P.833.50518)

Appendix 2

Diaries and Reminiscences

Clara, 1901

During the winter and spring of 1901, while Henry, Clara, and Edsel were staying with William and Jane in the house at 582 West Grand Boulevard, Clara kept the following diary. (A list identifying many of the personalities mentioned follows.)

January 1. Henry worked all day, went to Grandpa Ford's for dinner. Came home and had another six o'clock dinner. Had music a little dancing and quite a jolly time.

January 2. Edsel and I went out for a walk, met Mr. and Mrs. Gore, promised to go to their house to tea Friday. Went in the gas office and had a nice visit.

January 3. Went to Mrs. Blair's to supper, helped her hang lace curtains. After tea went to concert, heard Harold Jarvis sing and Miss Finley recite.

January 4. Went to Mrs. Gore's to tea. Had very nice time. Edsel and Helen had a fine time.

January 5. Took Henry a lunch. Then called upon Mrs. Brooks, Mrs. Wilson and Mrs. McElroy. Brought Mrs. McElroy home to supper. Had supper, a little music, then went to town.

January 6. Edsel and I went to Sunday school. Then went to Grandpa Ford's. Henry went out in the country. Called at McCormick's and had supper.

January 7. Took my skirt to Mrs. Knapp's to cut down, then packed up to move.

January 8. Rained this morning. Went to meet Eva who came home from Kate's. Then moved down to Grandpa Ford's, got there just as men got there with furniture.

January 9. Worked all day getting settled. Very tired tonight. Edsel found lots of his playthings that he had not seen for some time. Decorated his rocking horse with Xmas-tree trimmings.

January 10. Did some more settling today. Got things in pretty good shape.

January 11. Snowed all day. Edsel got soaking wet. He and Grandpa played checkers. Edsel cheated awful and beat every game. Went to bed so full of laughs he could not say his prayers.

January 12. Went downtown, got Edsel shoes and leggings. Went into Sheaffer's store to hear the music. After supper we tried to learn Grandpa to play cards. Henry got patents on entire machine.

January 13. Edsel and I went to Sunday School. Met Mrs. Gore, came home, had dinner, then Henry fixed Edsel's old sleigh to take him coasting, but Edsel would not go, said sleigh was no good. He was sent upstairs for punishment for his pride. He was sorry.

January 14. Snowed. Helped Jane wash. I started flannel skirt for myself. Jane started pair of mittens for Edsel.

January 15. Edsel started lessons for the first time this morning.

January 16. Blustering. Went out home. Found them all well. Pa making ice. Edsel had a big time helping Roy do chores. Henry came in while we were eating (downtown), also met him on streetcar while coming home.

January 17. Very cold. Done a little of everything today. Swept upstairs. Going downtown tomorrow. Jane is going to Joe Benton's.

January 18. Had dinner early today so we could get an early start. Annie came in about one o'clock so we could go.

January 19. Went downtown. Bought underwear and golf gloves. Changed jacket for Grandpa Bryant. Marve sick with grip. Henry bought Edsel new coaster.

January 20. Henry and Edsel went coasting on the boulevard. After dinner went out to Maggie's. Maggie brought to the car.

January 21. Washed as usual. James came in for Maggie's things. Will came in also.

January 22. Queen Victoria died today. Cut out dressing sack for myself. Edsel had hard time making E, made it too much like L.

January 23. Snowed. Maggie came in today. Edsel had big time coasting. Made new kind of salad dressing. Licking good.

January 24. Uncle George Ford died yesterday. Grandpa is not feeling well today. Coal stove went out and everything went wrong. Edsel says he will be glad when spring comes.

January 25. Grandpa is feeling better. Edsel and I went downtown. Met Henry on the crowded streetcar going home.

January 26. Went to Uncle George's funeral. Met Mr. and Mrs. McCormick. Saw Mr. and Mrs. Leslie go behind the house to count their money. They looked very funny.

January 27. Edsel and I went to Sunday School. Met Henry, went to vegetarian cafe for dinner, then went out home. Eva has bad cold.

January 28. Coal fire out again. Jane has tooth ache and swelled face. Sewed today.

January 29. Went downtown, changed Edsel's pants. Met Henry in streetcar. He had bad headache. Put brown paper and vinegar on his head and mustard plaster on back of neck.

January 30. Helped Jane wash, her face is better. Worked on my silk petticoat. Edsel made snow fort and decorated it with flags.

January 31. Ironed a little and packed grip for a trip to Kate's.

February 1. Spent half hour with Henry then took train to Kate's. Sam met us at depot. Found Kate in good health.

February 2. Kate and I visited most all day. Edsel had fine time with Uncle Sam feeding cows and lambs and giving pigs chocolate ice cream soda as he calls it.

February 3. Snowed all day. Wrote a letter to Henry. Felt pretty lonely. Kate said she wished it was not Sunday so we could play cards.

February 4. Sam, Frank and Edsel went for cutter ride to Jasper. Played cards all night. Edsel had bad attack of chillblains.

February 5. Kate baked bread, mince pie and biscuits. She did not feel well after dinner so I did up the work. Edsel dug snow nearly all the day. Kate grew worse at night. Had doctor and nurse there by twelve o'clock.

February 6. Kate's baby born at nine a.m. None of us had been to bed. Had breakfast at ten. Dinner half after two. Kate and baby doing fine. Sam telephoned from Jasper to Henry.

February 7. Did Kate's work. Got very tired. Baby very good.

February 8. Baby not so well, cried nearly all night and all day. Got him some soothing syrup. Sam and I washed and I baked bread. Am awfully tired. Baby better tonight.

February 9. Baby all right today. Took baby's picture with Kodak. Henry came. Edsel and Sam went to Jasper to meet him. We were glad to see him. He had a new automobile coat.

February 10. Took snapshots of Edsel and sheep. Slept three in bed. It was pretty hot.

February 11. Baked bread. Got great praise for my bread. My feet hurt so I can hardly stand on them.

February 12. Kate had a chill last night. Had Doctor all night. Better this morning.

February 13. Sam and I washed. Mrs. Johnson (nurse) hung out clothes. Sam made Edsel a sleigh and he is happy. Gets hitches and hauls snow.

February 14. Too tired to write anything.

February 15. Sam and Edsel went out to hunt a hired girl. Rode all over with horse and cutter and had a fine time.

February 16. Kate got up for first time today. Got a letter from Henry. It made me very lonely.

February 17. Kate got up to dinner feeling good. Sam was going to take Edsel and I for a cutter ride but could not go. Wrote to Henry and was very lonely.

February 18. Sam went for girl he had hired and she would not come. Played sick. Kate very disappointed. Sam found another that promised to come tomorrow.

February 19. Sam brought new girl and took home the nurse. Girl seems to be a willing girl.

February 20. At half after three telegram came said Mrs. Ford: Sick come at once. Very much worried. Letter came at five, Henry sick. Would give anything to get home tonight.

February 21. Sam took us to Jasper to take train. Very nervous about Henry. Got home, and before train had quite stopped, Henry got in. Was never so glad to see him. Because I expected he would be in bed.

February 22. Henry feeling some better. Just resting and getting used to being at home.

February 23. Wrote letter to Kate. Grandpa and Jane seem pleased to have us at home. Henry made toboggan of snow in backyard for Edsel.

February 24. Took Edsel to Sunday School, he was glad to get back again.

February 25. Jane baked bread from recipe I gave her and is delighted.

February 26. Will and family came in and Maggie came in also. Ate up all Jane's bread. Made her hot.

February 27. Went out home. Edsel had fun on Roy's toboggan.

February 28. Mr. and Mrs. Beebe came to spend the eve, played cards, had lots of fun. Edsel disappointed because they did not bring Irene.

March 1. Edsel and I went downtown. Got his hair cut and did some shopping.

March 2. Jane went downtown and I kept house.

March 3. Edsel and I went to Sunday School. Edsel got book as prize for going steady. Henry, Edsel and I took a nice walk.

March 5. Very cold. Stayed home and sewed.

March 6. Very cold. Sewed, played cards and I lost two games out of three.

March 7. Met Henry. He took us to dinner. Played cards. Beat this time. Grandpa very much pleased.

March 8. Very wet and sloppy. Stayed in all day.

March 9. Maggie came in, we all went downtown. I bought myself goods for shirt waist. Played five hand game of Pedro.

March 11. Got a letter from Kate. She asked me to send her a little hair brush for little King Edward.

March 12. Went downtown to automobile works and came back on belt line with Henry. Grandpa and I beat at cards with Henry's help.

March 16. Jane went out in country. I am keeping house.

March 17. Henry took Edsel to Sunday School while I got dinner.

March 18. Am all alone. Grandpa and Edsel gone to see Henry. Jane came back.

March 19. Did not do anything today.

March 23. Brought my geranium that Mrs. McElroy had kept all winter.

March 24. Went to Sunday School with Edsel. Then went out home. All took a walk through the fields to the cemetery. Had lots of fun.

March 25. Edsel tried to do his Grandpa's chores. Emptied ashes, filled wood box Then Jane stopped him. Made him feel bad.

March 26. Went downtown. Got Edsel's hair cut. After supper Edsel, Henry and I took walk. Wanted to have a little talk by our selves.

March 27. Jane, Edsel and I went to church. When we got back, Maggie and James were in and had dinner all ready. They went home at four o'clock. We all went for a walk.

April 1. Tried to fool Henry but could not.

April 2. Edsel, Jane and I went to hear recital of Little Lord Fauntleroy. It was very good.

April 5. Henry and Mr. Murphy went out with automobile to Farmington around to Orchard Lake on to Pontaic and back home. Started half after two, back at six.

April 6. Henry fixed me up a dose of brandy and rock candy for my cold. The dose made me laugh.

April 7. Jane, Henry, Edsel and I went to St. Joseph's church. We went to Sunday School in the afternoon. Had a very bad cold, coughed all the time in church.

April 8. Did not feel very good today.

April 11. Went downtown to get tickets for the Old Homestead. Henry bought me a pair of patent leather shoes and a pair of black silk hose.

April 13. Henry did not come home to supper, very lonesome.

April 14. Did not go to church or school. Went in woods for wild flowers but found none.

April 15. Helped Jane wash. Took a nap. Did a little mending.

April 16. Went to RR crossing to meet Henry, he had Edsel's tricycle all painted up fine. Edsel is delighted.

April 17. Had showers all day. I wrote a letter to Kate. Jane went downtown, brought me goods for shirt waist for birthday present.

April 18. Rained and snowed. Snowed an inch.

April 19. Weather good. Henry, Jane, Edsel and I went to Wonderland. Coaxed Grandpa to go but he would not.

April 20. Went downtown met Henry at Hudson's. Tried to change my shoes but could not. Got my money back.

April 21. Very windy and rainy. Edsel and I went to Sunday School, wind broke my umbrella that I got for Xmas. Feel bad about it.

April 25. Weather fine. Henry came home for dinner, took me and Edsel back on automobile.

April 27. Henry went to the flats with Fred, had a duck boat so Edsel and I could not go. They had to walk part of the way as water was too low to use boat. Edsel and I went out home.

April 28. Eva, Wallace and I went in woods for flowers. After dinner Eva went over to Maggie's. Henry is duck hunting.

April 29. Henry got home all safe. Brought home fish and ducks. He had quite a time walking across the bay. But had a good time.

April 30. Did my ironing and nearly roasted. Henry came home to dinner.

May 1. Henry came home to dinner, took Edsel and I downtown. I ordered me a walking skirt; and took Edsel to the dentist.

May 5. Went out to Sunday School, and after supper Jane, Edsel, Henry and I went out to John's. It was Robby's birthday.

May 7. Got ready to iron half past ten. Henry came with Mrs. McElroy on the automobile. She stayed to dinner. Henry came for her at eight o'clock. Had some nice music.

May 8. Did my ironing. Henry went to Indiana. Took Edsel and I as far as Wyandotte. We came home in the electric cars. Maggie came to get a hat but did not get any.

May 9. Maggie went home today. I intended going to Mrs. McElroy's but weather looked bad.

May 15. Went down to McElroy's on automobile.

Some of the names mentioned in Clara's diary of 1901

Grandpa: Henry Ford's father, William Ford.

Edsel: son of Henry and Clara.

Mr. and Mrs. Gore: neighbors of Henry and Clara.

Helen Gore: about Edsel's age.

Mrs. McElroy: close friend of Clara.

McCormicks: Dearborn farm neighbors of the Fords.

Kate: younger sister of Clara (Mrs. Samuel Raymond).

Eva: youngest sister of Clara (later Mrs. George Brubaker).

Jane: Henry's youngest sister (died in 1906 at age thirty-five).

Pa: Clara's father, Melvin S. Bryant.

Roy: Clara's brother, on the Bryant farm.

Joe Benton: friend of Jane.

Annie: wife of William Bryant, Clara's brother in Detroit.

William Bryant: Clara's brother, Martindale Street, Detroit.

Grandpa Bryant: Clara's father (Edsel's grandfather).

Marve: Clara's brother, living on farm.

Maggie: Margaret, Henry's sister (Mrs. James Ruddiman).

James: James Ruddiman, Margaret's husband.

Will: Henry's youngest brother, William D. Ford.

Uncle George: George Ford (1835–1901), son of Samuel Ford.

Mr. and Mrs. Leslie: Dearborn pioneer farm family.

Sam: Samuel Raymond, husband of Kate.

Uncle Sam: Edsel's uncle Samuel Raymond.

Jasper: small town south of Adrian, Michigan.

Mrs. Johnson: temporary nurse hired by the Raymonds.

Mr. and Mrs. Beebe: Detroit friends of the Fords.

Little King Edward: presumably a nickname for the Raymonds' first child, Milton.

Mr. Murphy: a wealthy lumber merchant who financed Henry's auto developments.

Hudson's: large Detroit department store.

Fred: Clara's brother Frederick H. Bryant (liked to hunt).

Wallace: perhaps a boyfriend of Eva Bryant.

John: Henry's brother in Dearborn.

Robby: Robert, son of John Ford, Henry's brother.

Wyandotte: a town ten miles southwest of Detroit.

Clara, July 11 to August 6, 1912: "My Trip Abroad," a gift of Rose (Flint)

July 11. Left Detroit on the six-ten train. Mr. and Mrs. Flint from Providence (Rhode Island) came over—spent the night and went with us to Hoboken the next morning to be with us until the last minute.

July 13. Left at ten A.M. Not one meal was missed by the party. Voyage all the way over was perfect, and we all voted that the German ship food service couldn't be better. Delighted with the food and German service.

July 20. Arrived Plymouth at one P.M. All seemed spellbound with the beautiful scenery, looked as if it had been painted. Our own motor car that we had ordered, with Mr. Perry our friend from Manchester, were there to meet us—got through with little trouble with customs officer. Started immediately for London. Got as far as Exeter that night after traveling many miles out of our way to see the country. Stopped at a quaint old hotel opposite the Exeter Cathedral, which was built in the ninth century.

July 21. Visited Cathedral in the morning. Drove to Bristol where we had tea, then on to Bath, stopped off to see the town where royalty used to go for mineral bathing, took photo of "white horse," then motored on to Ascot, where the noted Ascot races are run, stayed all night, took breakfast at a beautiful hotel called Berystede. Strolled about until twelve o'clock. Started run to London going through "Windsor Park," saw Windsor Castle. Went through Hampton Court Palace and Gardens. Edsel met Bill Chesbro of Detroit in the palace. Arrived at Picadilly Hotel about seven P.M.

July 23. Arose very late. Mr. Ford, myself, Edsel, Brother Marvin, Mr. and Mrs. Perry took breakfast in our private breakfast room, that we were lucky enough to have off our bedroom. Coffee very bad. Mrs. Perry and myself went shopping, then drove around saw Buckingham Palace and Victoria Memorial monument and many noted places. [While shopping in London, Clara purchased a scarf at Liberty and Company, a blouse at Peter Robinson, and two ties at Selfrige and Company.]

July 24. Started at noon traveling north. Stopped at a quaint little inn for tea in Deventry, built in 1610, then on to Kennelworth Castle which is now in ruins, then on to Warwick, my mother's birth city. Stopped at Warwick Arms hotel. Hunted up the sexton of the church, found record of mother's birth and marriage of grandparents. Church mother attended was built in 1620 and in good repair. After we found her old home and garden, stood on the stone steps leading to the garden and Edsel took my picture. The house was on Linen St. Also went through Warwick Castle. Then motored to Stratford on Avon. Went through Shakespeare's birthplace and Hathaway's home. Then on to Stratford, also the home of Marie Correli novelist. Then on to a little old town called Broadway and stopped at Lygon Arms hotel. Broadway is the home of Mary Anderson DeNavarro. Saw her home. Then drove on to Litchfield, went in the Cathedral said to be the most beautiful in England, took photographs of cathedral and had tea. Then on to Birmingham. Drove around and bought films. Then on arriving at "Newfield House," Mr. and Mrs. Perry's home, twelve miles from Manchester where we are staying a week. The Perry home is a fine old house with five acres of ground, fine old garden, orchard and bowling green where Mr. Ford had many a good game. Mr. Perry has presented Mr. Ford with a set of bowls to take home.

Mrs. Perry has her two little nieces with her, five and eight years of age. The dearest quaintest little things. They look and act just like the two little children in the Blue Bird. While staying with the Perrys we took short trips through the country and got back for night. One day we drove to "Chatsworth," the home of the Duke and Duchess of Devonshire. Went through their garden and greenhouses, which were hanging with all kinds of grapes, peaches and many other lovely things. Then we drove twenty miles farther and visited Welbeck Abbey, house of the Duke and Duchess of Portland. Their grounds and gardens were too beautiful to describe. I made a few notes for my own benefit. The Duke and Duchess were entertaining one hundred ex-convicts' wives on the lawn, they were having tea and a band was playing. Also three little orphans whom the Duchess is bringing up, were just leaving in a carriage with their nurse to a home which is provided on the estate for them. It is the most beautiful place we have visited. The stables, laundry and chicken house are like small castles.

August 5. Started back for London to attend the auto race at Brooklands. Drove two hundred and fifty miles, arriving at the Picadilly hotel at eight o'clock, have traveled fifteen days and have not seen a foot of bad road.

August 6. Attended race and had a splendid day. Mr. Ford gave silver cup to Ford winner.

Edsel, August 7 to August 25, 1912

Wednesday, August 7, Picadilly Hotel, London. Mother, Marvin and I ate breakfast alone, Mr. Perry and Father went out early. I walked up Regent St., bought two hats, a cap and collars. Had lunch at one. Left for Ireland. Arr. Gloucester 6:30.

Raining very hard. Mr. Perry met Mrs. P at depot. All had dinner. Walked over to old Cathedral. Hired hand organ to play. Retired early.

Thursday, August 8, Bell Hotel, Gloucester. Left town at seven A.M., had had our breakfast at six in our rooms. Still raining. Traveled fast to catch boat at Fishguard. Ran out of petrol eight miles from boat. Lost an hour, also our boat. Went to Fishguard Bay Hotel. Very nice, ate lunch at four P.M. Walked up very beautiful garden to a high bluff over the bay. Ate dinner at eight. Went down to the night boat. Watched them load our motor on boat. Boat name—Inniscarra. Retired.

Friday, August 9, on board SS Inniscarra. We arrived in Cork at 9:30, had breakfast at Metropole Hotel. Walked about town. Father walked off alone, waited for him until eleven, then drove out to Blarney Castle. Saw some girls kiss the stone— enough for me. Had lunch there. Went to Bandon then to Clonakilty. Found Aunt Ann's house, took pictures. Saw church and school. Drove on thru rain to Bantry on Bantry Bay. Stayed at Vickery's Hotel—rather poor. Saw much bog, lots of peat.

Saturday, August 10, Vicker's Hotel Bantry, Cork Co. After breakfast Father and I went thru Bantry Woolen Mills, bought cloth for suit. Started for Killarney. Went thru Glendariff. Most beautiful scenery we have seen, mountains, lakes, heather, took lots of pictures on Mt. pass. Drove thru tunnel, arrived Killarney at noon. Royal Victoria Hotel on Lake. After luncheon we walked into town. Saw lots of funny sights. Queer Irish boys. Walked back to hotel. Had dinner. Wrote letter. Retired.

Sunday, August 11, Royal Victoria Hotel, Killarney, Ire. Just before we left we met Mr. and Mrs. Orla B. Taylor in the hotel. They are from Detroit. Left for Dublin at eleven A.M. Sun shining. Roads not very good. Had lunch at Limerick. Raining as we started. Much colder. Had tea at Railway Hotel, Kildare. Looked at church and round tower. Arrived at Shelbourne Hotel, Dublin at eight P.M. Saw Taylors and Fred K. Stearns of Detroit in dining room. All sat in my room after dinner because of fire in fireplace.

Monday, August 12, Shelbourne Hotel, Dublin. We walked about Dublin, also visited our agents. I wrote a letter for father. Left on a Ford and Cadillac to Kingston, boarded S.S. Scotia, good passage, landed in Isl. of Anglesey at 5:30. Took train, arrive in London at eleven. Mr. Black met us. Went to Picadilly. Had lunch. Retired.

Tuesday, August 13, Picadilly Hotel. Same old Picadilly, know it pretty well by this time. Mr. Perry, Father and I went to steamship office, cancelled our rooms on Victoria House. Booked on George Washington sailing on Aug. 24. Went to Selfriges, Father bought hat. [On this same day, Clara purchased from Helena at 15 Chichester Street an "evening gown," a "costume," and a "coat," for 54 pounds or $270.] Went back to Hotel, bought some things, had tea, started for Brighton on two Fords. Horselin to come from Holyhead with Rolls Royce. Arrived Royal York Hotel Brighton at 8:30.

Wednesday, August 14, Royal York Hotel, Brighton. Arose fairly early, took a stroll on the Front, saw a hydro-aeroplane which had just landed from France. After breakfast we started on the Fords for Newhaven, sailed on S.S. Brighton at 11:45, smooth passage, arrived Dieppe 3:15. Went to Metropole Hotel. Rode Rolls Royce back to depot, met Mr. White's man. Then we walked along the seashore and chalk cliffs about three miles, back at eight P.M. retired early.

Thursday, August 15, Elysee Palace Hotel, Paris, France. Immediately after breakfast we left for Paris via Rouen arriving there at four P.M. Stopped at Elysee Palace Hotel on Champs Elysee near Arc d' Triumph. Mr. White came up, we had dinner in our sitting room. All stayed talking until eleven P.M.

Friday, August 16, Paris, France. Arose at eight, walked up to Arc d' Triumph and on Ave de la Grand Armie, had breakfast at ten. Mr. White and M. DePasse called, we all went to see De Passe store at Neuilly sur Seine. Back to hotel. Mr. Perry left for London. We went thru Napoleon's Tomb then on Bois de Bologne. Tea at Pre Catalin, coffee at 5:30 at Cafe de la Paix. Went by Louvre along Seine. Church de Madelline, Latin quarter and Luxenburg gardens. Dinner at Cafe Grand. Met Mrs. White there. Back to hotel at 10:30.

Saturday, August 17, Elysee Palace Hotel, Paris. Father, Marvin and I had breakfast downstairs. Whites joined us. We went to M. DePasse's store, then to Aris carburetor works, then to see diesel engine, looked at chronometers. Had luncheon with ladies, Cafe de la Paix, went to Palace of Versailles and Trianon Palace. Had tea at Trianon Palace Hotel, very beautiful, went to aviation school, saw about four flights. Met ladies, had dinner at Cafe in Luna Park. Saw some attractions, returned twelve P.M.

Sunday, August 18. We all very very tired, arose late. Mr. and Mrs. White came over, we went to Versailles thru the Palace. Then had late luncheon at Trianon Palace Hotel. Then went to Grand and Petit Trianon Palaces. The former used as design for Anna Gould's Paris house. Went to Porte de Buc Aviation school for Jarman bi-planes and R.E.P. monoplanes, only bi-planes flying, returned to Hotel at eight. Had dinner at Hotel at nine. Took walk down Champ Elysee to Obelisk and return.

Monday, August 19, Paris, France. Went to Mr. White's office then to Renault factory, made engagement for P.M. Then went to Bellview had lunch, then to Renault. Met Mr. DePasse, also Mr. Renault, went thru his shops. Then we went to Clement-Bayard, went thru that works. Then back to hotel, got the ladies, went out to Ahughiek-les-Bains. The casino had dinner. Returned.

Tuesday, August 20, Paris, France. Went to White's office, sent away cards to office employees at Ford Motor Company. Then went to Cafe on Champ Elysee for lunch. Went to accessories store, bought horns and lamps. Then to Nieuport aeroplane works, then to Charron automobile works. Went to N.D.L. S.S. Line Am. Express Co. and visited some jewelry shops. Returned to hotel for dinner.

Wednesday, August 21, Paris. Mr. White came over and we then went downtown thru some jewelry shops, bought two watches, two clocks, some toys, met the ladies at the hotel, went to Marguerres for dinner then went to Whites' house. Mr. White entertained us on the piano. Went home on taxi except Father and Marve who walked. [Receipts dated August 21 show that Henry purchased from Chaude at 36 Galerie Montpensier a clock, thermometer, and barometer combination for 230 francs or $46.]

Thursday, August 22, Paris. Father and I went to Rolls Royce store, then met Mr. White, drove down town to Eiffel Tower. Bought some things, met the ladies at Cafe de la Paix, had luncheon. Took Mrs. Perry to depot Gar-du-Nord. Returned to hotel, had dinner there for first time with the original party who left Detroit. Father and I sent some cards and letters. Retired. Had a bad headache—too much Paris. [Receipts dated August 22 show "Monsieur Henry Ford, Elysee Palace Hotel" to have purchased from Bijouterie-Joaillerie,

Alexandre, two silver Longines watches for 470 francs or $69; also, from E. B. Meyrowitz-Optician at 3 Rue Scribe two camera outfits, one costing 240 francs, the other 271 francs, totaling $102.20 for the two outfits. And "Madame H. Ford" purchased from Manalt-Hoschede of 8 Rue Volney a robe and blouses costing 405 francs or $81.]

Friday, August 23, Paris. We started from Paris at eleven A.M. for Cherbourg. Had very good luncheon at Golden Lion Hotel, Mr. Wolfe proprietor. Started at 2:30, had a puncture about four miles from Lisieux, changed wheels, as we arrived in Lisieux we bought spare tube and petrol. Started out, had another puncture, and just as we arrived back at garage another tire blew out. Bought two new tires, started out again, arrived at Normandy Hotel Deauville at ten P.M., had dinner and retired.

Saturday, August 24, Metropole Hotel, Deauville, France. Left hotel at nine, drove about Trouville, then to Hermanville to Mr. White's villa — "La Loges." Had lunch there, walked down to their cabin on shore, back and bought some salt-water taffy. Retired early.

Sunday, August 25, La Logesvilla, Hermanvilla, France. Started early for Cherbourg, arriving at one P.M. Had luncheon, waited until five P.M., boarded tender. Met George Washington at 7:30 P.M. Mr. Marshall Stephens met us at Cherbourg. Mr. Archer and Mr. Perry were on boat.

Louis Ives, February 17, 1926, to March 13, 1926

Wednesday, February 17. We left Rouge Plant North Yards 10 A.M. Mr. Rockelman, Ray Dahlinger and Harry Bennett bid us good-bye. Edsel went as far as Flat Rock. We all went through the Plant, very interesting. Mr. Ford trying to teach us a new dance step. Mr. F and I rode on the engine a good deal of the time as far as Ironton, where our Fairlane was transferred at 10 P.M. to the Norfolk & Western RR.

Thursday, February 18. This morning we passsed through the Coal Mines. Wonderful hills. So many small houses on these hills through West Virginia. Stopped at Litchburg. Mr. F and I run around the train. At Appoinatton, hundreds of school children came down to the train to see Mr. Ford. Wonderful sight. We stopped at Petersburg. Mr. F and I running uptown. Met four colored boys who sang and danced the Charleston. We brought them down to the train, they performed for the ladies. We had a dance before retiring.

Friday, February 19. Arrived at Charleston this morning. Sent postal cards. Mrs. F, Capt. Stokes, Mr. Burns who had driven down in a Lincoln Car and myself took a short ride through the town. Met Mr. Dembey at the dock. Left Charlestown Harbor about three P.M. Had a wild trip to Savannah, quite a storm, wind 35 miles per hr. Mrs. Ives had a little sick time. Arrived at Savannah twelve P.M. Tied up at the Municipal Dock. Large crowds gathered to meet us.

Saturday, February 20. Started ten A.M. for Mr. Ford's plantations 20 miles from Savannah. Mr. Burns with the Lincoln Car drove us with Mr. Cooper to this property. The names of these plantations are Cherry Hill, Richmond and Strathy Hall on the O'Geeche River, very interesting old places, beautiful old live oaks with Southern Moss hanging from the limbs. Mr. F found an old engine. Mr. Burns going to get it out of the ruins and send it home.

Sunday, February 21. Mr. F, Mr. Cooper and myself took a ride on the Belfast Road, saw a flock of wild turkeys. Mrs. Ford and Mrs. Ives went to church, this church was founded by John Wesley, the first Sunday School in the world was started here. We four had some wonderful music this evening. Mr. F with his fiddle, Mrs. I at the piano, Mrs. F and myself doing some very fine singing.

Monday, February 22. Mrs. F and Mrs. I went shopping with Mrs. Cooper in Savannah. We men went in a speed boat to a rice plantation. Here we found another old engine which Mr. F, I believe is going to have Mr. Burns send home.

Tuesday, February 23. Arrived at St. Catherine Island. We four went in a launch to see a plantation owned by some ladies, looked over the building and came back to the Yacht for lunch. After lunch we went back to the island. Met Mr. and Mrs. Oelmer, Mr. and Mrs. Cunningham and Mr. Cooper. The men walked over the Island (the ladies rode in a Ford Car to the Oyster Packing House). The ladies say Mr. Oelmer is "some" driver. The oyster business is very interesting. Capt. Oelmer, who whistles through his teeth when talking, has charge of the business for 35 years. We saw piles of oyster shells which are put back in the ocean so new oysters can grow on them.

Wednesday, February 24. We visited the Torreys at their Winter Place on Ossabaw Island. A very beautiful place, had dinner there. Went back to the Yacht to St. Catherine's Island Dock. After supper we were entertained by the black folks singing around a bonfire, they danced the buzzards dance.

Mrs. Ives took a picture of "Jiggs," a namesake of mine. A Birthday Cake was presented to me by Mr. and Mrs. Ford, on top was the figure 71 made with small candles.

Thursday, February 25. This morning Mr. F, Cooper and myself took a ride with Mr. Oelmer on the beach and through the woods. After dinner Mr. F and I went in the Speed Launch to see Mr. Howard Coffin at Sapelo Island. He has a fine place. We came back to the Yacht in 50 minutes, 30 miles. Mrs. Ford invited Mr. and Mrs. Cunningham and Mr. Cooper to supper. Afterward we adjourned to the deck and had some dancing. At 9:30 PM our guests departed and Capt. started our Yacht for St. Augustine.

Friday, February 26. Arrived at St Augustine 9:30 AM. The four of us went in a launch to the town as we did not tie up to the dock. We hired an old fellow with a horse and phaeton to drive us around. Called to see Mr. Hewitt, who lives in a house supposed to be the oldest in the U.S. He deals in old antiques. Mr. F bought some. We started 3:00 PM for Palm Beach, a young lady tried to interview Mr. F but did not succeed, much to her displeasure. We visited a Historical old fort.

Saturday, February 27. Arrived at Palm Beach 11:00 AM. Anchored 16 miles away from the shore. The four of us went in the launch through the river to the Hotel Royal Poinciana, had dinner there, took a taxi and went to the Alligator Farm. Quite a sight, to see gentlemen and ladies pushed around in basket carts propelled by blacks. We came back to the Yacht about 6:00 PM. The Capt. started at once for Miami.

Sunday, February 28. Arrived at Miami 2:00 AM. Anchored outside until 8:00 AM. A pilot came and we went inside and tied to a dock. The Firestones came to meet us and we all went to their home which is very fine situated on the bank of the ocean. We were shown some fine saddle horses. We drove around the city, then back to their home for supper. After dinner we all drove out to Coral Gables and back to the boat. The

Firestones came on board for a visit and when they left we set sail for Cuba, about 6:00 PM.

Monday, March 1. All day on the Gulf, a little rough but fine weather. Mima a little sick. Sent a radio to Antoinette on the Gulf Stream. Water here is 80 degrees. Arrived in Havana 6:00 PM, after passing by the Old Morro Fort. Capt., Mr. and Mrs. Ford, Mima and I took a launch and went ashore. We had quite a nice walk through the city, very quaint place. Mrs. Ford bought some fruit, the name is Mimao. The weather is ideal, like June in Dearborn.

Tuesday, March 2. After breakfast on the Yacht we went ashore. Mrs. F and Mrs. I went sight seeing. Mr. F and I visited some stores. Mr. F bought me a straw hat. After lunch on the Yacht, Mr. F and myself went ashore and called on Mr. Facisco. We went out to a sugar plantation and on our way back we called on Mr. Baarque, the Chief Justice of Cuba, at his home, a beautiful place. He showed us his chapel where his family worship. The chapel is situated on his and the children's premises. All the homes are on the same grounds.

Wednesday, March 3. Ladies went shopping this morning, Mr. Ford, Facisco, Clark and myself drove around the city, saw a place where they make rum. Mr. Ford, Clark and myself looked over some property which Mr. F thinks of buying. We had dinner at Hotel Inglatira. This afternoon our party had tea with Mr. Baarque and his interesting family.

Thursday, March 4. Ladies this morning went shopping, bought some baskets. They went into a Cathedral 300 years old. Mr. F, Clark, Facisco, a doctor and myself visited a sugar plantation. We went through the sugar mills which were very interesting. Suggested to Mr. Ford to have some of the sugar without bleaching process sent to the Highland Park Store to be retailed, as an experiment twenty bags was ordered sent to the states.

We had dinner at the manager's house, was quite unique, as they served bread without butter and four kinds of liquors.

In the afternoon the Baarque family came on the Yacht for tea. We had some dancing. We left for Fort Myers about 10:00 PM.

Friday, March 5. All day on the gulf, beautiful weather, smooth sea. We all had a good rest. Anchored off Fort Myers for the night. Decided to go to-morrow to Boca Grande.

Saturday, March 6. All day here at Boca Grande Harbor, waiting for an immigration officer for inspection. Did not come until 10:00 AM, Mr. F Bore.

Sunday, March 7. Stayed here at Boca Grande Harbor, had a jolly time telling stories, etc. After luncheon we took the launch and went to Boca Grande. Walked over the Golf Links and back to the hotel. Here we met Mr. John Russell, Mr. and Mrs. Jere Hutchins, Mr. and Mrs. Will Hudson, Mr. and Mrs. Young of John Hopkins. They told us Mr. and Mrs. Loomis, Mr. and Mrs. Walker and Sadie Burnham were here last Thursday, sorry to have missed them. We went back to the Yacht, had dinner, Mr. F gave us some music on the phonograph. Got a charlie horse in my right leg while running on my toes with Mr. Ford.

Monday, March 8. We started in the launch for the Fords' Winter Home near Fort Myers, a beautiful ride up the Caloosa Hatchee River. Mr. F and I got out of the car about four miles from their home and walked the rest of the way. Mr. F fed me up on grapes and orange fruit.

The Fords' place joins Mr. Edison's, a fine place with grapes and orange trees loaded down with fruit and other wonderful tropical growths. Mr. Firestone and family called on us. We had a nice visit with the Edisons at their home. Mrs. Ford, Mima and myself drove to town, Mima bought a hat. We returned, bid the Edisons, Firestones good-bye. Motored up quite a distance on the shore where the Capt. picked us up in the launch. We arrived on the Yacht, 7:00 PM.

Tuesday, March 9. This morning Mr. F, Capt. and myself took the speed launch and went to Sanibel Island. In the afternoon we all went to the island to gather shells, got some very fine ones. We returned and as we were at supper, one of the sailors fell overboard; he was rescued. We started on our way about 7:30 PM for Pensacola, where we will leave the Yacht for good. Sent a radio message to Antoinette.

Wednesday, March 10. On the way to Pensacola, Mrs. Ford and Mrs. Ives spent most of the day sorting shells. In the afternoon we saw a school of Porpoises swimming along the side of the Yacht. We had some fine music, singing old songs; Mima at the piano, we all enjoyed it. This is our last night on the Yacht, we hate to leave it as we have such wonderful and lovely times. We went to bed about 10:30 PM.

Thursday, March 11. Arrived at Pensacola 8:00 AM, very stormy, passage about 370 miles across the Gulf. We took a launch ashore, quite a gathering of people to see us, past an old "Cutie" reporter, without an interview. Mr. Multon and his partner who has charge of the Ford Interest took Mr. F and myself for a ride, visited a Saw Mill and the US Navy Station. Our party boarded the Fairlane about 3:30 PM. After dinner three colored waiters from a dining car on our train came into our car and sang some songs. Arrived at Atlanta sometime in the night.

Friday, March 12. Left Atlanta 7:30 AM, arrived at Rome 9:30 AM. Miss Berry, Mr. Keowan and Secretary met us at the depot. We drove to the school and around the grounds. We went to the chapel to see the service, very interesting; the boys on one side, the girls on the other, they sang very nice, especially the boys in the gallery. Some of the boys and girls made short talks, telling about their experiences. After the exercises we went to the dining hall and had a fine dinner, the girls came around our table and sang to us. They showed us the spinning wheel and the way to make cloth. In the afternoon we drove around the grounds, saw the cows and other interesting things. We went to the gymnasium, the boys and girls came to see us dance the old dances, we had a jolly time. After the dance we went to Miss Berry's home for tea. Met her lovely old mother and her charming sisters.

Mr. Ford left some dance books, writing his name in them. As we were leaving the boys and girls gathered around our car and sang God Be With You Til We Meet Again. Pulled out of Rome 7:30 PM.

Saturday, March 13. Arrived at Cincinnati early this morning, snow on the ground very cold. Arrived in Detroit 4:45 PM. Ray was here to meet us. Arrived home much to the surprise of Antoinette and Nelson.

[Notes: Antoinette and Nelson were children of Louis and Mima Ives of Dearborn. Fred Rockelman was general manager of the D.T.&I. Railroad. Harry Bennett was in charge of Ford Motor Company Security. Perry Stokes was captain of the *Sialia*. R. L. Cooper was a land purchasing agent for Ford in Savannah. Mr. Burns was one of Ford's chauffeurs. Howard Coffin was chief engineer of Hudson Motor Company in Detroit. Marscho Faschio was a Cuban sugar plantation owner whom Henry had visisted on his previous Cuban trip in March 1917.]

Excerpts from the reminiscences of
Reverend Hedley C. Stacey, recorded in June 1952.

In 1925, I went to Dearborn, and I was there for twenty-six years. I went to Christ Episcopal on Michigan Avenue; it was the original church. Mr. and Mrs. Ford were parishioners. As a matter of fact, Mr. Ford's father was on the vestry of the church, and the Fords were very active in the church. So was Mr. Ford's sister Margaret Ruddiman. The father and mother took a great deal of interest and had a great deal to do in the building of the church. As long as they lived, they were very interested and very active. In fact, Mr. Ford told me he had gone to church school there and carved his name on the pew. I really got a great kick out of that when he would tell me how, while he was supposed to be listening to the service, he and a couple of his pals were really working with their knives. He got a great kick out of it, I know.

The Fords were regular subscribers. They were subscribers when I became rector there and continued up to the time of their deaths. I met them very soon after I got to the parish. In fact, it was the first Christmas when we made the very first contact, because we spent an evening with them. Of course, as everybody knows, Mr. Ford thought an awful lot of Mrs. Ford. She had quite an influence on him, within limitations.

Mrs. Ford was interested in an old ladies' home in Detroit, and a couple times a year she'd ask me if I would go down and talk with them, so we had that regular trip together, down to Detroit to talk with these dear old ladies. I also taught services in the home on Michigan Avenue; it was Mrs. Ford's Home for Wayward Girls. In fact, the last time I rode into Detroit was when Mr. Ford rode with us, which was unusual. That was just a couple years before he died. He decided that he just wanted to go down, and we made the trip together. Of course, it caused quite a bit of excitement in the home to have Mr. Ford there.

Well, my impressions of Mr. Ford are personal and very happy. He used to come around the rectory, sometimes alone, pick me up in his car, and we would go out driving together. We'd either drive together or sit in the house and talk for a couple of hours. Mr. Ford didn't talk too much about religious things, although he was definitely interested. I remember one conversation where for a couple hours he discussed the subject of immortality. He had his own ideas about that. He was never clear or defined about his ideas, but he did seem to have an idea on the Hindu idea of reincarnation. He thought it was quite possible to perhaps come back again, but it was quite vague and indefinite. He had no tangible substance, none whatever, that he expressed to me, but he had a deep religious sense; that is to say, you know, I think he believed in God.

I always thought that he had a very strong mystical element about him; I always felt it. I have often wondered if he was really interested in spiritualism, although he never indicated in any direct way, but I was very conscious that he felt that there were spiritual influences. He never stated it in technical terms at all. I think that in his contact with nature, he was undoubtedly a very religious man at that particular time. He would have a religious experience with the wonders of nature and glory and all that sort of thing. I think he was very sensitive to that element. I would say he was very intuitive. I think that he would admit that his difficulty was that his intuitions were from a type of idealism, but he was blocked when he got to practical things. That would explain why many times his actions would differ definitely from his statements.

Frankly, I don't think Mr. Ford had much use for the institutional churches, the set churches. He liked the freer churches, a community church. He was much more interested in the community church than he was in the Episcopal Church as an Episcopal Church.

He talked to me one time about changing my church, and at one time I was called up and asked if I would prepare some general figures as to what a seven-day-a-week church and parish house would cost, thus establishing a real religious institution that operated seven days a week. He seemed to be anxious at that time to build, in memory of his father and mother, a church that would be a community church. Of course, I was a priest in the Episcopal Church, and that was outside my scope. I talked to the bishop about it, but we just couldn't do it.

I think Mr. Ford had on his mind a type of church that was a community church, that had a preschool idea with it, yet with definite religious instruction elements. It would be a teaching church. At least once a year, he would come to me directly and say, "When are we going to build the church?" But he never did pledge any money to the building of the church, although he talked constantly of building it. For instance, we had to sell the old church on Michigan Avenue in order to get $50,000 toward building a new church. I asked him if he would not be interested in keeping or preserving the old church which was his father's and mother's church. I did suggest in a letter I wrote to him in Georgia that it would be a lovely thing if he would purchase that property, and we would maintain it as a memorial to his father and mother. Mr. Ford wrote me back and said that he was not interested in a memorial. It just broke my heart.

[Henry was willing to give land for a new church.] However, for twenty years, Mr. Ford and I disagreed as to the location he wanted to give. Finally, he consented to the corner of Cherry Hill and Military, and we got a title free and clear. Ford contributed, but not a very large amount; the total contribution was $15,000. The church cost us possibly $300,000.

Mrs. Ford's attitude was definitely favorable. She's told me many times, "I don't understand why Henry doesn't build that church for his mother and father. He ought to do it." In fact, I can say this in all honesty, it was the influence of Mrs. Ford finally that got us the deed of the present property. She called me up one day after they came back from Georgia, after his first illness, and said, "Mr. Stacey, what is the difficulty hindering yourself in regard to that property so that the church can be built?"

I said, "It is the difficulty of location."

She said, "What do you want?"

I said, "I want the corner of Cherry Hill and Military."

She said, "Why can't you get it?"

I said, "Lady, you'll have to answer that question."

"Well," she said, "I will call you back."

Not very long after that, she called me back and said, "Mr. Stacey, you are going to have the deed to the property. How much do you want?"

I said, "Oh, about three and a half acres."

There was a tree there that Mr. Ford was very interested in; he wanted it preserved. He also thought that it would be a very nice tree, near which we should build the rectory, and I could sit under the tree. In order to give us that tree, they added additional acreage. He wanted us to have the rectory right by the tree so that we could sit under the tree and enjoy ourselves.

Mr. Ford did not have enough chance to help in the actual plans for the building; he was ill. Mrs. Ford did have an opportunity to see the new church, and she liked it very much. Mrs. Ford called me up when she was in the hospital. She said she had been thinking about further contributions to the church. I was to have tea with her that afternoon, but a relative in Adrian died. That ended that, because in a very short time she passed on. I never had a chance to go back and complete that talk, and we never got what she had in mind, the contribution that she was going to make to the new church.

She was talking to me about a memorial church out near the Ford Cemetery for a couple of years. The question was what to do with the cemetery, what was going to happen to it with that industrial encroachment and the buildings around there. At one time, there was a serious conversation of moving the graves, just Mr. Ford's. In fact, I was asked whether I would consent to the establishment of the monument right next to the church on Cherry Hill. At that time, Mrs. Ford was very much taken up with the idea to have it right there on the property next to the church.

Difficulties arose in regard to the cemetery itself. There was quite an involvement of the other people in the cemetery. They found that it was practically impossible to ask to move Mr. Ford, and any such relatives that they thought of, anywhere else. They came down to the fact that it had to be maintained where it was, and Mrs. Ford talked to me several times as to the best way of preserving the sanctity of the place there. She decided that a nice church and a parish house built in connection with this cemetery would be one of the nicest ways of preserving the whole business, and that, as far as I know, was the origin of what would be St. Martha's. Mrs. Ford called me in a couple of times, and we'd talk about the kind of church she wanted, but the plans were not actually completed when she passed on, but they were near enough that they could carry out her ideas.

I couldn't say that Mrs. Ford came to me for spiritual help while Mr. Ford was ill in 1945. We talked of religious things and we sent each other books. Two or three times a year, if I would find a book that I didn't think she would have access to, or a nice little devotional book, I would send her a book. Many times she said that she and Henry in the evenings would open these books and read. She would write me letters saying, "I was reading aloud to Henry the other night, and we came across this. I wonder if you noticed this little chapter or passage in the book."

Mrs. Ford never did express any interest in an institutional church. She was more orthodoxly religious. Many times she would express her sorrow because they couldn't attend the little church, because if they went there two or three times, people got to know it and then there were the crowds. In the early days, Mr. and Mrs. Ford would come to the church parties, but when the parish got larger and the number got greater, they ceased to attend.

We attended the old-fashioned dances. In the early days when the dances were in the Engineering Lab, it was strictly informal. We didn't become formal until they moved into the new Lovett Hall; then it became a tux affair. We always had refreshment after the dance. We always wished the Fords good night, but there was no receiving line. Yes, sir, they were really happy affairs; we enjoyed them very much.

I remember there were occasions when in the time of the depression, Inkster (a town neighboring Dearborn) was in a very bad condition, and I was interested in that. I remember we got a meeting which Mrs. Ford attended. I suggested that the way to handle that at that time was that people should take a family and be interested in that family, to see them through, not just to give them a basket or ten dollars. Mrs. Ford asked me for a family; I think there were eight children. I gave her the biggest family I had. She laughed about it very much. The families were supplied with clothes and all that.

Mr. Ford arranged for the three men who could work, the father and two sons, to get jobs right away. They would take them to the plant and have jobs which alleviated the situation for the family. That was a time nobody could get a job. They told me to contact Mr. Bennett and see that the men were employed; that helped that situation plenty. Afterward, they took over the whole business of Inkster and handled it until they got on their feet. Actually, my contacts were strictly with Mr. and Mrs. Ford in that respect and then, of course, with Mr. Bennett's office for the actual operation. When something needed to be done, I'd get in touch with him, and that's all there was to it. He attended to it.

One time Mr. Ford came to the house, and he always called me doctor. I wasn't a doctor, but he always called me doctor. He said, "Doctor, suppose a colored person came to your church. What would you do?" I said, "Mr. Ford, we do have colored people at our church. They are just as welcome at the church as white people or any other people. We make no distinction. We invite them to come, and if they come, we make them feel very much at home, I hope." Mr. Ford liked that response.

I remember one time when Mr. Ford discussed with me personally this question of wages and told me the results of his investigation after he had started to pay what was then the largest wages ever dreamed of to workingmen. He wasn't quite sure that it was so good for them in the final analysis; he said he found out, on investigation, that as fast as he raised wages, the cost of living would go up, and within a year or so, the cost of living had overtaken the raise—rent and produce and so on. He said that was one of the things he had found out, and he established commissaries in order to get the goods to people at a reasonable cost that wouldn't gobble up all the raises they ever got.

Mr. Ford never discussed with me the idea of his tying in closely with soybean production for food. Of course, he was very interested in food. He'd always try to persuade me to eat carrots and soybeans. He tried to put me on a diet. In fact, he used to take a carrot out of his pocket, hand me one, and say, "Here, chew it, it'll do you good." He didn't feel that he should bother much with medical advice. You ought to be eating in such a way that you wouldn't need medical advice. All the ills that he would trace to the body would be blamed on diet. I never mentioned to him if I had a headache or didn't feel well.

He talked to me about exercise. He was always challenging me to do anything, to catch hold of a pole and pull myself up a dozen times and so on. He could do more than I could ever do in that way. He was showing his youth in that sort of thing.

The thing that interested me [about the Fords] was that they never seemed to realize their own greatness or the influence they had. They never seemed to have any sense of money influence or of being the Henry Fords. They would say that they went down to such and such a place, so-and-so and so-and-so, and how kind they were to them, and this, that, and the other. I used to say, "Well, why shouldn't they be? You know, you could buy and sell those people a dozen times." Mrs. Ford used to laugh very heartily and say, "I never thought of that."

I would say definitely that Mr. Ford was a man of moods. He was a victim of moods. I would say that I don't think that a mood lasted any length of time. It was because some other influence would come upon him, and his mood would change like lightning. He was adaptive, but also he was very susceptible to pressures. Of course, I would never ask Mr. Ford for anything, never, not for one single thing; I never asked for anything. He found it very difficult to be in a company of people, because he was suspicious that people wanted him for the things that he had to give. He wanted what he had, and it cramped his social life. He found it very difficult to move in circles, that is certain circles, without, if not immediately on the spot, being asked for twenty cars or this, that, and the other.

There was one incident when a young Persian came to see me. He wanted to sell Mr. Ford a prayer clock, and undoubtedly it was very, very valuable. He had tried to get in down there, and he couldn't, so he came directly to me. He introduced himself. He had lots of credentials and all that and asked me if I couldn't get in to see Mr. Ford for him. I said, "No, I do not make it a practice to intercede for anybody." He burst out with this statement, "Well, Mr. Stacey, as far as I can see, it would be much easier to see God than to see Henry Ford." I agreed with him.

I found that you could very rarely change Mr. Ford's ideas. I think that very rapidly an idea would become fixed, and he wasn't very easily persuaded to the contrary. Once that idea caught him, it was fired, although he himself, in and of himself, would change the idea in the wink of an eye; however, it wouldn't be from outside pressure but from his own thoughts. I never heard him apologize. He felt that mistakes belonged to the norm of life, that that's the way you learn, and that you shouldn't be afraid to make them. I don't think he felt that there was a need of apology. It should be accepted as part of your education.

The thing that always amazed me about Mr. and Mrs. Ford was that lack of sense of the wealth that they possessed. They retained a native simplicity that awed me more than the fact that money as money didn't mean a thing to them. It was just something to use to carry out ideas. That's all. It would put something to work. Otherwise, he didn't care who had it. Mrs. Ford had the same attitude toward money. She had an absolute horror of extravagance. She thought a good deal of the people who suffered did so because they just didn't handle their money right. They just were too extravagant and went way beyond their means. She always maintained a very, very frugal sense. I think they both in that respect retained the normal frugality of the farmer, the man of the earth. I think that that was essential in Mr. Ford's background and thought. I don't think he ever got away from that. Mrs. Ford also retained that feeling very definitely.

Mrs. Ford discussed the Oxford movement with me, but Mr. Ford did not. They knew Frank Buchman and that group. When they brought them to the inn, I attended two or three affairs. Frankly, I wasn't in sympathy with them, although I did realize the magnificent ideal that they had. I never felt that it was too practical. Well, Mrs. Ford felt that they were out for good; they wanted to do people good. It ran on the lines of their own thinking that the ills of the world would certainly be met along those spiritual lines. If people were moral and honest and kind and sought out things that were the best, naturally, it would certainly help the world's problems.

Appendix 3
Clara's Kitchen

Clara Bryant Ford was no slouch at cooking. Being the oldest daughter in a family of eleven living on a farm, she without doubt had gained training at an early age. When she married Henry Ford in 1888, her mother, Martha, gave her the *Buckeye Cookbook* to keep Henry happy. While living in small apartments in Detroit between 1891 and 1909, and having no garden plot to tend, Clara indulged in the pleasure of cooking for her family. Later, when wealthy, she continued to concern herself with cooking by collecting recipes and often expecting her cooks to provide more tasty foods than they knew how to prepare.

Cookbooks found in her kitchen after she died were the following:

Women's City Club
Detroit Times "Homemakers Club"
Boston Cooking School Cook Book
The Settlement Cook Book
Junior Goodwill Cook Book
The Country Kitchen
Miss Minerva's Cook Book
Lowney's Cook Book
Symphony in Cookery
Chafing Dish Possibilities
The Old Vanity Fair Recipes
The Butterick Cook Book
The New Cookery
The Malone Cook Book
The Savannah Cook Book
Feeding the Professor

Some of Clara's favorite individual recipes which were saved include the following, many of them in her own handwriting.

Citron Recipe

Pare the citron. Cut slices one and one-half inch thick and then into one and one-half inch strips, leaving the full length of the fruit. Take out the seeds with a small knife. Weigh. To each pound of fruit add an equal amount of white sugar. Make a syrup of the sugar, using one pint of water to 10 pounds of sugar. Simmer gently. Then put the citron in the syrup and boil one hour or until tender.

(This recipe of Clara's was published 10/16/49 in The Detroit News)

Stuffed Squab with Wild Rice

Boil rice well, wash thoroughly, put butter in pan, cook sliced onion & celery together, add rice. Clean squab, stuff with mixture, tie legs, place in roasting pan, rub with olive oil, salt, pepper, cover. Cook one hour at 400 degrees.

(This recipe is in Clara's handwriting)

To Coddle an Egg

Boil a small quantity of water in a small sauce pan. When boiling drop egg into water — remove from flame — cover — & leave for 3 to 4 minutes.

(These instructions are in Clara's handwriting)

Apple Pudding

2 cups cooked cream of wheat
2 cups milk
3 apples cored & sliced
3 eggs
1 cup sugar
a little nutmeg

Mix cream of wheat with milk, beaten eggs and sugar.
Pour 1/3 cream of wheat into a buttered baking dish, cover with apple rings, sprinkle with sugar & nutmeg, dot with butter, repeat twice. Bake in moderate oven 1/2 hour, serve hot or cold.

(Written in Clara's handwriting)

Apple Pudding.

2 cups cooked Cream of wheat

2 " milk

3 apples cored + sliced

3 eggs

1 cup sugar

a little nutmeg

Mix cream of wheat with milk,
beaten egg (+ sugar,
pour 1/3 cream of wheat into a
buttered baking dish, cover with
apple rings, sprinkle with sugar
+ nutmeg, dot with butter,
repeat twice, bake in moderate
oven 1/2 half hour
serve hot or cold.

25% Soy Bean Bread

24 ounces Bread Flour
8 ounces Soy Bean Flour
20 ounces Milk (or 7 ounces Evaporated Milk and 13 ounces water)
2 tablespoons Honey
1 tablespoon Sugar
1 tablespoon salt
1 teaspoon Malt
1 beaten Egg
3 cakes yeast
2 tablespoons Crisco

Scald milk, pour into bowl and add the honey, sugar, salt, malt and egg. When this mixture is luke warm, break into and dissolve well the three cakes of yeast. Add this to the flour which has been put into a large bowl and when mixed, work in the melted Crisco thoroughly. Turn on board and kneed until elastic. Return to bowl, cover with a damp cloth, place in a warm temperature of about 80 degrees and let rise for one hour and twenty minutes.

Punch or cut down and let rise again for thirty minutes.

Cut into two 1 pound 12-ounce loaves or any size loaves desired, rolling each into a ball as it is cut in order to close the pores. Then start with the first ball and shape into loaves, place in pans and let rise for thirty minutes, in a temperature of 90 degrees.

Bake in a moderate oven for one hour and thirty minutes.

(This recipe is typed and its source is unknown)

Pineapple Muffins- 2 Doz.

One cup sugar, 1/2 cup butter, 4 eggs, 3 cups white bread flour, 3 teaspoons baking powder, 3 cups milk, pinch salt.

When muffin pan is ready for oven put small amount of dough in each section.

Then a tablespoon of grated pineapple in each section, then fill each section with dough.

(This recipe came from Longfellow's Wayside Inn, in South Sudbury, Massachusetts)

Grandma Taylor's
English Christmas Pudding

For Mrs. Henry Ford —

1 pound of suet, chopped fine
1 pound of raisins
1 pounds of currants
1 pound of sugar
1 pound of bread crumbs
1 pound of sifted flour
1 tablespoon full mixed spices — cloves, cinnamon & nutmeg.

Beat 4 eggs into one pint of milk & stir in extract of lemon —
1 teaspoon of baking powder.
Boil in cloth bags — 4 hours.
(Submitted by Mrs. Orla B. Taylor, Detroit, Michigan)

Fig Pudding

1/2 pound figs chopped fine
1 tea cup grated bread crumbs
1 cup sugar
2 tablespoons of melted butter
4 eggs
5 ounces of candied orange & lemon peel
Steam 2 1/2 hours.

Pudding Sauce

Cream until very light —
1/2 cupful of butter milk
1 cup sugar
1 egg well beaten
1 teaspoon of vinegar
1 tablespoon marachino cordial

Turn — with upper part of a small double boiler, and stir constantly until clear like honey.
Do not let it boil.
This sauce has an elusive flavor that is delightful.
(These two recipes submitted by Mrs. Orla B. Taylor of Detroit)

Spinach Loaf

2 cups finely chopped spinach
1 cup finely cut onion,
1 cup celery cut into small pieces
1 cup bread crumbs or grape-
nuts. 2 eggs, or 1/2 lb cottage cheese
or both. 2 lbs melted butter
1/2 teas salt, mix well,
place in buttered baking pan
bake slowly 35 minutes
Very Good

Chocolate Pudding

3 tablespoons butter
2/3 cup sugar
1 egg
1 cup milk
2 1/4 cups flour
4 1/2 teaspoons baking powder
2 1/2 squares chocolate
1/2 teaspoon salt
Vanilla

Beat well and steam 1 hour. Serve with whipped cream, plain, or any sauce white or chocolate.

(This recipe mailed to Clara from Mrs. Milton D. Bryant, Clara's sister-in-law, in Traverse City, Michigan)

Pear Conserve

Wash the peel of one lemon and one orange. Cook until tender. Turn off the water. Chop the peel and add 4 pounds of cored pears chopped through the meat grinder, three pounds of sugar, the juice of three lemons, one can of shredded pineapple, one half pound of seedless raisins, one large orange, and one cup of water (two of water if the pears are not juicy). Cook several hours very slowly. About a half hour before removing them from the fire, add one pound of chopped nut meats.

(This recipe was written by Clara on a piece of scrap paper)

Date Sticks

2 eggs
1 cup powdered sugar
2 tablespoons (round) flour
1 level teaspoon baking powder
1 pound dates
1 cup walnuts

Spread as thin as possible in buttered tins and bake in moderate oven 20 to 30 min.

May be served as dessert smothered in whipped cream if spread thicker in tins and taken up with spoon after it is baked.

(This is another recipe in Clara's handwriting)

Mrs. Ives' Conserve

4 qt currants
1 pineapple
4 oranges
4 lb sugar
pulp of oranges, all 4
grated rind of 2
cook all together hard 20 min.

(Mrs. Louis Ives was a very good Dearborn friend of Clara)

Green Mango Pie

Peel and cut up green mangoes and stew until tender with sufficient sugar to sweeten.

Line pie tin with crust, add stewed mangoes, a little nutmeg and lump of butter. Put on top crust and bake.

(This recipe was submitted by Mrs. C. W. Stribley of Fort Myers, Florida)

Charolette Harbor Hotel Cake
(Marshmallow Cake)
(Recipe to serve 50 people)

14 Oz. Butter
28 Oz. sugar
28 Oz. flour
8 whole eggs
1 pt. milk
Cinnamon
Vanilla
4 Oz. chocolate

Cream butter, sugar, & eggs. then add flour, milk and chocolate.

Filling
1/2 pt. whites of eggs
2 1/2 (cups)? granulated sugar
2 pt. water
2 Oz. gelatine
Small amount of vanilla flavor & pinch of cream of tartar.
Cook sugar and water to boiling point, 350 degrees, and add boiling sugar in small stream and then gelatin and flavor. Whip until nearly cold.
(Recipe submitted by Mrs. Evelyn D. Rea of Fort Myers, Florida)

Molded Salad

1 pk lemon flavored gelatine. 1 2/3 cup boiling water, 2 tablespoons vinegar, 1 tablespoon sugar. 1/4 tablespoon salt, 1/2 cup diced celery, 1/4 cup chopped sweet pickle. 1/2 cup chopped pimentoes, 1 cup diced asparagus.

Pour boiling water on gelatine stir till dissolved. Add vinegar, sugar, salt, cool until thick add other ingredients. Pour into mold rinsed in cold water. (Serve with) lettuce & mayonaise. You can add more water & vinegar.
(This recipe was written by Clara on Fair Lane stationery with a note "Jeane — very good")

Blackberry Pot Pie

Take wild blackberries put in pan & cover with sugar.
Then take flour, salt, baking powder, and mix with cream. Then drop from spoon wild berries and cover & cook.
Let berries cook before putting in batter. Eat with butter.
(Recipe is written by Clara on a scrap of paper — source unknown)

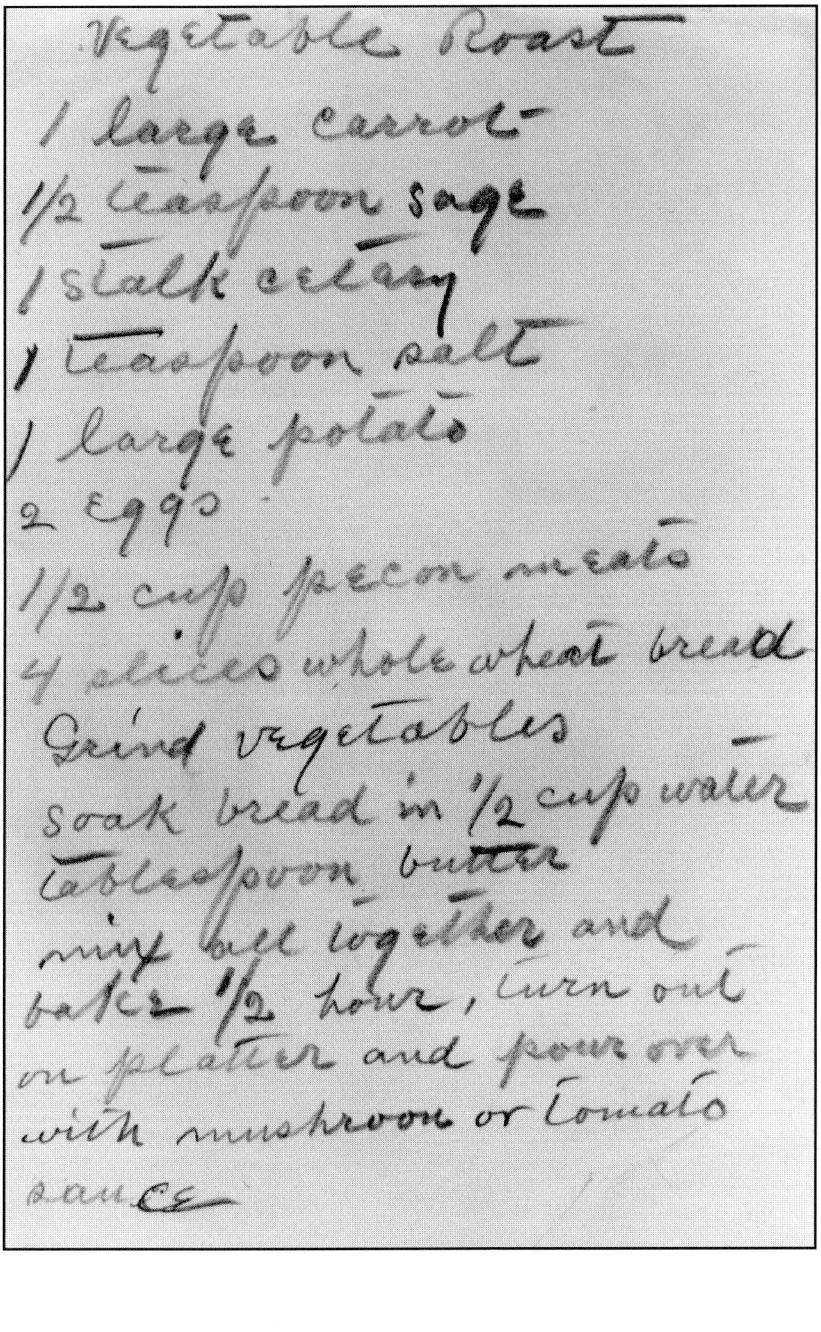

Vegetable Roast

1 large carrot
1/2 teaspoon sage
1 stalk celery
1 teaspoon salt
1 large potato
2 eggs
1/2 cup pecan meats
4 slices whole wheat bread
Grind vegetables
soak bread in 1/2 cup water
tablespoon butter
mix all together and
bake 1/2 hour, turn out
on platter and pour over
with mushroom or tomato
sauce

Cream Sponge Cake

4 yolks of eggs
3 tablespoons cold water
1 cup sugar
1 1/2 tablespoon corn starch in cup, (add) flour to fill cup
1 1/4 teaspoon baking powder
1/4 teaspoon salt
4 whites of egg beaten stiff & dry. 1 teaspoon lemon flavoring.
Very good
(Recipe on small sheet of paper in Clara's handwriting)

Hungarian Recipe

Black cherries, pour juice off, put in skillet with brown sugar & butter. Cook until thick. Butter a casserole, put cherries in bottom, then bread that has been soaked in milk. Then more cherries & more bread. Then make custard.
(Recipe in Clara's handwriting — source unknown)

Edison Cake

1 Cup Butter
2 1/2 Cups Granulated Sugar
6 Yolks of Eggs
2 Teaspoons Vanilla Extract
1/2 Teaspoon Rose Water
3 1/2 Cups Sifted Flour
3 Teaspoons Baking Powder
1/4 Teaspoon Nutmeg
1 Cup Milk
6 Whites of Eggs

Mix as any cake in the order given, folding in the whites last. Bake for one hour in cool oven.
(This recipe was typed — source unknown)

Canned Corn

18 cups corn
1 cup sugar
1/2 cup (scant) salt
Enough water to prevent burning
Boil 1/2 hour and seal in glass top jars
(Recipe appears to be Clara's writing on slip of paper)

Maple Mousse

3 eggs
1 cup maple syrup
cool till thick
add
2 cups cream whipped
put through sieve & freeze
(One of Clara's favorite desserts)

Devil Cake

1/2 cup butter
1 1/2 cup sugar
3 eggs
1/2 cup milk
1 1/3 cups flour
3 teaspoons baking powder
2 squares baker's chocolate
1 teaspoon vanilla

Cream butter and sugar, add yolks of eggs, add milk alternately
with flour & baking powder, melted chocolate, then milk.
(Another of Clara's favorite recipes)

"Kisses"

1 cup nut meats broken fine
1 teaspoon of vanilla
5 egg whites, 1 lb. pulverized sugar
Beat (egg whites) until stiff enough to stand.
Add vanilla beat more, add nuts.
Put on paper, no greasing. (Bake at ?)
When cold take off paper and serve.
Do not bake too hard.

Mrs. Henry Ford
*(This recipe is in Clara's handwriting, is signed by her, and with an
added note: "Sorry to be so late")*

Appendix 4

Ford Motor Company Chronology, 1903–1964

These particular items are selected from other more complete chronologies because of their close association with the contents of this book.

1903

June 16. Ford Motor Company is organized with John S. Gray as president and Henry Ford as vice president and chief engineer, receiving one-fourth of stock for car design.

July 23. Company sells its first car, a two-cylinder Model A, assembled at the Mack Avenue Plant in Detroit.

1904

August 17. Ford Motor Company of Canada is incorporated near Windsor, Ontario.

December. Production begins at Piquette Avenue Plant in Detroit.

1906

October 22. Henry Ford becomes president of Ford Motor Company following the death of John S. Gray.

1908

October 1. First Model T is made available to the public.

1910

January 1. Manufacturing operations are transferred to Highland Park, Michigan.

1911

January 9. Henry Ford wins Selden patent case in New York.

April 1. Industry's first branch assembly plant is completed in Kansas City, Missouri.

October. First overseas plant is established in Trafford Park, Manchester, England.

1913

April 1. First experiments with moving assembly line begin at Highland Park Plant.

1914

January 5. A $5.00 daily wage for eight-hour day replaces $2.34 wage for nine-hour day for male factory workers.

January 6. At least 10,000 men clamor for work at Highland Park Plant.

1915

January. Start of purchasing of land for the Ford Rouge Plant.

December 10. One-millionth Ford car is produced.

1916

October 25. Henry Ford Trade School opens at Highland Park.

1917

April 1. Construction begins on Rouge Plant at Dearborn.

July 2. First Ford truck is introduced for sale.

September 4. Henry Ford II, son of Edsel and Eleanor Ford, is born.

October 1. Fordson tractor production begins in Dearborn as a product of Henry Ford & Son (not Ford Motor Company).

1918

July 11. First of sixty Eagle boats for U.S. Navy is constructed at the Rouge Plant in Dearborn.

1919

January 1. Edsel B. Ford succeeds his father, Henry Ford, as president of Ford Motor Company.

July 9. With minor Ford Motor Company stockholders bought out, Ford Motor Company and Henry Ford & Son are reorganized as family-owned corporations with Henry, Edsel, and Clara Ford as sole owners.

July 20. Benson Ford, son of Edsel and Eleanor Ford, is born.

1920
July 1. Detroit, Toledo & Ironton Railroad is purchased by Henry, Edsel, and Clara Ford (not Ford Motor Company).

1922
February 4. Lincoln Motor Company is purchased by Ford Motor Company for $8 million. Edsel Ford is named president.

1923
December 31. Record production year: 1,923,360 Ford cars and trucks are produced in the United States.

1924
June 24. Ten-millionth Ford Model T is built.

1925
January 15. Ford Airport in Dearborn is dedicated.

March 14. William Clay Ford, son of Edsel and Eleanor Ford, is born.

1926
June 11. First Trimotor Ford plane flies from Ford Airport.

1927
May 26. Last Model T is produced after more than 15 million.

November 1. Model A production begins at Rouge Plant.

1928
February 14. Tractor production is discontinued at Rouge Plant to be continued later in Cork, Ireland.

1929
March 28. Rouge Plant employment rises to 100,000 while Highland Park employment diminishes.

July 1. Detroit, Toledo & Ironton Railroad is sold for $36 million.

December 1. Minimum wage of $7.00 a day becomes effective.

1931
April 14. Twenty-millionth Ford car is built.

1932
February 20. End of production of Model A vehicles after a total of 4,813,617 are produced.

March 9. First Ford car built with a V-8 engine.

1933
January 8. Final Trimotor plane is completed. Total of 198 are built.

1934
May 26. Ford Rotunda is opened as exhibit at Chicago World's Fair.

1935
October 5. Lincoln-Zephyr vehicle production is started.

1936
January 15. Ford Foundation is established.

May 16. Ford Rotunda is opened to the public in Dearborn.

1937
January 18. Twenty-five-millionth Ford car is built.

May 26. "Battle of the Overpass" between U.A.W. organizers and Ford security guards.

1938
October 8. Mercury vehicle production begins.

December 19. Henry Ford II is elected a director of the company.

1939
April 30. "Road of Tomorrow" is exhibited at New York World's Fair.

June 15. First Ford-Ferguson tractor is built at Rouge Plant.

October. Lincoln Continental is introduced by Edsel Ford.

1940

November 20. Six-cylinder Ford car production is started.

1941

March 1. First Ford Army Jeep is driven off Rouge assembly line.

April 18. Ground is broken for Willow Run Aircraft Plant near Ypsilanti, Michigan.

April 28. Benson Ford is elected a director of the company.

June 20. Closed-shop contract is signed with U.A.W.-C.I.O. covering 123,000 employees.

August 15. First Ford-built Pratt & Whitney aircraft engine is produced at Rouge Plant.

December 12. Company adopts wartime seven-day week.

1942

February 10. All civilian car production is halted.

November 28. First complete B-24 bomber is flown from Willow Run.

1943

May 26. Edsel Bryant Ford dies.

June 1. Henry Ford I is reelected president.

December 15. Henry Ford II is elected vice president.

1944

January 23. Henry Ford II is elected executive vice president.

April 24. Forty-two B-24 bombers are flown from Willow Run in one day.

December 7. Total of 7,000 B-24 bombers have been completed at Willow Run at a maximum rate of 432 per month.

1945

April 28. Standard five-day work week is resumed.

June 28. War production totals include 8,600 bombers, 278,000 Jeeps, and 57,000 aircraft engines.

July 3. Ford civilian passenger-car production resumes.

September 21. Henry Ford II is named president of the company.

1946

July 1. Ernest R. Breech is named executive vice president.

March 16. Frank Campsall, secretary to Henry Ford and a director of the company, dies.

July 30. A crowd of 50,000 honor Henry Ford on his eighty-third birthday with a celebration at Ford Field in Dearborn.

1947

April 7. Henry Ford dies at his home in Dearborn at age eighty-three.

April 18. Henry Ford's will is made public.

1948

January 30. Benson Ford is elected vice president and general manager of Lincoln-Mercury Division.

June 4. William Clay Ford is elected a director of the company.

December 27. Edsel B. Ford II, son of Henry Ford II, is born.

1949

September 28. Retirement plan for company employees is introduced.

1950

September 29. Clara Bryant Ford, age eighty-three, dies at Henry Ford Hospital in Detroit.

1951

March 5. Ford Motor Company purchases Fair Lane, the Dearborn home of Mr. and Mrs. Henry Ford.

1952

August. Henry Ford Trade School closes after thirty-six years of operation.

1953

May 7. Ford Archives are dedicated at Fair Lane.

May 12. William Clay Ford is elected president and manager, Special Products Division.

June 16. Ford Motor Company celebrates the fiftieth anniversary of its founding.

1955

April 18. Benson Ford is appointed vice president and group director of Mercury and Special Products Division; William Clay Ford is appointed vice president and group director of Lincoln Continental Division.

October 4. William Clay Ford unveils the new Continental Mark II luxury automobile.

1956

January 17. Ford Motor Company common stock amounting to 10 million shares is placed on public sale.

December 12. A gift of 210 acres of the Fair Lane estate together with $6 million in cash to the University of Michigan is announced by Ford Motor Company.

December 12. Transfer of Ford Archives from Fair Lane to the Ford Rotunda is announced.

1957

June 6. Donation of seventy-five acres of the Fair Lane Estate to the Dearborn Board of Education for Henry Ford Community College is announced.

1962

November 9. Ford Rotunda, with the exception of the north wing housing the Ford Archives, is destroyed by fire.

1964

September 15. Ford Archives, appraised at $4,485,000, is donated by Ford Motor Company to the Edison Institute.

References

Research Center Accessions

The accessions are individual collections of papers donated to the Research Center of Henry Ford Museum & Greenfield Village by individuals or institutions to be saved for research purposes. The largest of the accessions pertain to Ford Motor Company and other projects and personal interests of Henry Ford. Related accessions, of which there are hundreds, are likely to bear some relationship to automobiles or to automotive personnel.

Fair Lane Papers, Accession 1, Boxes 1–187. (1861–1950.) The entire contents of these 187 boxes were found at Fair Lane in 1951 following the deaths of Henry and Clara Ford.
———Box 3. William Ford, Sr., deed to Henry Ford, fifty-one acres (homestead property) for $4,000, dated February 1902.
———Box 12. Certification of marriage, William Ford and Mary Litogot Ahern.
———Boxes 18–24. Clara Ford's diaries.
———Box 33. Will of William Ford, Sr., dated June 10, 1896.
———Box 35. Fair Lane operations: Clara's records — personnel, salaries, gifts, family activities, 1914–1950.
———Boxes 53–54. Bryant family correspondence.
———Boxes 103–8. Clara Ford's correspondence, brochures, travel guides, and miscellaneous notes regarding trips, domestic and abroad, 1912–1945, including European souvenirs and language training in French and German.
———Box 135. The Peace Ship.

————Box 136. Neutral Conference in Continuous Mediation.

————Box 137. The Principles of the Oxford Group, Sherwood Sunderland Day, University of Oxford Press.

————Box 162. Garden clubs.

Henry Ford Office Records, Accession 2, Boxes 1–42. (1907–1916.) These are the personal records of Henry Ford, consisting of miscellaneous correspondence, architectural estimates, canceled checks, pay vouchers, and bank statements.

Henry Ford Office, General, Accession 23, Boxes 1–82. (1861–1948.) Contained in these boxes are materials removed from Henry's office in the Engineering Laboratory following his death in 1947. This accession includes a great variety of subjects such as awards, memberships, birthday and Christmas greetings, etc.

————Boxes 7, 17. Correspondence and notes relating to Wayside Inn in Massachusetts.

————Box 13. Copy of Records Secured in Detroit and Pontiac, also in Middle and Western Massachusetts & New York State. Collected by Gladys M. Salta. More than 200 entries including births, marriages, deaths, wills, and land transactions pertaining to various Bryant and Bogert families.

————Box 27. Ford family genealogy sheets tracing descendants of William Ford and Rebecca Jennings, including their son John Ford, Henry's grandfather.

————Boxes 28–31. Ford family history and genealogy including Irish correspondence.

————Box 28. Ford family tree correspondence conducted by Raymond Laird. Notes, topographical, historical, and genealogical on the Ford family, by Charles A. Webster of Ireland, who was retained by Henry Ford to research the history of the Ford family.

————Boxes 33, 35. Bryant genealogy as traced by Gladys M. Salta, who was commissioned by Clara Bryant Ford to research the Bryant and Bogert families in the 1920s.

Buckberry Notes, Accession 42, Box 1. In this box are manuscript materials gathered for a book on the history of the Ford Motor Company. Included is a list of Ford dealers who in 1945 had been in business continuously for more than twenty-five years beginning January 15, 1903.

Henry Ford Office Correspondence, Accession 62, Boxes 1–122. (1911–1919.) Arranged alphabetically within years.

Papers of the Neutral Conference for Continuous Mediation, Accession 79, Boxes 1–52.

Milton D. Bryant Papers, Accession 102, Boxes 1–7. Correspondence among various members of the Bryant family.

George R. Brubaker Files 1917–1928, Accession 185, Boxes 1–6. Office files and correspondence concerning Henry Ford & Son tractor business.

Henry Ford Office Correspondence, Accession 284, Boxes 1–40. (1920.) Ford Motor Company Dealership Records, Accession 387. Bound in several large volumes rather than boxes, these records list dealers by state and by date between 1912 and 1920.

Henry Ford Farms, Accession 445, Boxes 1–19.

"I Knew Him When" (Alfred Monnier on Henry Ford). *Detroit Free Press*, February 24, 1929. Small Accession 496, Box 8.

Legal—Edgar LeRoy Bryant Case, Accession 513, Boxes 1–14. Suit against Clara Ford Estate. (1901–1947.)

Edward L. Bryant Personal Papers, Accession 526, Boxes 1–7.

Office of Henry & Clara Ford — Estate, Accession 587, Boxes 1–198. L. J. Thompson, financial and property records. (1901–1955.)

Estate of Clara J. Ford, Accession 588, Boxes 1–6. (1951.)

"Knowing Mrs. Henry Ford," Hazel Peckinbaugh Dunlap, Accession 872 (Small Accessions Box 20). Typed manuscript, 30 pages, 1962.

Bryant Family History, Accession 889, Box 1.

Frank Hill Research Papers, Accession 940, Box 8. Baptism records of Clara Bryant.

Auction Catalog of Fair Lane Furniture, Accession 1460, Box 38 (Small Accessions).

Leonard B. Willeke Papers, Accession 1605. (1916–1924.) Willeke was an architect working for Henry and Edsel Ford.

Bryant Family Chart, Vertical File, Research Center.

William F. Metcalf, M.D., Collection, Accession 21. Center for Health Information Resources, Henry Ford Health System, Detroit.

Reminiscences

These are oral histories, most of them bound in hard covers and filed in the library of the Benson Ford Research Center of the Henry Ford Museum & Greenfield Village as Accession 65. As with other accessions, they are available for study in the library but are not to be taken from the library.

Ablewhite, H. S. Head of the Sociological Department of Ford Motor Company under Harry Bennett from 1941 to 1945, later in charge of Henry Ford Museum. He tells of Clara's effect on the museum. 126 pages.

Apple, Floyd F. Spent twenty-five years working in the powerhouse at Fair Lane after being employed by Ford Motor Company from 1922 to 1925. He tells of powerhouse operations, upkeep of grounds around Fair Lane, and the personalities of the Fords. 42 pages.

Barthel, Oliver E. Automotive pioneer with Charles B. King in 1885. He met Ford shortly after and relates how Ford and King worked together on automotive problems, each producing his own car. 86 pages.

Beebe, Faye I. Next-door neighbor and friend of the Ford family. She describes social activities of the two families. 12 pages.

Brand, Mary Louise. Daughter of Fred Gregory, who purchased land for Henry Ford. She describes the history of the Fair Lane area, the building of Fair Lane residence, and land purchases for the Rouge Plant. 33 pages.

Buhler, Rosa, and J. D. Thompson. Buhler, maid from 1933 to 1950, and Thompson, head butler from 1936 to 1950, have combined their memories to provide a colorful and intimate story of the Henry Ford family at home. 77 pages.

Cordell, Harold M. Assistant secretary in the Henry Ford office from 1921 to 1929. He was close to Henry Ford and tells of the origin of Henry Ford Museum & Greenfield Village. 113 pages.

Cutler, Edward J. An artist, draftsman, and architect responsible for the design and reconstruction of historical buildings erected in Greenfield Village. 194 pages.

Davis, Mr. and Mrs. Clarence. Relatives of Henry Ford. They describe the Ford family as they first settled in the Dearborn area. They discuss Ford's boyhood and personal recollections of the Fords in their leisure moments. Henry Ford's ideas on food, diet, health, war, and other facets of his complex personality are discussed. 90 pages.

De Caluwe, Alphonse. Belgian who worked at Fair Lane from 1921 until 1951. He was head gardener for Clara from 1924 until her death. He provides many anecdotes concerning Clara's manner of handling her workers.

Finzel, William. Friend of the family of Clara Bryant Ford. His recollections deal with the Henry Ford and Bryant families, old-time dancing, old-time music, and fiddler contests. 12 pages.

Ford, Burnham. Son of William Ford, Jr. He operated a Ford dealership at Flat Rock, Michigan.

Ford, Clyde M. Cousin of Henry Ford, Dearborn's first Ford dealer, and later first mayor of Dearborn. He tells the history of Dearborn Township, the Fords in Dearborn, and the accomplishments of Henry Ford. 60 pages.

Fries, William H. Associated with Detroit University School for many years. His wife was a close associate of Clara Ford. He describes the personal nature of Henry and Clara Ford. 5 pages.

Gleason, Fred. Son of John Gleason, who owned the steam engine Henry Ford operated when a young man. He tells of his sister, Christine, who refused Henry Ford's marriage proposal. 30 pages.

Henry, Inez. Student and later staff member of the Berry Schools of

Mount Berry, Georgia. She discusses the Fords on their frequent trips to the school and their reactions to the philosophy of education practiced at Berry Schools. 47 pages.

Holmes, George H. He describes the Dearborn area in the 1880s and 1890s, the birth of Henry Ford in 1863, the courtship of Henry and Clara Ford, Ford as a young mechanic, the local reaction to Ford's first car, and Ford's interest in Greenfield Village.

Keown, M. Gordon. Graduate of Berry Schools in 1904 and director from 1942 to 1944. His memoir provides a history of Berry Schools and an account of the relationship between the Fords and Martha Berry. 59 pages.

Liebold, Ernest G. Trained as a banker, became cashier of Henry Ford's Highland Park State Bank, and in turn became Ford's general secretary with financial responsibility for essentially all of Henry and Clara's personal business for more than twenty years. 1,536 pages.

Litogot, Edward B. Nephew of Henry Ford's mother, Mary Litogot, he worked at the printing trade in Detroit until 1930, when he was employed by Henry as printer for Greenfield Village. He discusses Ford's interest in Greenfield Village and relatives of Ford. 36 pages.

Loskowske, Fred W. General foreman of Ford Farms under Raymond Dahlinger from 1914 until 1950. He relates his experiences during the construction of Ford Airport, Greenfield Village, welfare gardens, and various village industries. 123 pages.

McIntyre, John. Powerhouse engineer at the Ford family residence. He has recorded his impressions of the Ford family and their interests. He gives an account of the last days of Henry Ford and the power failure at the time of his death. 34 pages.

Mielke, William. Electrician who joined Henry Ford & Son in 1916. He describes operations at that location and at the Ford Dairy Farm, events at Fair Lane and at the Engineering Laboratory. 163 pages.

Monnier, Edward F. Describes school days with Clara Bryant, the courtship of Clara and Henry Ford, and Henry's early interest in mechanics. 16 pages.

Morse, Elba. Director of the Bay Cliff Health Camp for physically handicapped children located near the Huron Mountain Club. She describes the visits to the camp by the Fords and the assistance given to the townspeople by the Fords. 20 pages.

O'Donnell, Dr. David. Practiced medicine in Detroit and had the Henry Ford family as patients during the last decade of the nineteenth century and the early years of the twentieth century. He tells of the birth of Edsel Ford. 6 pages.

Prindle, Charlotte M. Descendant of a pioneer Detroit family. She describes the city at the turn of the century, Henry Ford's first car, and Henry and Clara Ford as friendly neighbors. 12 pages.

Pring, William Walter. Joined Henry Ford in his first two unsuccessful automobile companies from 1899 to 1902. He describes the Detroit Automobile Company, Henry Ford, Henry M. Leland, the Henry Ford Company, and Cadillac Motor Car Company, 1902–1905. 68 pages.

Prunk, Grace (Brubaker). A favorite niece of Clara Ford. Interviewed by Richard Folsom in 1987, typescript filed in the Fair Lane Archives.

Rankin, Robert. Became Clara's chauffeur in 1938 and from 1945 drove for both Henry and Clara Ford. His recollections are rich in anecdotal material. 75 pages.

Rosenfield, John. Touches briefly on his work with the Ford Farms from 1917 to 1925 and his observations of Clara and Henry during the years he was gateman at Fair Lane estate from 1925 to 1950. 10 pages.

Ruddiman, Edsel A. Lifelong friend of Henry Ford, he speaks of their school days at the Scotch Settlement School and their later work together on the dietary quality of soybeans. 9 pages.

Ruddiman, Mrs. Stanley. Close friend of both Henry and Clara Ford from 1915 until their deaths. She presents the viewpoints of the Fords on world peace, religion, politics, and finance. She recounts the revival of old-fashioned dancing, the founding of the Edison Institute, and the home life and personal tastes of the Fords. 149 pages.

Sack, Israel. Antique dealer. He tells of antique dealers in Boston, furnishing the Wayside Inn for Henry Ford, and his cooperation with Henry Ford in establishing the Henry Ford Museum. 44 pages.

Scott, Mrs. Louis C. (Nettie Bryant). Daughter of Clara's uncle Nelson, ten years younger than Clara. Clara spent much time at Nettie's house in the early years. Nettie tells of Clara's courtship with Henry and of incidents when they were together later.

Searle, Frederick. Tells of Edsel Ford as his student at the Detroit University School and of the origin, philosophy, students, faculty, curriculum, and results of the Henry Ford Trade School, of which he was superintendent from 1917 until 1946.

Simpson, Mr. and Mrs. Lewis. Lewis Simpson assisted in the design of the Fair Lane residence. The Simpsons speak of W. H. Van Tine, the construction of Fair Lane, and its architectural features. Included are personal glimpses of the Fords. 25 pages.

Smith, Dr. F. Janney. Became a staff member of Henry Ford Hospital in 1915. He describes the hospital, its origins, administration, professional staff, patients, and personalities from 1915 until 1954. Ford's ideas on health, diet, and medicine are discussed. 28 pages.

Snow, Clara. Longtime resident of Dearborn, she was an intimate friend of Henry and Clara Ford, was a member of the old-time dance group, and participated with Clara Ford in the Dearborn Garden Club and the Woman's National Farm and Garden Association. She describes the Fords in these various relationships. 64 pages.

Stacey, Rev. Hedley G. Rector of Christ Episcopal Church in Dearborn, sometimes spiritual advisor to Clara Ford. He speaks of the religious life of the Ford family. 47 pages.

Stakes, Capt. Perry T. Master of steam and motor vessels of all oceans unlimited and first-class pilot of inland waters from Boston to New Orleans and of the Great Lakes. Stakes was hired by Henry Ford to captain the yachts *Sialia I* and *II*. He tells of trips taken with the Fords and their friends from 1919 until 1927. 27 pages.

Strauss, Frederick. Tells of Henry's apprentice days at James Flower Brothers and the Detroit Dry Dock companies. He describes Ford's early gasoline engine experiments, the Ford workshop in 1899, the Park Place shop, and the building of the 999 and the Arrow. The formations of Ford Motor Company and predecessor companies are also recounted. 92 pages.

Voorhess, Charles. Employed by Henry Ford on Ford Farms in 1913, becoming power engineer at Fair Lane and at the Dearborn Engineering Laboratory. Henry Ford personally kept him busy on a variety of electrical projects. 194 pages.

Waddell, H. Rex. Secretary to Henry and Clara Ford following the death of Frank Campsall in early 1946. 56 pages.

Wandersee, John. Hired as a sweeper in 1902 by Henry Ford. He tells of the formation of the Ford Motor Company, the metallurgical developments with which he became closely associated, and his impressions of Henry Ford during those early days. 72 pages.

Williams, John H. Became a member of the staff of Fair Lane as house boy in 1922. He describes Ford family routines, social entertainment, travel, recreation, religion, and other aspects of daily life. 50 pages.

Wilson, Rufus. Henry Ford's personal chauffeur from 1919 to 1945. He reveals many facets of Ford's complex personality, including Ford's own driving habits. 48 pages.

Wolfe, A. G. From 1907, lived on the Ford Dairy Farms, where his father was in charge. He attended the Henry Ford Trade School and was employed in the Experimental Department of Ford Motor Company. He describes Ford's interest in farming, construction of Fair Lane, experimental vehicle design and testing, the Ford family on vacations, and the Ford cemetery. 226 pages.

Zarembski, Frank. Employed in Greenfield Village, where he made shoes for Henry Ford. 9 pages.

Zaroski, Joseph. Henry Ford's barber during the last ten years of Ford's life. He relates many anecdotes about Henry's attitude toward money, politics, war, and religion. 29 pages.

Articles

Breur, Elizabeth. "An Interview with Mrs. Henry Ford." *Ladies Home Journal,* September 1923.

Bryan, Ford R. "Patrick Ahern, Henry Ford and Fair Lane." *Dearborn Historian,* vol. 22, no. 1, Winter 1982.

Bryant, Edward L. "The Bryant Homestead and the Martha-Mary Chapel." Five volumes. Dearborn Historical Museum, 1965.

Collins, Frederick L. "There's a Great Wife behind Every Great Man: Mrs. Henry Ford." *Delineator,* April 1927.

Folsom, Richard. "Ford Residences." Dearborn Historical Museum, 1982.

"Ford Was Mender of Bicycles." *Boston Post,* January 12, 1914.

Harlow, Alvin F. and Doris. "The Woman Who Had Great Faith." *Woman's World,* January 1935.

"Henry Ford Estate Tour Guide." University of Michigan–Dearborn, 1990.

Mitchell, Jerald A. An Interview with Florence Crews Houtz. April 13, 1991. Private manuscript.

Ruddiman, Margaret Ford. "Memories of My Brother Henry Ford." *Michigan History.* Michigan Historical Commission, Lansing, September 1953.

"Wayne County Michigan Land Records, Early Land Transfers, Detroit and Wayne County Michigan." W.P.A. Vital Records Project, Michigan State Library and D.A.R., Louisa St. Clair Chapter, 1940.

"The Woman Who Has Been Henry Ford's Inspiration." *True Experiences,* February 1940.

"Women's Committee for the Development of Fair Lane." *Dearborn Historian,* vol. 4, 1963.

Books

Barras, Clara. *The Life and Letters of John Burroughs,* Vol. 2. Boston: Houghton Mifflin, 1925.

Bennett, Harry (as told to Paul Marcus). *We Never Called Him Henry.* New York: Fawcett Publications, 1951.

Bryan, Ford R. *Beyond the Model T.* Detroit: Wayne State University Press, 1990.

————.*The Fords of Dearborn.* Detroit: Harlo Press, 1987.

Burroughs, John. *Under the Maples.* Boston: Houghton Mifflin, 1921.

Bush, George A. *Henry Ford's Peace Expedition: Who's Who.* Copenhagen: I. Cohen's Printing House, 1915.

Clancy, Louise, and Florence Davis. *The Believer.* New York: Coward-McCann, 1960.

Dahlinger, John. *The Secret Life of Henry Ford.* Indianapolis: Bobbs-Merrill, 1978.

Dearborn Township Census. 1840–1880.

Detroit City Directory, 1880–1884. Detroit: J. W. Weeks.

Detroit City Directory, 1885–1915. Detroit: R. L. Polk.

Fair Lane. University of Michigan–Dearborn, October 1979.

Ford, Henry, with Samuel Crowther. *My Life and Work.* Garden City, N.Y.: Doubleday, 1923.

Greenfield Township Census. 1884.

The Henry Ford Peace Expedition. Copenhagen: I. Cohen's Printing House, 1915.

Illustrated Historical Atlas. County of Wayne. H. Belden & Company, 1876.

Irwin, Ann Davis. *Generations: A Family Life.* Ann Arbor, Mich.: After Thoughts, 1989.

Marquis, Samuel S. *Henry Ford: An Interpretation.* Boston: Little, Brown, 1923.

Miner, Jack. *Jack Miner and the Birds.* Chicago: Reilly & Lee, 1925.

Moreland, Faye Witt. *Green Fields and Fairer Lanes.* Tupelo, MO: Five Star Publishers, 1969.

Nevins, Allan. *Ford: The Times, the Man, the Company.* New York: Charles Scribner's Sons, 1954.

Nevins, Allan, and Frank Ernest Hill. *Ford: Expansion and Challenge, 1915–1932.* New York: Charles Scribner's Sons, 1957.

O'Callaghan, Timothy. *Henry Ford's Airport and Other Aviation Interests.* Ann Arbor, Mich.: Proctor Publications, 1993.

Olson, Sydney. *Young Henry Ford.* Detroit: Wayne State University Press, 1963, 1997.

Snider, Clara J., and Michael W. R. Davis. *The Ford Fleet, 1923–1989.* Cleveland: Freshwater Press, 1994.

Sorensen, Charles E., with Samuel T. Williamson. *My Forty Years with Ford.* New York: W. W. Norton, 1956.

Twork, Eva O'Neal. *Henry Ford and Benjamin Lovett.* Detroit: Harlo Press, 1982.

Index